Making Monsters

Making Monsters

The Uncanny Power of Dehumanization

DAVID LIVINGSTONE SMITH

HARVARD UNIVERSITY PRESS

Cambridge, Massachusetts & London, England

2021

First printing

Library of Congress Cataloging-in-Publication Data
Names: Smith, David Livingstone, 1953– author.
Title: Making monsters : the uncanny power of dehumanization /David
    Livingstone Smith.
Description: Cambridge, Massachusetts : Harvard University Press, 2021. |
    Includes bibliographical references and index.
Identifiers: LCCN 2021011261 | ISBN 9780674545564 (hardcover)
Subjects: LCSH: Humanity—Psychological aspects. | Respect for persons. |
    Power (Social sciences) | Toleration. | Hate. | Lynching.
Classification: LCC HM1131 .S554 2021 | DDC 179/.9—dc23
LC record available at https://lccn.loc.gov/2021011261

For Ruby

That which has happened is a warning. To forget it is guilt. It must be continually remembered. It was possible for this to happen, and it remains possible for it to happen again at any minute. Only in knowledge can it be prevented.

—KARL JASPERS

CONTENTS

PREFACE

Something Like a Darkness

"They did not know that the [Tutsi] were human beings, because if they had thought about that they wouldn't have killed them. Let me include myself as someone who accepted it. I wouldn't have accepted that they are human beings."[1] Elie Ngarambe, a Hutu man, spoke these words to US political scientist Daniel Jonah Goldhagen in 2008. Ngarambe was talking about his role in the 1994 Rwanda genocide, during which he bludgeoned and hacked Tutsi women, men, and children to death.

Goldhagen confessed his perplexity at how anyone could perform the horrendous acts that were everyday occurrences during the Rwanda genocide. "I find it hard to understand," he said, "and I want to understand, how people could approach other people who are begging for their lives, and screaming in pain, and chop them." In doing so, he expressed same sort of mute incomprehension that many of us experience when reading about these events, or about the horrors of the Nazi extermination camps, or about any of the all-too-frequent episodes of collective brutality that deface human history.

Struggling to adequately describe the state of mind that allowed him to butcher his neighbors, Ngarambe responded, "That is a hard question to answer. Because even though you did it, you know they had the same flesh as you." He then added,

> It was very sad when a baby would cry. I did not kill children, but at some point you felt guilty. You would see an infant who's just learning to smile, and it smiles at you, but you still kill it. It was a cloud that came into people's hearts and covered them, and everything became dark. You are holding a machete over

someone who is weak and saying, "Please, I will give you money. Please forgive me." Or a woman would say, "I am a beautiful woman. Please take care of me." But instead, you kill them. This genocide, when we look back and think about it, it is beyond our ability to understand. I cannot explain it. The only answer I can give is that it was like being in a fog, something like a darkness.

In the first statement, Elie Ngarambe claimed that he did not think of those that he killed as human beings. This may sound strange. How can one human being regard another human being as not really human? Was he insane? There is no reason to think Ngarambe was suffering from schizophrenic delusions that compromised his grasp of reality. He was, in all likelihood, a psychologically normal man, albeit one who participated in one of the most hideous bloodlettings of the twentieth century.

The claim that Elie Ngarambe really believed that fellow Rwandans were subhuman creatures may strike you as preposterous—so preposterous that you might jump to the conclusion that his testimony was just a pathetic alibi that was intended to excuse the inexcusable. Or you might think that he meant it to be taken metaphorically, perhaps as meaning that he did not have empathy for the people that he butchered, rather than literally. But I am going to argue in the chapters to follow that both of these alternatives are mistaken. Instead, I submit that Elie Ngarambe, like so many others who have acted similarly, meant his words to be taken literally as a true description of his state of mind.

The act of conceiving of other human beings as subhuman creatures is not limited to a single culture or just one historical period. It can be traced across thousands of years of human history and found in many far-flung regions of the globe. The evidence is overwhelming that we human beings periodically view other members of our species as not really people at all, but rather as less-than-human beings that it is morally permissible, or even obligatory, to harm or to kill.

It is because dehumanization is so entangled with and implicated in the worst atrocities that human beings have ever perpetrated upon one another that investigating it is an important—indeed, an urgent—task. But strangely enough, there has not been much research into the nature of dehumanization. Most academic disciplines have all but ignored it and have treated dehumanization as though it were already well understood. Only social psychology can boast of anything like a substantial research literature dealing with what goes on in people's heads when they think of other people as less than human.

It was the paucity of research into dehumanization, conjoined with its great importance, that inspired me to write my 2011 book *Less Than Human: Why We Demean, Enslave, and Exterminate Others*, which remains the only interdisciplinary study of the subject in the English language (or, to the best of my knowledge, any other language). Writing it, I worked my way through relevant literatures in a number of disciplines—history, philosophy, anthropology, and psychology, among others—to pull together, order, and analyze all the information I could find about this disturbing phenomenon. In *Less Than Human* I sought to answer three fundamental questions (as well as a number of important but less weighty ones) about dehumanization. First, I wanted to figure out exactly what dehumanization is, and to distinguish it from related phenomena such as objectification, racism, and xenophobia. Second, I wanted to develop a theory of how dehumanization works, using the best psychological tools currently available. And third, I wanted to establish why dehumanization occurs, by determining what if any function it has.

I believe that I made considerable headway in answering all three of these questions, and I continue to stand by much of what I wrote in *Less Than Human*. However, over the intervening years I became dissatisfied with certain aspects of the analysis and decided that my story was both incomplete and, in some respects, misleading. The book that you are reading now rectifies these deficits and presents an account of dehumanization that is far more powerful and subtle, one that captures the peculiar phenomenology of dehumanization far more effectively than its predecessor did.

In *Less Than Human*, I argued that when we dehumanize others we conceive of them as *appearing* human when they are *really* subhuman. I now think that this story is not exactly right. What actually occurs when we dehumanize others is much stranger and more toxic. I now believe that when we dehumanize others, we conceive of them as being both human and subhuman—that is, *wholly* human and *wholly* subhuman—at the same time. I am aware that this statement may sound bizarre or nonsensical. Logically speaking, it is no more possible for a being to be wholly human and wholly subhuman than it is for an object to be completely red and completely green at the same time. But forcing human psychology into the procrustean bed of logic is a fool's errand. A logician may tell you that contradictions are always false, but human experience is no stranger to contradiction, and contradiction lies at the core of dehumanization. One need only revisit Elie Ngarambe's words to see this weird contradiction at work. He insists, in the first quotation, that he did not think of his victims as human, but also states, in the second quotation, that those whom he murdered "had the same flesh"—that is, were beings of the same kind—as himself.[2]

The tension between conceiving of the other as human and conceiving of them as less than human is a very important feature of dehumanization, and understanding this unlocks many of its otherwise puzzling characteristics. It explains why dehumanized people are so often represented as monsters, demons, or predators, why they are so often regarded as uncanny affronts to the natural order, and why they are so often treated with a particular kind of gratuitous cruelty and degradation. Understanding the paradoxical character of dehumanization also gives us purchase on a pair of crucial methodological problems. It casts light on the vexing problem of how to distinguish genuine dehumanization from superficially similar phenomena, such as the use of animalistic slurs, and it also suggests a way to track the "silent" forms of dehumanization that do not involve explicitly labeling others as subhuman beings.

It was already beginning to dawn on me when writing *Less Than Human* that to understand dehumanization one needs to understand a lot more than *just* dehumanization. Since then I have come to appreciate this insight much more fully. It is impossible to really grasp how and why we are able to dehumanize others without considering the function of the concept of the human, the evolutionary background to human ultrasociality, the cognitive psychology of the uncanny, and theories of belief formation, to name just a few. And because dehumanization stands at the interface between the political and the personal, to address it fully requires one to explore the interface between political processes and human behavior, and in particular it requires one to address the nature of propaganda and ideology. I discuss all of these topics and more in *Making Monsters*, with the aim of fashioning a deep, rich, and subtle account of dehumanization.

Very many people have contributed to the thinking that informs this book. In some cases, the contributions have been extensive. In others, a chance remark, a criticism, or a suggestion in passing has proven to be important to the line of inquiry that I have pursued. I would especially like to thank Nancy Bauer, Paul Bloom, Scott Carden, Tommy Curry, Noel Dominguez, Stefanie Fishel, Lori Gruen, Michael Hauskeller, Bryce Huebner, Wulf Hund, Ioana Hulbert, John Jackson, Robin Jeshion, Jonathan Kaplan, Kristian Kemtrup, Suzy Killmister, Maria Kronfeldner, Edouard Machery, Katie MacKinnon-Burks, Kate Manne, Colin McAleer, Mari

Mikkola, Mark Moffett, Daniel Mosely, Harriet Over, John Protevi, Hogan Sherrow, Jason Stanley, Eric Schwitzgebel, Damion Scott, Johannes Steizinger, Lynne Tirrell, Shelly Lynne Tremain, Charlotte Witt, and Saskia Wolsak. Very special thanks go to Peter Swirski for his painstaking reading and insightful comments on the developing manuscript, to Ioana Hulbert for much of the research that went into the "Pollution" section in Chapter 11, and to Ditte Marie Munch-Juricic, whose work was vital to the discussion of perpetrator abhorrence in that same chapter. I would also like to thank Andrew Kinney at Harvard University Press for giving me the green light for this project, Paul Vincent for stellar copyediting, and the editorial and production team in general for turning a roughly hewn manuscript into a polished book. Finally, I need to thank the person who has by far been the most significant influence on my life, both intellectually and emotionally. I am hugely grateful to my spouse, Subrena Smith, whose insights, inspiration, and care have been vital to my research trajectory and to bringing this book to completion.

Making Monsters

CHAPTER ONE

What Is Dehumanization?

I begin with a "what" question. What exactly are we talking about when we talk about dehumanization? The answer to this seemingly simple question is not straightforward.

Scholars use "dehumanization" to denote a motley ragbag of loosely connected phenomena, and the situation is not any better outside the ivory tower. "Dehumanization" and "dehumanize" are used to describe a spectrum of situations, institutions, behaviors, and attitudes extending all the way from the tedium of the assembly line to the horrors of Auschwitz. In this foggy semantic atmosphere, it is easy for those who are interested in figuring out what dehumanization is, how it works, and what its functions are, to talk past one another. Given this, it is important to be clear about what one means by the word "dehumanization" right from the start. There is no point in asking what "dehumanization" really means, because it really means a lot of different things. Instead, we should be asking whether some conceptions of dehumanization are preferable to others, and why they are preferable, and for what purposes. My goal in this chapter is to begin to articulate a particular approach to understanding dehumanization, and to explain why I prefer it to some of the alternatives that are currently on the table.

I begin by describing two examples of dehumanization—the lynchings of Henry Smith and Sam Hose in late nineteenth-century Texas and Georgia, respectively—and then use these examples to sort through and evaluate conceptions of dehumanization. I have chosen these examples rather than others because they are unambiguous (it is difficult to imagine that there are many people who would deny that they are examples of dehumanization) and also because, given their abominable cruelty and brutality, they graphically convey why the phenomenon of dehumanization is worthy of careful and sustained attention.

Strange Fruit

On February 1, 1893, a twenty-seven-year-old mentally disabled man named Henry Smith was tortured and burned to death. Smith, a Black farm worker in Paris, Texas, was accused of raping, mutilating, and murdering a White policeman's four-year-old daughter.[1] He had been apprehended a little over a hundred miles to the east in Arkansas and taken back to Paris in handcuffs to be lynched before the eyes of ten thousand spectators.[2]

The crime for which Smith was arrested, and the gruesome spectacle that followed it, was covered widely by the national media. The *Saint Paul Daily Globe* reported "the city was wild with joy over the apprehension of the brute" and the citizens were determined that "the punishment of the fiend should fit the crime."[3] Schools, businesses, and even saloons were closed in honor of the festivities, and the reporter noted that "everything was done in a business-like manner." A specially commissioned excursion train brought onlookers from as far away as Dallas to watch the macabre spectacle. First, Smith was paraded around the city on a carnival float, where he was displayed as a king on his throne, holding a make-shift scepter. Then,

> his clothes were torn off piecemeal and scattered in the crowd, people catching the shreds and putting them away as mementos. The child's father, her brother, and two uncles then gathered about the Negro as he lay fastened to the torture platform and thrust hot irons into his quivering flesh. It was horrible—the

man dying by slow torture in the midst of smoke from his own burning flesh. Every groan from the fiend, every contortion of his body was cheered by the thickly packed crowd of 10,000 persons. The mass of beings 600 yards in diameter, the scaffold being the center. After burning the feet and legs, the hot irons—plenty of fresh ones being at hand—were rolled up and down Smith's stomach, back, and arms. Then the eyes were burned out and irons were thrust down his throat.[4]

Then the crowd placed Smith on a mound of cottonseed hulls doused with kerosene and burned him alive. Such public burnings of Black men soon came to be known as "barbecues."[5] The *Globe* continued, "The Negro rolled and tossed out of the mass, only to be pushed back by the people nearest him. He tossed out again, and was roped and pulled back. Hundreds of people turned away, but the vast crowd still looked calmly on."[6] Finally, when the burning was over, and only the charred remains of a corpse remained, trophy hunters picked through the ashes for pieces of bone, buttons, teeth or even pieces of charcoal to take home with them as souvenirs.

The question of Smith's guilt is irrelevant to this discussion (bearing in mind that, as the heroic anti-lynching campaigner Ida B. Wells observed, all such allegations should be regarded as suspect).[7] What is most important for the purposes of this book is the language that Smith's tormentors and their sympathizers so frequently used to describe him, and the relationship between that discourse and his ghastly execution.

In the report in the *Saint Paul Daily Globe*, Smith was described as a "fiend" and a "brute," terms that appeared very often in newspaper coverage of the incident. He was described in other media outlets as a "Black beast" (*San Antonio Gazette*),[8] a "bestial negro" (*St. Louis Republic*),[9] an "incarnate monster" (*New Orleans State*),[10] an "unnatural monster" (*Texarkana News*).[11] The *Globe* went so far as to call

Smith "the most inhuman monster known in current history,"[12] and in his own account of the burning, eyewitness Junius M. Early described Smith as "a being in human shape."[13] Reverend Atticus Haygood, a Methodist bishop and former president of Emory University, informed his readers that the murdered child was "torn asunder in the mad wantonness of gorilla ferocity."[14] And Henry Vance, the murdered girl's father, described Smith as having a "brawny muscular body surmounted by a small head, developed wholly in the direction of the animal passions and appetites; devoid of any humanizing sensibilities . . . a fiend incarnate."[15]

These characterizations of African Americans were not unusual. The Black people—especially Black men[16]—who were victims of mob violence in retribution for their real or imagined crimes were routinely described as subhuman animals, predatory apes, or demons in human form. Lacking paradigmatically human sensibilities, and endowed with superhuman strength and insatiable sexual appetites, they were imagined as rampaging monsters terrorizing White society—monsters that needed to be kept in their proper place, ideally in chains.

In the spring of 1899, just six years after Henry Smith was tortured and incinerated, Sam Hose, a twenty-one-year-old Georgia man, was accused of murdering his employer, raping his employer's wife, and injuring their children. Descriptions of Hose were virtually indistinguishable from those that had been used to characterize Smith six years previously. He was a "fiend incarnate," a "monster in human form," a "black brute whose carnival of blood and lust has brought death and desolation," and a "fiendish beast," and his punishment was every bit as horrific.[17] Fresh from Sunday morning church services, the God-fearing citizens of Palmetto, Newnan, and Griffin—small, rural communities that are now parts of Metropolitan Atlanta—as well as four thousand spectators who arrived on packed excursion trains, dragged this young man to the center of town, chained him to a tree, and began to mutilate his body. According to civil rights historian Phillip Dray, "The torture of the victim lasted almost half an hour.[18] It began when a man stepped forward and very matter-of-factly sliced off Hose's ears. Then several men grabbed Hose's arms and held them forward so his fingers could be severed one by one and shown to the crowd. Finally, a blade was passed between his thighs, Hose cried out in agony, and a moment later his genitals were held aloft."[19]

Hose was then set alight. He was burned to death very slowly in order to prolong his agony. At one point, as the flames gradually consumed his living body, he somehow managed to break free of his chains, but was thrust back into the flames by members of the surrounding crowd. After the flames died down, men removed the heart and liver from his incinerated corpse, cut them into small pieces, and broke his bones into fragments, all to sell to trophy hunters who paid top dollar and fought over the souvenirs. "Those unable to obtain the ghastly relics direct," one journalist wrote, "paid their more fortunate possessors extravagant sums for them." The report elaborated, "Small pieces of bones went for 25 cents, and a bit of the liver crisply cooked sold for 10 cents. As soon as the negro was seen to be dead there was a tremendous struggle among the crowd, which had witnessed his tragic end, to secure the souvenirs. A rush was made for the stake, and those near the body were forced against it and had to fight for their freedom. Knives were quickly produced and soon the body was dismembered."[20] Hose's ears, nose, and penis, which were cut off before the fire started, were especially prized items. A set of his knuckles was displayed for sale in the window of an Atlanta grocery store.[21]

The atrocities committed against these two men, as well as thousands more like them, seemed to fit with their status as subhuman beings. It is common for people to slaughter and barbecue nonhuman animals, to display their body parts in butcher shops, and to preserve pieces of their bodies—a boar's head, a deer's antlers, a rabbit's foot—as trophies or good luck charms.[22] Black life, like animal life, was cheap in the American South, and killing Black people was considered to be morally inconsequential. "Back in those days," recalled one White southerner, "to kill a Negro wasn't nothing. It was like killing a chicken or killing a snake. The Whites would say, 'Niggers jest supposed to die, ain't no damn good anyway—so jest go on an' kill 'em.'"[23] And another remarked, in a letter to the editor of *The Crisis,* that according to the Bible, "The negro originated from an animal. And we Southern people do not care to equal ourselves with animals." Consequently, "The people of the South do not think any more of killing the black fellows than you would think of killing a flea."[24]

Black men were not just seen as animals. The extremes of rage and contempt, the efforts to degrade and humiliate the victims, and the pleasure that the White mob took in causing them the maximum amount of suffering in the name of "justice" before letting death free them from their torment are not typical of how human beings treat the animals that they hunt and eat. Smith and Hose were demonized as what would be called a century later "superpredators"— fiends who are devoid of conscience and intent on satisfying their insatiable appetites for rape, murder, and mayhem. This vision of Black brutality is clearly expressed (to give one among very many examples) in an article about Smith's lynching that appeared in the *Memphis Commercial:*

> Their [the lynch mob's] deed was not provoked by one crime alone. The growing frequency and fiendishness of these crimes by negroes keep the people of every southern community in a perpetual condition of suppressed terror and rage. The lust of the negro spares no victim. The little innocent so brutally murdered and mangled at Paris is but one of many such who have died to gratify the beastly lusts of the negro. The awful fact

stares nearly every southern community in the face that it is infested with a race of ravishers whom no law can check and no punishment appall.[25]

According to South Carolina congressman Benjamin Tillman, "the poor African" whose savage instincts had previously been held in check by the firm but benign influence of his White overlord now "became a fiend, a wild beast seeking whom he may devour, filling our penitentiaries and our jails, lurking around to see if some help-less White woman can be murdered or brutalized."[26] The Black man, it was said, is "the most horrible creature upon the earth, the most brutal and merciless," "a monstrous beast, crazed with lust. His ferocity is almost demoniacal. A mad bull or tiger could scarcely be more brutal."[27] These men's alleged depredations on White women were "indescribably beastly and loathsome . . . marked . . . by a diabolical persistence and a malignant atrocity of detail that have no reflection in the whole extent of the natural history of the most bestial and ferocious animals."[28]

One of the most influential and notorious of these representa-tions was the description of the character named Gus in Thomas F. Dixon Jr.'s 1905 novel *The Clansman: A Historical Romance of the Ku Klux Klan*, the book that inspired the twentieth-century revival of the Ku Klux Klan, and from which the notorious 1915 motion pic-ture *The Birth of a Nation* was adapted. Gus, a former slave who bru-tally rapes a fifteen-year-old White girl, is described as having "gleaming apelike" eyes, and his "thin spindle-shanks supported an oblong, protruding stomach, resembling an elderly monkey's, which seemed so heavy it swayed his back to carry it. The animal vivacity of his small eyes and the flexibility of his eyebrows, which he worked up and down rapidly with every change of countenance, expressed his eager desires."[29] As Gus stalked his female prey, his "thick lips were drawn upward in an ugly leer and his sinister bead eyes gleamed like a gorilla's. A single fierce leap and the black claws clutched the air slowly as if sinking into the soft White throat."[30]

It is important to understand that even those Black men who were not accused of committing violent crimes—those who were seen as peaceful, or prudent, or merely subservient—were suspect. It was regarded as a truism that even if Black people did not behave violently, they all "had it in them" to do so, because criminality was assumed to be a permanent and unalterable condition of their nature. Thus, one contributor to the *Paris News*, commenting on the Smith affair, insisted that it is false to claim that the Negro "is intellectually and morally degraded as the result of slavery" and asserted what was then (as now) the widely accepted view among Whites that "the negro is what he is physically, intellectually and morally by the unalterable law of heredity. He was designed by the great Creator to form a link in the long chain of created beings."[31]

In invoking the "long chain of created beings," this author had in mind the ancient and pervasive idea of the "Great Chain of Being"—the idea that the entire cosmos is ordered as a vast hierarchy, in which every kind of being, whether mineral, plant, animal, or human, is ranked.[32] I will have much more to say about the centrality of the concept of the Great Chain of Being in Chapter 6. For now, what is important is that this way of thinking introduces the notion that there are "higher" and "lower" kinds of beings, that the higher beings count for more, in a moral sense, than the lower ones do.

White people ranked Black people lower than themselves on the hierarchy; so low, in fact, that they often considered them as an alien species—a kind of humanoid ape—or at best as primitive, simianlike human being. In either case, Whites commonly believed that Black people's proper place in the natural order was beneath themselves. Supposedly, although the irredeemably animal nature of Black people could be tamed and trained, it could never be extinguished, and Black people would always slide back into primal savagery as soon as the reins on their behavior were relaxed.[33]

Choosing a Conception of Dehumanization

As I have already mentioned, the word "dehumanization" has come to mean very many different things to many different people, both in the vernacular and in the writings of scholars and researchers. To impose some order this explanatory chaos, I make a distinction between *conceptions* of dehumanization and *theories* of dehumanization. Conceptions of dehumanization are ideas about what dehumanization is—ideas about what sorts of phenomena the term "dehumanization" names. Theories of dehumanization are ideas about how dehumanization works—its psychological, political, and social dynamics. I will start with conceptions because conceptions are more basic than theories, insofar as they pin down what it is, exactly, that theories of dehumanization are theories of. Once we have settled on a conception of what dehumanization is, we will be in a position to theorize it.

My conception of dehumanization is simple. We dehumanize others when we conceive of them as subhuman creatures. These creatures might be nonhuman animals such as lice, rats, snakes, or wolves, or they might be fictional or supernatural beings such as demons and monsters. But in all cases, they are, in a sense that I will explain later on, "beneath" the human, even if, as is often the case, they are thought to possess greater-than-human powers. On my account, then, dehumanization is a kind of attitude. It is something that happens inside people's heads. Of course, dehumanizing attitudes often give rise to derogatory speech and cruel or callous actions. But these forms of speech and these kinds of actions do not constitute dehumanization. Rather, they are results of dehumanizing attitudes. There is a lot that needs to be unpacked in order to make this short definition maximally clear, and it will take many pages to do so anywhere near fully, but for now, stating it baldly is a good enough start.

There are reasons why I have settled on this conception of dehumanization, rather than any of the others that are available. I prefer it to the others because it satisfies four conditions that I think any serviceable conception of dehumanization ought to fulfill.

First, I want a conception of dehumanization that specifies the social and psychological forces that produce and sustain certain forms of cruelty and injustice, one that addresses the most hideous things that human beings do to one another—paradigmatically, genocidal violence, but also war, racial oppression, and other atrocities. That does not mean that my conception of dehumanization only pertains to the extremes of human violence. It can also address more subtle, everyday kinds of bias. But it minimally should encompass the worst that human beings have inflicted on one another.

Second, I want a conception of dehumanization that picks out a slice of reality that is not adequately covered by other terms and concepts—one with specific content and utility. There is no point in developing a theory of dehumanization that could just as well be described as a theory of racism, or a theory of sexual objectification, or a theory of "othering," or any number of other things. To my mind, an account of dehumanization ought to open a conceptual door that has hitherto remained closed, or left only slightly ajar. It ought to tell us something new about our world and ourselves, or connect the dots between what we already know to reveal an unsuspected pattern.

Third, I want a conception of dehumanization that lends itself to scientific explanation, broadly construed. One that allows us to infer the causal processes and mechanisms that underpin it, that is at least in principle amenable to testing, and that draws on theoretical and observational research. This is vital because, no matter how elegant, or enthralling, or prima facie plausible a theory is, it also needs to provide a true account of what is going on when people dehumanize one another. There are pragmatic reasons for this as well as explanatory ones. If you want to dismantle something, it is often essential to know how that thing is put together. If we want to put an end to dehumanization, as we all should, we need to have an accurate understanding of its structure, its inner workings, and the forces that perpetuate it. This means that, at the very least, a good account of dehumanization should be consistent with our best current science, and ideally it should draw upon and extend well-established scientific accounts of human behavior.

Fourth and finally, I want a conception of dehumanization that accords with at least some of the most important vernacular uses of the term, and that does not exclude paradigmatic cases. The treatment of prisoners at Auschwitz and the lynching of African Americans are two such cases. A theory of dehumanization that does not apply to these does not deserve to be taken seriously.

Having explained, albeit briefly, what I think dehumanization is, I want to sharpen this by explaining what I think it is *not*. I want give you a sense of the conceptual landscape—the various, competing conceptions of dehumanization that are found in the scholarly literature, and give my reasons for thinking that my view of dehumanization is preferable to any and all of them. That is not to say that the alternatives are incorrect. People use the word "dehumanization" as a label for a range of different phenomena. Rather, my objective is to show why my account best comports with the four desiderata discussed above.

Dehumanization Is Not Just Derogation

Some people think that dehumanizing people is nothing more than thinking of them as substandard human beings. On this view, people can be thought of as human and yet be dehumanized. The philosopher Robin Jeshion adopts a version of this approach. She distinguishes between what she calls "weak" and "strong" psychological notions of dehumanization: "On the weak psychological notion, dehumanizing thought involves regarding others as having lesser standing along a moral dimension, as being unworthy of equal standing or full respect as persons. On the strong psychological notion, the dehumanizing form of thinking involves conceiving of others as creatures that are not human at all, often as creatures that are evil or a contaminating threat, and that need to be wiped out."[34]

When we dehumanize others in the first, weak sense we consider them to be defective human beings, but when we dehumanize them in the second, strong sense we exclude them from the human family altogether. Jeshion sees the weak and strong forms of dehumanization as lying along a continuum and adopts the term "dehumanization" for both to emphasize their continuity. "At the psychological level," she writes, "I think there is no really hard and fast demarcation between the two. Thinking of others as lesser humans slides far too naturally into thinking of them as subhuman."[35] In contrast, I reserve the term "dehumanization" for the strong, psychological sense. Jeshion also uses "dehumanization" in a derivative sense to refer to the actions that are prompted by dehumanizing forms of thought.

My conception of dehumanization is more fine-grained than Jeshion's, which sets it apart from other forms of derogation. Put differently, on my view dehumanization is a special form of derogation, and one that is especially toxic. I also hesitate to endorse Jeshion's notion of dehumanizing actions, because this does not differentiate dehumanizing attitudes from their effects (acts of violence or the use of animalistic slurs). Of course, I agree that there are close connections between dehumanization and other kinds of derogatory attitudes. As will become clear in the chapters to follow,

I think that there is a close and important relationship between regarding others as lesser human beings and regarding them as less-than-human beings. However, I also hold that we should be careful not to obscure or minimize the difference between these two kinds of attitudes.

Descriptions of the lynchings of Smith and Hose suggest that something more than merely derogatory attitudes toward Black people (dehumanization in Jeshion's weak sense) was involved. Although it is possible to perform such hideous acts without believing that the victims are not truly human, it is harder—at least for most of us—to do so. Conceiving of people as belonging to a different and inferior species liberates deadly aggression far more effectively than does merely regarding them as inferior human beings. And this, in my view, justifies setting dehumanization, as I conceive of it, apart from other, less radically derogatory attitudes.

Dehumanization Is Not Rhetorical

Dehumanization is not a way of speaking to or about others. To dehumanize someone is not the same as using animalistic slurs against them. Of course, people often express their dehumanizing attitudes by referring to others as animals, but, as I remarked in the previous section, it is important not to confuse the verbal expression of an attitude with the attitude itself.

The idea that dehumanization is a rhetorical practice is quite common. It is the idea that we dehumanize others by referring to them as less-than-human creatures. For example, the social psychologist Daniel Bar-Tal writes that dehumanization is "labeling a group as inhuman, either by using references to subhuman categories, for example, 'inferior' races and animals, or by referring to negatively valued superhuman creatures such as demons, monsters, and satans. In both cases, members of the delegitimized group are depicted as possessing inhuman traits."[36]

Common though it is, there are good reasons to reject this way of understanding dehumanization. If dehumanization is equated with certain kinds of speech—if dehumanization is nothing more than speaking to or about a person or group in a certain way—then although members of the White mobs that lynched Henry Smith and Sam Hose presumably thought of them as less than human, it was only by hurling slurs at these men that they dehumanized them. And if dehumanizing people is nothing more than calling them sub-human creatures, then the men who tortured Smith did not dehumanize him unless they also slurred him in a certain way. Further, if dehumanization is just a form of derogatory speech, then the man who hacked off Hose's penis and held it aloft to the cheering crowd did not at that moment dehumanize his victim if he did not also (at that very moment) speak of him in a derogatory manner.

Consider also the thousands of White spectators who did not soil their hands with blood but who looked on approvingly as these events were taking place, the women and men who delighted at the victims' screams and who inhaled the aroma of their burning flesh, the grocer who proudly displayed Hose's knuckles in his Atlanta shop, and the many, many others who experienced vicarious pleasure reading eyewitness accounts of the lynchings in newspapers or who listened excitedly to the gramophone recording of Smith's dying agonies. Should we say that these people did not dehumanize Smith and Hose unless they also called them animals? It seems obvious that if anything exemplifies dehumanization, these things do.

Animalistic Slurs Do Not Always Express Dehumanizing Attitudes

I have made the point that it is possible to dehumanize others without ever expressing this verbally. It is also true (and in fact, it is very common) to use animalistic slurs to characterize others without dehumanizing them. We are all familiar with insults like "pig" or "bitch," spoken in anger or contempt. People who use words like these to characterize others rarely believe that their targets are really less than human. They use these words to express their feelings about the person, or to hurt them, rather than to describe the other person as a subhuman entity. As Jeshion says, and I agree, slurs are dehumanizing only insofar as they encode dehumanizing thought.[37]

Sometimes animalistic language gets used strategically to induce dehumanizing attitudes in others. Consider dehumanizing political propaganda, a topic that I discuss in Chapters 9 and 10. Propagandists who paint verbal pictures of others as dangerous animals, or who represent them in graphic media as animals, do not have to believe that these people are really subhuman beings. Sometimes, even though they are aware that the members of some hated, feared, or despised group are as fully human as they themselves are, they try to get the consumers of their propaganda to think of these others as subhuman. For example, sometimes animalistic language is used to induce dehumanizing attitudes in soldiers, for the purpose of legitimating the act of killing. As one US veteran who confessed to committing wartime atrocities during the Vietnam War described it: "When you go into basic training you are taught that the Vietnamese are not people. You are taught they are gooks, and all you hear is 'gook, gook, gook, gook' . . . and once the military has got the idea implanted in your mind that these people are not humans, they are subhuman, it makes it a little bit easier to kill 'em. . . . All of them are considered to be subhuman."[38]

There are also examples of prosecuting attorneys characterizing defendants as animals to nudge juries toward a guilty verdict in death penalty cases. Prosecutor Michael Thompson told the jury during the sentencing phase of *State of Texas v. Kerry Max Cook* that what "separates us from . . . lower portions of [the] animal kingdom . . . is totally absent from the mind of Kerry Max Cook," and then went on to compare capital punishment in this case with the act of euthanizing an animal. "[I] have hunting dogs myself," he remarked, "occasionally something happens to that animal that you have no alternative but to put them to sleep. That is a situation in this case." The defendant, Cook, was convicted but ultimately exonerated after being incarcerated for forty years, twenty of which were spent on death row.[39] For reasons that will soon become clear, this prosecutorial strategy is probably most effective when there is also a racial element at work.

These considerations show that you cannot just "read off" dehumanizing attitudes from the words that people use. If you think that this can be done, then you misunderstand the relation between dehumanization and derogatory language by committing a category mistake. The term "category mistake" was coined by British philosopher Gilbert Ryle for the error of attributing a characteristic to a thing that things of that kind cannot have. For example, I would be committing a category mistake if I were to say that Thursdays are fuchsia, or that the number 37 paid me a visit last night, because days of the week are not the kinds of things that can be colored and numbers are not the kinds of things that can occupy spatiotemporal locations.[40] These are very obvious examples, but many category mistakes are more subtle. When people assume too tight a connection between dehumanization and slurs, they commit the category mistake of confusing a cause with its effects. Suppose you were to mistake the symptoms of a cold—runny nose, sore throat, headache, and so on—for the cold itself. You would be wrong if you thought of a cold as nothing but a bundle of symptoms. Cold symptoms do not *constitute* a cold. They do not make it the case that one has a cold. What makes that case is being infected with a rhinovirus, and the unpleasant symptoms—the sore throat, stuffy nose, and so on—are *consequences* of the illness rather than the illness itself. Anyone who thought that having a cold is nothing but having a bundle of cold symptoms would be making the same kind mistake as a person who thinks that using animalistic slurs makes it the case that one dehumanizes people. The use of animalistic slurs is often a "symptom" or consequence of dehumanization, but it is not dehumanization itself. And just as a cold can be asymptomatic (one can be infected with a rhinovirus without experiencing any of the common cold symptoms), it is possible to have dehumanizing beliefs about others without ever saying that they are subhuman animals.

All that being said, the way that people speak about others is a very important indicator of their beliefs about them. We attribute beliefs, desires, and other mental states to people on the basis of what they say, on the assumption that what people say more often than not expresses what is going on in their minds. That is why the way that people talk about others—specifically, their implicit or explicit characterization of those others as subhuman creatures—can reveal dehumanizing attitudes. In other words, we "diagnose" dehumanization by interpreting their verbal "symptoms," just as we infer that someone has a rhinovirus infection when we find that they have a sore throat and runny nose. These symptoms are not diagnostically foolproof, but they are diagnostically important, and this is no less true of the use of animalistic slurs to diagnose the presence of dehumanization. The signs and symptoms of dehumanization, which include both the words that people utter and their nonverbal behavior, help us make inferences about dehumanizing attitudes, even though (as when diagnosing an illness) these inferences are fallible. In both cases, the more information one has at one's disposal, the more securely one's conclusions will be grounded.

The gap between dehumanizing attitudes and their verbal expression—the fact that either can be present in the absence of the other—has very important methodological ramifications for a theory of dehumanization. It implies that a good theory of dehumanization should enable one to distinguish between cases in which a person's speech truly indicates that they think of others as less than human and cases where their speech does not really express an underlying dehumanizing attitude. And a good theory of dehumanization should also have the resources to detect "asymptomatic" forms of dehumanization—that is, cases where dehumanizing attitudes are betrayed by subtle and indirect cues rather than being explicitly embodied in speech or action. I know that this sounds like a very tall, and perhaps unrealistic, order. But as this book proceeds, I am going to do my best to show that it is attainable.

Dehumanization Is Not Just Metaphorical

Sometimes we think of people figuratively as nonhuman animals. For instance, if you think of someone who disgusts you as a pig, you are probably not thinking that they are literally a pig. Instead, you are probably thinking that this person has despicable characteristics that are conventionally associated with pigs, such as gluttony, dirtiness, or selfishness. The use of animal imagery to represent human characteristics is deeply ingrained in our artistic and literary traditions, and in ordinary habits of mind.

Because we are accustomed to thinking of people as animals metaphorically, it is easy to assume that dehumanizing attitudes are metaphorical too. Put differently, when people dehumanize others, they do not really think of them as subhuman animals. Instead, they think of them as fully human beings with subhuman-like characteristics.

I reject this view. I believe that that when people dehumanize others, they really do conceive of them as subhumans, and that when these dehumanizing attitudes are expressed in speech, they are meant to be literally descriptive. When Nazis conceived of Jews as vermin, and when White supremacists thought of Africans as apes, they really meant that Jews and Africans are less than human.

I am aware that this may sound crazy to you. Nazis and White supremacists were and are, for the most part, sane human beings. How could any sane person mistake a human being for a rat or an ape? Rats are small, furry, four-legged rodents with bare tails, whereas *Homo sapiens* are much larger, furless, two-legged, tailless primates. So the notion that a cognitively intact human being could believe that Jewish humans are really creatures like rats or that Black humans are really creatures like apes seems to make no sense at all.

If you think that this is crazy, you have my sympathies. The whole idea does seem very strange. In the chapters to follow, I will do my best to dispel the aura of implausibility surrounding the seemingly outrageous idea that human beings can conceive of other human beings as creatures that are less than human.

Dehumanization Is Not Objectification

Some writers on dehumanization think of it as a way of *treating* others rather than, as I do, something that goes on inside the dehumanizer's head. On this view, to dehumanize someone is to treat them in a degrading way. Degrading treatment includes targeting them with slurs, but also a lot more. Broadly speaking, degrading— and thus, dehumanizing—treatment has the aim of harming other human beings. But this cannot include just any harm, because that would make dehumanization include too much, and make "dehumanization" just a synonym for bad behavior. Advocates of this conception of dehumanization hold that only some harmful behaviors are dehumanizing ones, and they try to spell out the ways in which specifically dehumanizing behavior can be distinguished from harmful behavior in general.

The most common strategy for doing this is to equate dehumanization with what is called "objectification." The roots of the idea of objectification are in Immanuel Kant's moral philosophy. Kant asserted that there is something about human beings that sets them apart, morally, from all nonhuman entities. He claimed that nonhuman things have value only as "means," by which he meant that their value lies solely in the uses to which they can be put. In contrast, he believed that we humans have intrinsic value. We are special because have value in and of ourselves. Our value is built into the kind of beings that we are, rather than in the uses to which we can be put.

With these assumptions under his belt, Kant argued that treating human beings in purely instrumental ways—that is, valuing them only insofar as they can provide things for us—amounts to treating them in an object-like way, and thus "objectifying" them.

Although the term "objectification," as used in contemporary philosophy, dates from long after Kant's death, it is clear that he had something very much like it in mind.[41] For example, he claimed in his 1797 *Doctrine of Right* that when a person has sex for pleasure he "makes himself into a thing, which conflicts with the right of humanity in his own person."[42] To Kant recreational sex was deeply degrading and immoral, because it involves using one's partner merely as a means for erotic enjoyment.

To properly understand the Kantian notion of objectification, it is important to understand his notion of what an "object" is. In the Kantian framework, the category of objects includes both inanimate things and nonhuman animals. Most of us would balk at the idea that a beloved dog falls into the same moral category as, say, an ironing board. Not so Kant, who claimed that human beings are special because they are capable of reflecting on themselves, a feature of the human mind that "raises him [that is, the human being] infinitely above all the other beings on earth," and this makes human beings "altogether different in rank and dignity from things, such as irrational animals, with which one may deal and dispose at one's discretion."[43]

In the late twentieth century, feminist thinkers adopted the notion of objectification to cast light on women's sexual exploitation at the hands of men, which they often refer to as "sexual objectification." "To be sexually objectified," wrote Catherine MacKinnon, "means having a social meaning imposed on your being that defines you as to be sexually used . . . and then using you that way." When they are sexually objectified, women are, in the words of the philosopher Rae Langton, "treated as merely bodies, as merely sensory appearances, as not free, as items that can be possessed, as items whose value is merely instrumental."[44]

Objectification is not just a psychological attitude. It is not just a way of thinking about others, because when we objectify others, we *use* them. Objectification is right out there in the world, embodied in behaviors, institutions, norms, and representations in the mass media. As MacKinnon pointedly observes, "Objectification is different from stereotyping, which acts as though it is all in the head. . . . The problem goes a great deal deeper than illusion or delusion. Masks become personas become people, socially, especially when they are enforced."

The connection between objectification and dehumanization is mostly implicit in feminist writings, and when dehumanization is mentioned explicitly it is usually only in passing. There are, however, some exceptions. One of these is MacKinnon's essay "Are Women Human?," in which she alludes to social practices that she believes underpin a socially constructed subhuman status of women:

If women were human, would we be a cash crop shipped from Thailand in containers into New York's brothels? Would we be sexual and reproductive slaves? Would we be bred, worked without pay our whole lives, burned when our dowry money wasn't enough or when men tired of us, starved as widows when our husbands died (if we survived his funeral pyre), sold for sex because we are not valued for anything else? Would we be sold into marriage to priests to atone for our family's sins or to improve our family's earthly prospects? Would we, when allowed to work for pay, be made to work at the most menial jobs and exploited at barely starvation level? Would our genitals be sliced out to "cleanse" us (our body parts are dirt?), to control us, to mark us and define our cultures? Would we be trafficked as things for sexual use and entertainment worldwide in whatever form current technology makes possible? Would we be kept from learning to read and write?[45]

Clearly, the scope of the concept of sexual objectification is a lot narrower than the scope of concept of dehumanization. But what can we say about the relation between dehumanization and objectification per se? Sexual objectification is a special case of objectification, so if objectification is a kind of dehumanization, sexual objectification is a more circumscribed variety of dehumanization.

Because I regard dehumanization as a state of mind rather than as a way of treating people, I do not think that objectification—be it either sexual or nonsexual—should be identified with dehumanization. It is possible to dehumanize a person without treating them as an object, and it is also possible to treat a person as an object without dehumanizing them. In fact, there are putative examples of objectification that are remote from anything that could reasonably be characterized as dehumanization. One of these is the treatment of the human body in medical contexts, especially surgery.[46] Surgeons treat their patients as flesh-and-blood machines that need fixing, but this is far removed from thinking of them as dangerous or despicable animals. If you think that Henry Smith and Sam Hose were dehumanized, it is quite a stretch to include a patient undergoing open heart surgery under the same conceptual umbrella. And as Martha Nussbaum observes, we can even affectionately objectify our loved ones: "If I am lying around with my lover on the bed and use his stomach as a pillow there seems to be nothing at all baneful about this, provided that I do so with his consent (or, if he is asleep, with a reasonable belief that he would not mind), and without causing him pain, provided as well, that I do so in the context of a relationship in which he is generally treated as more than a pillow."[47]

The idea of affectionately dehumanizing someone is incomprehensible, so objectification and dehumanization cannot be the same thing.[48] And even if this were not the case, equating dehumanization with treating others as objects makes nonsense of the claim that Henry Smith and Same Hose were dehumanized. They were not treated as objects. Smith was, ironically enough, tortured and executed on a platform emblazoned with the word "Justice"—but notions of justice, however misappropriated, are simply irrelevant to the treatment of objects. You cannot punish a stone or wreak vengeance on a tree.

Dehumanization Is Not Degrading Treatment

Treating others like objects is not the only way to treat them badly. Smith and Hose were subjected to the most horrific abuse imaginable, but they were not treated as objects. Some scholars think of dehumanization as bad or "inhumane" treatment that is not restricted to objectification. Using the term "bestialization" rather than "dehumanization," legal and political philosopher Jeremy Waldron sets out this idea as follows:

The "higher than the animals" sense of human dignity gives us a natural sense of "degrading treatment': it is treatment that is more fit for an animal than for a human, treatment of a person as though he were an animal, as though he were reduced from the high equal status of *human* to mere animality. It can be treatment that is insufficiently sensitive to the differences between humans and animals, the differences in virtue of which humans are supposed to have special status. So for example a human is degraded by being bred like an animal, used as a beast of burden, beaten like an animal, herded like an animal, treated as though he did not have language, reason or understanding, or any power of self-control. Or it could include treating a person as though he did not have any religious life or sense of religious obligation, or as though the human (or *this* human) were one of those animals who are indifferent to separation from offspring or mate. It might also include cases of post-mortem ill-treatment: eating human flesh, for example, or failing to properly bury a human, or dragging a corpse.[49]

Leaving aside the dubious implicit claim that these are appropriate ways to treat nonhuman animals, this notion of dehumanization is problematic. It is certainly possible to engage in violent, harmful, or degrading behavior toward others without denying their humanity, and the most skilled torturers are effective because they are exquisitely sensitive to what causes human beings the greatest agony.[50]

It is also possible to think of others as less than human without ever treating them cruelly. It is beyond dispute that people who are abused or brutally oppressed are very often dehumanized, but it is important to correctly understand the relationship between the dehumanization and the abuse. The act of dehumanizing others facilitates atrocities. It stands to these atrocities as cause stands to effect and, because causes are by definition distinct from their effects, dehumanization cannot be identified with the atrocities themselves and their harmful effects.

If dehumanization is solely a matter of how people are treated, then this rules out the principle that one can have dehumanizing beliefs that do not translate into action. But think again of the thousands of people who observed Henry Smith being lynched and who thought of him as less than human, as well as the countless others who saw him as a black beast and who relished reading horrific newspaper reports of the lynching. These people did not treat Smith in any way at all, as they had no contact with him, and yet it is more than reasonable to say that they dehumanized him.

Dehumanization Is Not Conceiving of Others as Inanimate Objects

One of Australian psychologist Nick Haslam's notions of dehumanization bears some relation to feminist conceptions of objectification. Haslam proposes that there are two kinds of dehumanization. One of them is the act of thinking of others as lacking those characteristics that distinguish human beings from other animals. Haslam calls this "animalistic dehumanization." The other is thinking of others as lacking characteristics that distinguish human beings from inanimate objects. He calls this "mechanistic dehumanization." When people are mechanistically dehumanized, Haslam argues, they are seen as inert, cold, rigid, fungible, and lacking in agency, and therefore as object- or robot-like.[51]

Although there is clearly some connection between this idea of dehumanization and the notion of sexual objectification, there are also some striking differences. Mechanistic dehumanization is all about how we conceive of others, whereas sexual objectification pertains to how we treat others. Also, the idea of an "object" is quite different in the two cases. In Haslam's theory, the mechanistically dehumanized person lacks characteristics associated with animacy. But the sexually objectified person is not supposed to lack animacy. Rather, she is seen as being a nonsubject (even sex robots are supposed to simulate animacy). The sexually objectified person may be seen as lacking agency, as Haslam's mechanistically dehumanized people are, and perhaps as inert, but certainly not as cold or rigid.

Even though Haslam and I both conceive of dehumanization as a kind of mental state, his notion of animalistic dehumanization is not the same as mine either. I have defined dehumanization as conceiving of others as subhuman creatures. This definition does not say anything about the manifest attributes of dehumanized people. It does not say that dehumanizing others is the same thing as seeing them as possessing traits that are associated with subhuman creatures, as Haslam's definition of animalistic dehumanization does. My account is about how we *categorize* people, rather than about their observable characteristics—their deep nature rather than their observable phenotypes. This may sound like a trivial point—a distinction without a corresponding difference—but it is actually quite important. I will explain why in considerable detail later on in this book. For now, I will merely note that what we take a thing to really be does not necessarily correspond to how it appears to us. In other words, human psychology allows that the appearance of a thing does not have to correspond to what it really is. In Chapter 2, I will argue that dehumanization is not primarily a matter of attributing subhuman *traits* to a person, as Haslam believes. Instead, it is about attributing a subhuman *essence* to them.

Dehumanization Is Not a Kind of Harm

Another idea is that we dehumanize others by subjecting them to treatment that harms them by damaging or obliterating their distinctively human characteristics. This perspective is prominent among feminist writers that equate dehumanization. They point out that sexual objectification / dehumanization usually injures the women who are its targets. For example, Andrea Dworkin, who implicitly links objectification with dehumanization, explains: "When objectification occurs, a person is depersonalized, so that no individuality or integrity is available socially or in what is an extremely circumscribed privacy. Objectification is an injury right at the heart of discrimination: those who can be used as if they are not fully human are no longer fully human in social terms; their humanity is hurt by being diminished."[52]

Likewise, Linda LeMoncheck, whose book *The Dehumanization of Women: Treating Persons as Sex Objects* explicitly equates objectification with dehumanization, describes dehumanization as treating a person in ways that prevent the development of, diminish, or snuff out their paradigmatically human characteristics. She writes that the dehumanized person "is effectively reduced to realizing only those capacities that things, bodies, or animals have. Thus, one can beat others to the point of irrationality, or drug or hypnotize persons so that they are no longer self-aware or self-determining."[53] On this view, dehumanization is a kind of harm, and acts that bring about these kinds of injuries are dehumanizing acts.[54] This is distinct from the more commonplace idea view that dehumanization is often harmful. To say that dehumanization is harmful is to say that it causes harm (that is, that harm is one of its effects). But as I have underscored several times already, causes and their effects are, by definition, distinct from one another, so saying that dehumanization causes harm is implicitly saying that it is not the same thing as the harm that it causes. But rather than claiming that dehumanization *causes* harm, LeMoncheck has it that dehumanization is *a kind of* harm. Dehumanization is, so to speak, made out of harm.

Mari Mikkola is the philosopher who has most thoroughly developed the notion of dehumanization as harm. She argues, "An act or a treatment is dehumanizing if and only if it is an indefensible setback to some of our legitimate human interests, where this setback constitutes a moral injury."[55] For Mikkola, "human interests" are those factors that contribute to the well-being of members of our species. Not all such setbacks are indefensible. Imprisoning a serial rapist is certainly a setback to his legitimate human interests (because freedom from imprisonment is important for human well-being), but it is a justified setback. To be morally injurious, a setback has got to "damage the realization and acknowledgment of the person's value." Unlike many other feminist philosophers, Mikkola does not equate dehumanization with objectification. She argues that it is an open question whether objectification is always a bad thing (see my remarks in the section on objectification above), but dehumanization is by definition morally impermissible.

Mikkola's analysis of dehumanization differs from my account in two key respects. First—and very importantly—Mikkola approaches dehumanization from an ethical rather than an empirical perspective. Her account turns on evaluative terms such as "indefensible setbacks," "legitimate human interests," and "moral injury," whereas my approach is psychological and mainly descriptive. A wide range of processes, not just the psychological ones that I describe as "dehumanization," might underwrite the sorts of phenomena that count as dehumanization in Mikkola's framework. So, for her, the psychological specifics are irrelevant to whether or not an act counts as dehumanization, whereas for me, whether or not something counts as an instance of dehumanization is entirely a matter of its psychological specifics.

Second, as I have already discussed, I prefer a view that distinguishes dehumanizing attitudes from dehumanizing actions. Consequently, I do not see dehumanization as requiring the commission of injurious acts. There is no doubt that dehumanization, in my sense, very often facilitates acts that bring about dehumanization in Mikkola's sense (for example, some White Americans' dehumanizing belief that Black men are predatory beasts contributed to the lynching of Henry Smith and Sam Hose, which was dehumanizing in Mikkola's sense). But conceiving of Black men as dangerous animals was not a necessary condition for terrorizing, torturing, and murdering them, and these behaviors could occur in the absence of this belief. The belief was not sufficient for the practice either. There must have been very many White people (then as now) who harbored dehumanizing beliefs about Black people without ever doing violence to them.

Dehumanization Is Not Conceiving of Others as Mindless or Less Human Than Oneself

Psychologists Nicholas Epley and Adam Waytz describe dehumanization as a deformation of "mind perception" (a term borrowed from the psychologist Daniel Wegner).[56] Epley and Waytz write, "The central feature of all existing psychological accounts is a failure to attribute a mind to other humans, treating others as if they lacked the capacity for higher order reasoning or conscious awareness and experience. . . . Dehumanized others lack the capacity to think—like animals—or to feel—like objects."[57] As they see it, we dehumanize others to the extent that we regard them as possessing "lesser minds."[58] It is easy to conflate this take on the nature of dehumanization with the notion of objectification. After all, inanimate objects are mindless, and it is no doubt true that some people think of objectification as a kind of attitude. But in the canonical feminist literature, objectification is described as a social and political phenomenon rather than as a psychological one. Objectification is cemented into social institutions, norms, and practices. That is not to say that these theorists deny psychology any role in the objectifying process, only that they insist that objectification is not something mental. The fact that Epley and Waytz think of dehumanization as something that is in the head rather than out there in the world sets them apart from these objectification theorists.

Although I also conceive of dehumanization as a kind of psychological state, I do not accept the view of dehumanization as mind denial. One reason is that does not fit with paradigmatic cases of dehumanization. Consider the Nazi dehumanization of Jewish people. During the Third Reich, German ideologues clearly and explicitly characterized Jews as monstrous, subhuman beings. But the Nazis did not think of Jews as in any way mentally handicapped. Quite the opposite: they considered them to be diabolically intelligent. Adolf Eichmann, one of the prime architects of the Holocaust, claimed that Jews possess "the most cunning intellect of all the human intellects alive today" and are "intellectually superior to us."[59]

Another reason why I cannot accept the mind-denial account is that it involves the idea that when we dehumanize others we think of them as being less human than ourselves rather than as beings that are less than human. This might seem like a trivial difference, but in fact it is a crucial one. There is qualitative difference between placing others categorically outside the realm of the human and regarding them as inferior human beings. Thinking of someone as less human than oneself requires a conception of humanness as something that one can have more or less of, rather than something that one either has or does not have, completely, with no middle ground in between.

Nicholas Haslam—the psychologist mentioned earlier who has written most extensively about dehumanization—and Jacques-Philip Leyens, who pioneered the study of "infrahumanization" (roughly, implicit dehumanization), both believe that we naturally think of humanness as something that a being can have more or less of. In fact, the idea that there are degrees of humanness is ubiquitous and goes virtually unquestioned in the psychological literature on dehumanization. As the psychologist Susan Fiske puts it, "Recognizing or denying another's humanity *varies by degrees*, along simple, predictable, and apparently universal dimensions" (emphasis added).[60] In contrast, I do not think that we conceive of humanness in this way. Instead, I think that we tend to conceive of others as either fully human or as not human at all. I will unpack and justify this claim later on, once I have laid down some crucial conceptual and theoretical foundations.

Dehumanized People Need Not Be Considered as Globally Inferior

Thinking of others as subhuman does not entail thinking of them as inferior in every respect. In fact, dehumanizers often believe that those whom they dehumanize have physical or mental powers that are superior to their own, as we saw in the case of Adolf Eichmann. A glance at the stereotypes that were historically imposed on oppressed groups leaves no room for doubt that members of dehumanized populations are often considered to be stronger, faster, less sensitive to pain, more sexually voracious, more violent, more ambitious, or more intelligent than their oppressors. They may be seen as "superpredators" (African Americans), "bloodthirsty savages" (Native Americans), or members of a powerful conspiracy intent on destroying the Aryan race (Jews). Even today, Black patients are often given less pain medication than their White counterparts for the same complaints, perhaps because of the entrenched stereotype that Black people are relatively insensitive to pain. Whites often see and treat Black children as older than they actually are, and imagine that Black men are larger and more physically formidable than they actually are.[61] Sometimes dehumanized people are even thought to possess supernatural powers. We see this in medieval Christian beliefs about Jews, who supposedly consorted with the devil and were practitioners of the black arts. The general idea was mentioned in one of the earliest references to dehumanization as a psychological phenomenon. The philosopher David Hume remarked in his 1739 *Treatise of Human Nature:* "If the general of our enemies be successful, 'tis with difficulty we allow him the figure and character of a man. He is a sorcerer: He has a communication with daemons; as is reported of Oliver Cromwell, and the Duke of Luxembourg: He is bloody-minded, and takes a pleasure in death and destruction."[62]

Adam Waytz and his colleagues Kelly Marie Hoffman and Sophie Trawalter coined the term "superhumanization bias" for the tendency for dehumanizers to attribute superpowers to the people they dehumanize. They define superhumanization as "the representation of others as possessing mental and physical qualities that are supernatural (transcending the laws of nature), extrasensory (transcending the bounds of normal human perception), and magical (influencing or manipulating the natural world through symbolic or ritualistic means)."[63] Others, such as the political scientist Daniel Jonah Goldhagen, reserve the term "demonization" for a pattern of dehumanization in which the feared and hated others are "deemed inhuman creatures, willfully malevolent, a Christian secular incarnation of the devil or his minions."[64]

Dehumanization Is Not Necessary for Committing Atrocities

The most important reason why we need to understand how dehumanization works is its role in facilitating violence and its contribution to indifference to the suffering of the victims of violence.

There is a plethora of examples speaking to the relationship between dehumanization and violence. For example, the seventeenth-century Anglican clergyman Morgan Godwyn wrote that colonial slaveholders ranked their African slaves as subhuman animals and treated them accordingly—by which he meant the slaveholders treated their slaves in ways that would be morally impermissible for the treatment of human beings but permissible for the treatment of livestock. Much the same idea was expressed more than two centuries later by William J. Northen, governor of Georgia between 1890 and 1894, when he wrote that "During my recent canvass of the State, in the interest of law and order I was amazed to find scores, and hundreds of men, who believed the negro to be a brute . . . and his slaughter nothing more than the killing of a dog."[65]

The claim that dehumanization fosters violence is sensible. But some people go further, and make a far stronger claim. They say that dehumanization has got to be in place in order for the most horrific forms of violence to occur, or that dehumanization is enough to spark horrific acts of violence. I do not agree with this. It is certainly possible for people to perform hideous acts of cruelty against others without dehumanizing them. And it is likewise possible for people to dehumanize others without doing violence to them. History supports both of these claims.

From the late twentieth century onward, psychologists such as Herbert Kelman and Albert Bandura explained the connection between dehumanization and violence by proposing that dehumanization fosters "moral disengagement," which makes it permissible to commit acts of violence against those whom we regard as subhuman.[66] However, unlike most dehumanization theorists who have addressed this topic, I do not believe that moral disengagement is the mechanism linking dehumanization with atrocity. In fact, I think that the precise opposite is true. Dehumanization fosters violence precisely because it fans the flames of an immensely destructive kind of moral engagement (I will have much more to say about this in Chapter 8).

Now, having surveyed the conceptual territory and contrasted my preferred conception of dehumanization with its main competitors, I am positioned to argue why we should accept that dehumanization, as I describe it, really does exist. That is the mission of Chapter 2.

CHAPTER TWO

Dehumanization Is Real

You who are reading these words right now may not have any difficulty accepting that psychologically intact human beings (as contrasted with those who suffer from psychotic delusions or those described as "sociopaths") are able to think of other human beings as subhuman. But there are many people who have a hard time accepting that this is a fact. It sounds so strange to them, so inconsistent with their commonsense assumptions of how human minds work, that they are apt to dismiss it as impossible. Perhaps you are such a disbeliever. This would be understandable. So far, I have only explained to you what I take dehumanization to be; I have not given you compelling reasons to accept that it ever occurs.

In this chapter I aim to explain why any reasonable person should accept that dehumanization, in the precise sense that I have specified, at least *sometimes* occurs. That it sometimes occurs shows that dehumanization cannot be ruled out on the grounds of its impossibility, because if something is impossible, it cannot occur even once. Of course, showing that dehumanization sometimes occurs says nothing about how frequently it occurs. It might be very rare, or very common, or something in between. However, if dehumanization at least sometimes occurs, it follows that we should open our minds to the possibility that anything that looks like a case of dehumanization (for example, the characterizations of Black men as beasts that I described in Chapter 1) may really be a case of dehumanization.

Passing Strange

In her book *Saracens, Demons, and Jews: Making Monsters in Medieval Art,* art historian Debra Higgs Strickland looks at how medieval European Christians represented those whom they feared or despised as monsters: Jews, Muslims, Tatars, and Black Africans. She shows that European artists represented the monstrousness of these people by endowing them with physical deformities or observable animalistic or demonic traits. Strickland discusses a late thirteenth-century bestiary's depiction of the archetypal Jew as a monster:

> The creature in question is a manticore, described in the text as a ferocious, blood-red, high-jumping, man-eating creature with the face of a man, the body of a lion, and a hissing voice. What is notable about . . . the manticore, however, is his pointed Phrygian hat,[1] grotesque Jewish profile, and long beard. The figure is shown with the remains of a human leg clenched tightly in its three rows of teeth, forming a menacing grimace not unlike those of Christ-torturing Jews in passion imagery. . . . The image is otherwise rich in contemporary associations: not only does it suggest a conflation of monstrosity and barbarity as in other "Jewish monster" images, it capitalizes on the association already established in medieval art between the Jews and the red color of infamy. Furthermore, the manticore's cannibalism easily translates into a reference to contemporary ritual murder accusations.[2]

Christians were well aware that Jews did not possess the physical characteristics of manticores. They did not have lions' bodies or multiple rows of teeth (although they were sometimes supposed to possess various animalistic attributes, such as horns and a tail, and were thought to exude a foul odor).[3] This is why scholars most often interpret representations of Jews as monsters or demons in medieval art as symbols of sinfulness and evil. However, Strickland argues that their monstrous characteristics were meant to represent not merely their degenerate and sinful character, but also their inner subhumanity.

Why think that? We know that the Jewish infidel was, for many Christians, "considered to be the highest of animals but nevertheless subhuman."[4] Jews were thought to be demonic—in a literal rather than merely a figurative sense. "That is," observes Strickland, "not only do the Jews and demons physically resemble each other. . . . they are cut from the same cloth," by which she presumably means they are the same kind of subhuman entity.[5] We see this idea expressed in the writing of Peter the Venerable, an influential thirteenth-century bishop, whose tract *Against the Inveterate Obduracy of the Jews* seethes with dehumanizing, anti-Semitic rhetoric. The bishop opined in this text, "Really I doubt whether a Jew can be human."[6]

It is easy to convey the idea of Jewish subhumanity in words. It took Peter the Venerable only nine of them. But how do you convey the idea that Jews are less than human using painted or sculpted images, which were the main media of anti-Semitic propaganda for the illiterate medieval? Images capture only the outward appearances of things, so the idea of inner subhumanity must be portrayed as outer subhumanity—hence the medieval depictions of Jews and other racialized infidels as having monstrous, demonic, or deformed bodies. The same applies to visual propaganda produced in recent times, which encourages the dehumanization national, racial, or ethnic groups by endowing them with animalistic or demonic physical characteristics.[7] However, some medieval artists used a technique that allowed them to get around this constraint, and to hint at the idea that although the infidels might look like real human beings, this appearance is deceptive. They represented dehumanized others as visually indistinguishable from ordinary human beings, while including subtle hints, the medieval equivalent of dog whistles, indicating that, despite appearances, these infidel others are really subhuman monsters. Strickland calls these "crypto-monsters." A crypto-monster is, in her words, "a monster that does not look like one, who visually passes for an ordinary human being."[8] For example, in an eleventh-century text entitled *Marvels of the East*, which is concerned with the "monstrous races" (subhuman beings that were reputed to live in the most far-flung and inhospitable regions of the earth), there is an illustration of two Ethiopians engaged in conversation. They are pictured as having light-colored skin and normal human proportions, all of which Europeans would have found congenial. Dark skin and physical deformity were, during the Middle Ages, cliché visual markers of monstrosity. But here, as elsewhere, we have an image of beings that are clearly supposed to be subhuman (they are members of a "monstrous race") but who do not display stereotypical subhuman characteristics. Only their loincloths and the wild landscape behind them hint their monstrous status.[9] The lesson to be learned from this illustration, and others like it, is that to the medieval mind (and, I will argue, the modern mind as well) one can be a monster without looking like one. One can be inwardly subhuman while appearing outwardly human.

The idea of Jewish subhumanity goes back at least to the thirteenth century, and it has persisted across the centuries up to the present (I will discuss this in detail in Chapter 10). The idea that Jews are members of an alien species was a repetitive theme in the burgeoning anti-Semitic literature of the late nineteenth century. Theodor Fritsch, a prominent and virulently Judeophobic journalist and publisher of the day, wrote in 1884 that he could see "no trace of any real human trait" in the Jew, and that there is "a clear distinction between human beings and the Jew."[10] Likewise, the philosopher Ludwig Klages described his "discovery" that "the Jew is not a human being at all."[11] The view of the Jew as *fundamentally* other ruled out the possibility of Jews assimilating into Christian civilization. Short of divine intervention, Jews could not be transubstantiated into human beings, any more than Black people could choose to become White.[12]

The impression that there was a "Jewish problem" that could not be solved by ordinary means was already well established by the 1920s, when the National Socialist Party coalesced out of various racist and nationalist elements in German society. The Nazis greatly amplified this simmering attitude, with Hitler taking the lead. "As early as May, 1923," writes German historian Joachim Fest, "during a speech in the Krone Circus, Hitler had cried out, 'The Jews are undoubtedly a race, but not human. . . .' But when he began organizing his many scraps of ideas and feelings into something resembling a coherent system, they took on a different cast. Henceforth, when he denied that the Jews were human, it was not just the ranting of a demagogue but deadly earnest and fanatical belief."[13]

Jews were often seen as counterfeit humans. This idea was concisely expressed in the German proverb "Yes the Jew has the form of the human / However it lacks the human's inner being," which was transformed by the distinguished and influential jurist and political philosopher Carl Schmitt in 1933 into the Nazi slogan "Not every being with a human face is human" and repeated endlessly in Nazi propaganda thereafter.[14] Schmitt and his ilk characterized Jews as cosmetically human. On the inside, where it really matters, they were something other.

Black Beasts

We discover a very similar pattern of thinking when examining the history of White people's attitudes toward Black people. I showed in Chapter 1, using the examples of two nineteenth-century lynchings, how some White Americans characterized Black people as sub-human animals. But the question remains: Did these people *really* think that Black people were subhuman animals—livestock or pets when enslaved, predatory beasts when freed—or was their use of animalistic slurs just a degrading way of speaking about them? This question does not only pertain to White people's denigration of Black people. It concerns every case of ostensible dehumanization.

There is extensive historical documentation, accumulated over centuries, of people describing other people as less than human. Despite this, some historians find it difficult to believe that these descriptions were intended literally. In part, this skeptical attitude has to do with an inconsistency. Those who describe others as sub-human also often treat them in ways that are relevant only to human beings. For example, dehumanized people are often held to be mor-ally responsible for their actions. They are punished, often very cruelly, for moral infractions that they are accused of committing. But we don't regard nonhuman animals as moral agents. Only human beings are regarded as moral agents. That status is reserved for human beings. And dehumanizers often take pains to humiliate their targets, whom they also describe as vermin. But lice and rats are not the sorts of beings that can be humiliated. So (the reasoning goes), if people seem to believe that others are less than human but treat them in ways that are appropriate only to human beings, this must show that they do not *really* believe that these others are subhuman.

This line of reasoning is often found in the literature on the en-slavement and oppression of Black people. For example, Win-throp D. Jordan devotes a section of his important book *White over Black* to a discussion of seventeenth- and eighteenth-century Eu-ropean colonists' descriptions of Africans as soulless, subhuman brutes. But after laying this out, he goes on to assert, seemingly in stark contradiction to the evidence that he presents, that:

American colonials no more thought Negroes were beasts than did European scientists and missionaries; if they had really thought so they would have sternly punished miscegenation for what it would have been—buggery. Yet the charge that White men treated Negroes as beasts was entirely justified if not taken literally. Egalitarian defenders of the Negro were laying bare an inherent tendency of slavery with the only terms they knew how to employ. It was recognition of this tendency which moved Samuel Sewall to try (unsuccessfully) "to prevent Indians and Negros being Rated with horses and hogs" by the Massachusetts legislature.[15]

In Jordan's view, references to Africans as mere animals must have been intended metaphorically rather than literally. It couldn't have been true that colonists thought of slaves as subhuman because "even in the plantations, the Negro walked and hoed and talked and propagated like other men. No matter how much slavery degraded the Negro, every daily event in the lives and relationships of Negros and White men indicated undeniably that the Negro was a human being. White men feared their slaves' desires for freedom, they talked with their Negroes, and they slept with them. These were human relationships continually driving home the common humanity of all."[16]

The historian C. L. R. James seems to be making a similar point in his book on the Haitian Revolution, *The Black Jacobins:*

The difficulty was that though one could trap them like animals, transport them in pens, work them alongside an ass or a horse and beat both with the same stick, stable them and starve them, they remained, despite their black skins and curly hair, quite invincibly human beings; with the intelligence and resentments of human beings. To cow them into the necessary docility and acceptance necessitated a regime of calculated brutality and terrorism, and it is this that explains the unusual spectacle of property-owners apparently careless of preserving their property: they had first to ensure their own safety.[17]

Jordan found it so difficult to accept that White colonists really did consider enslaved people to be subhuman that he did not give other, contrary, information enough evidential weight. Just a few pages after the passage just quoted, James mentions an eighteenth-century memoir that characterized Black slaves as only half-human.[18] And although it is certainly true that, as Jordan says, opponents of slavery held that Africans were human beings who were treated as livestock, this is irrelevant to the question of whether the slaveholders, as well as other Whites who were friendly to that institution, considered Black people to be soulless beasts. The historical evidence that many of them thought this is overwhelming—so overwhelming that Jordan has difficulty maintaining his own skeptical position, which leads him to contradict his own thesis when he states,

> The discouragingly expensive mortality among the Negroes, especially in the West Indies and also in the rice swamps in South Carolina, tended to make Negroes seem almost non-human. Even in an age thoroughly accustomed to the hovering omnipresence of early death, the enormous toll of Negro life must have caused many White men to withdraw in silent horror, to refuse to admit identity with a people that they were methodically slaughtering year after year. The cruelties of slavery inevitably produced a sense of disassociation. To the horrified witness of a scene of torture, the victim becomes a "poor devil," a "mangled creature." He is no longer a man. He can no longer be human because to credit him with one's own human attributes would be too horrible.[19]

The tension between humanity and subhumanity is plentifully evident in racist writings about Black people. Often, White supremacist writings refer to Blacks both as men and as beasts, sometimes in the space of a single sentence. For example, Hegel characterized the African as an "animal man," a man who exists "in a state of animality."[20] We also find nineteenth- and early twentieth-century writers describing Black people as "men" but also claiming that they are not descendants of Adam and Eve, and therefore not human beings (in the religious version)[21] or that they belong to a different, and inferior, biological species than Whites do (in the scientific version).

Those who claim that White colonists did not really think of Black people as beasts are refuted by an ocean of explicit, unambiguous historical documentation showing that White people often did not accord Black people human status.[22] For example, when the German traveler Johan Christian Hoffman visited what is now South Africa in 1691 and wrote down his impressions of the indigenous inhabitants, he described them as "more as monstrous apes than as righteous humans," adding that "because of their brutishness they have almost nothing that resembles a human."[23] From at least the late seventeenth century, and right through the nineteenth century, it was not unusual for White colonists to deny that Africans possessed souls, and thereby to deny their standing as human beings. This is why Lydia Maria Child began chapter 6 of her 1833 abolitionist book *An Appeal in Favor of That Class of Americans Called Africans* with the words "In order to decide what is our duty concerning the Africans and their descendants, we must first clearly make up our minds whether they are, or are not, human beings."[24]

There is also testimony from Black Americans who were well aware that many Whites considered them to be lower animals. For example, in an 1853 speech to the New York City Anti-Slavery Society, Sojourner Truth informed her audience that during her childhood "I thought I was a brute, for I heard people say that we were a species of monkeys or baboons; and as I hadn't seen any of those animals, I did not know but they were right." If it were not the case that the humanity of Black people was often called into question, then Frederick Douglass's remarks on the subject in his 1854 speech on "The Claims of the Negro, Ethnologically Considered" would be bizarre. "The first general claim that may here be set up," Douglass asserted, "respects the manhood of the Negro," which, he maintained, "is fiercely opposed." He goes on to discuss, as an illustration of this view, an article from the *Richmond Examiner* that argued that although even poor Whites possess the inalienable right to liberty and the pursuit of happiness, "the Negro has no such right—BECAUSE HE IS NOT A MAN!"[25]

The distinction between what Douglass called "the man admitted and the man disputed" is upheld in much of the scientific and religious literature of the day. An 1860 article by the distinguished Louisiana physician and apologist for slavery Samuel Cartwright proposed that the serpent of Eden was not a reptile but was instead "an animal formed like man," namely, "a negro gardener" who was not a descendant of the first human couple, created in God's image, but rather a member of the so-called pre-Adamic races, as are all of his Black descendants. Although Cartwright was not entirely clear about whether Black people are human beings, some of his intellectual heirs were more outspoken. A Nashville clergyman named Buckner H. Payne, writing under the pseudonym "Ariel," was quite explicit that the gardener in the Garden was a subhuman beast. Black people exist today only because one of their ancestors "entered the ark *only as a beast.*" So, "the negro is not a *human* being—not of Adam's race." Not too long after, a Pennsylvania Lutheran minister named Gottlieb Hasskarl authored a book that was intended to establish (among other things) that the Black person is "inevitably a beast."[26]

Finally, in this particular exegetical lineage, we come to the writings of Charles Carroll. Carroll wrote a book entitled *The Negro: A Beast* and another entitled *The Tempter of Eve*, published in 1900 and 1902, respectively, by the American Book and Bible Society, in which he defended Payne's theory that Black people are not human beings.[27] In the first of these, Carroll argued on both religious and scientific grounds that Black people are not members of the species *Homo sapiens* but are instead a kind of ape, and in the second he argued that the serpent of Eden was in fact a Black man, and that Black people are not human beings. Carroll expressed the view that had been circulating in North America since the seventeenth century, that Negroes did not possess souls, and therefore were excluded from the universe of moral obligation. According to at least two early twentieth-century reviewers, Carroll's claims were avidly taken up by large numbers of poor southern Whites, and his two books have been described as "enormously influential."[28]

These views did not remain unchallenged, but the more mainstream positions weren't always clear about the human status of Black people either, and most of them were equally unpalatable. A number of scholars embraced polygenesis—the view that each of the races evolved separately from the others (usually with the addendum and that Whites are morally, intellectually, or aesthetically superior to all the others). The notion that Black and White people were distinct species—in a strict biological sense—was apparently first explicitly advanced by Edward Long, a virulently racist British colonial administrator in Jamaica, and was taken up by various others after that.

One of the best sources of information about views on race that were current among American scientists in the mid-nineteenth century is a massive (nearly eight hundred pages long) collection of essays entitled *Types of Mankind or Ethnological Researches*, which contains contributions from leading intellectual figures of the day, including the biologist Louis Agassiz, the physician Josiah Nott, and the Egyptologist George Glidden. This influential tome went through eight editions in three years, and was even mentioned by Charles Darwin, who was critical of it.

It is clear from many passages that the distinguished contributors to *Types of Mankind* were convinced that human races are separate species. For example: "It will be seen . . . that we recognize no substantial difference between the terms *types* and *species*— permanence of characteristics belonging equally to both. The horse, the ass, the zebra, and the quagga, are distinct *species* and distinct *types:* and so with the Jew, the Teuton, the Sclavonian, the Mongol, the Australian, the coast Negro, the Hottentot, &c.; and no physical causes known to have existed during our geological epoch could have transformed one of these types or species into another."[29]

These "race experts" claimed that the human races are so different from one another that "differences between distinct races are often greater than those distinguishing [nonhuman] species."[30] Today, we are mostly inclined think of the notion of the human as a species concept: all human beings, no matter how varied, are of the same fundamental kind. But for the nineteenth-century polygenecists, "human" denoted a genus, to which belonged various species—and mixed-race individuals were regarded as hybrids. Nott, who was perhaps the leading scientific expert on race during the mid-nineteenth century, opined in an influential article on race mixing that "*at the present day the Anglo-Saxon and Negro Races are, according to the common acceptation of the term, distinct species, and that the offspring of the two is a hybrid.*"[31] In defiance of easily ascertainable facts, nineteenth-century scientific racists often claimed that the offspring of interracial unions produce only infertile offspring.[32]

It is worth noting in this connection that there was also a strand in Nazi race theory that conceived of Jews not as a pure albeit inferior race, but as an inchoate mixture of races, a "mongrel" race, which rendered them especially degenerate and depraved. As one article in the Nazi newspaper *Der Stürmer* put it, "The Jews are bastards. They show the racial characteristics of the white, yellow, and black peoples. . . . Their revolting body odor also brands them as a foreign race. Their sneaky gait and posture suggest the apes. Many Jews have a small, receding forehead and a skull like a gorilla. As the poodledachshundpincher is a bastard among dogs, so the Jew is a bastard among peoples."[33]

Those who regarded Black people as a distinct species did not merely regard them as other. They regarded them as inferior. They assigned each of the races a position on a natural hierarchy—the Great Chain of Being that I mentioned in Chapter 1 and will discuss extensively in Chapter 6—with Whites at the top, most perfect and closest to God, and Blacks at or near the bottom. South African Bushmen were "the lowest and most beastly specimens . . . are but little removed, both in moral and physical character, from the orang-outan" and "are described . . . as bearing a strong resemblance to the monkey tribe."[34] These differences between the races were considered to be static and immutable—fixed for all time by the Creator. Nott wrote baldly that "there is a genus, Man, comprising two or more species—that physical causes cannot change a White man into a Negro, and to say that this change has been effected by a direct act of providence is an assumption which . . . *is contrary to the Great Chain of Nature's laws.*"[35]

On one hand, there is evidence that slaveholders accepted that Black people were human beings, and on the other there is evidence that *the same people* believed that Black people were subhuman. Faced with this inconsistency, it is easy to conclude that those men and women who described Black people as less than human must not have meant it to be taken literally. But this conclusion is too hasty. It is uncontroversial that many White people—including many who were committed to the abolitionist cause—believed that Black people were subhuman "savages." And, as Gustav Jahoda commented in his classic book *Images of Savages*, "One might wonder whether these mid-twentieth century writers might not have been influenced by their feeling that no one could possibly have been unsure about the humanity of savages."[36]

I think that it is a mistake to interpret the historical record through a binary lens. We do not have to assume that White slaveholders and their racist heirs either regarded enslaved Africans as fully human or regarded them as entirely subhuman. To do so is to make the mistake of insisting that their attitudes were logically coherent. It is instructive to compare the either/or perspective with the subtler position expounded by the preeminent historian of slavery David Brion Davis. Recounting Fredrick Law Olmstead's description of an overseer who remarked after brutally beating an enslaved teenage girl, "I wouldn't mind killing a nigger more than I would a dog," Davis raises the question: "Does this mean that blacks who were treated like animals were literally seen as 'only animals,' or as an entirely different species of humans? The answer is clearly no, except perhaps in some extreme cases and for very brief periods of time—as for example in the post-emancipation lynching era, when many black men accused of raping White women were hanged or tortured, dismembered, and burned alive, occasionally before immense cheering crowds of Southern White men, women, and children."[37]

Davis then suggests that when Whites dehumanized Blacks, they were in a *contradictory state of mind*, stating that

> since the victims of this process are perceived as 'animalized humans,' this double consciousness would probably involve a contradictory shifting back and forth in the recognition of humanity. When Henry Smith . . . was tortured and killed in 1893 before a Texas mob of some ten thousand Whites, many in the crowd no doubt saw him momentarily as "nothing but an animal" as they watched hot irons being pressed on his bare feet

and tongue and then into his eyes, and heard him emit "a cry that echoed over the prairie like the wail of a wild animal."[38]

Davis's insight that dehumanizers think of those whom they dehumanize as *both* human and subhuman is true to the historical record and the phenomenology of dehumanization. And it undermines the objection that dehumanization cannot be real because those who seem to regard others as subhuman animals also refer to them, implicitly or explicitly, as human beings.

CHAPTER THREE

In the Blood

My task so far has been to explain what dehumanization is and to show, using historical examples, that any reasonable person should accept that dehumanization is a real phenomenon. I hope I have managed to convince you that we really are capable of conceiving of other people as less-than-human beings, and that this is something that it is important to understand. My next task is to begin to tease out just what it is about the human mind that makes this peculiar phenomenon possible. Of course, psychology does not provide us with the whole story of how dehumanization happens. We also need to take account of political and social processes. But psychology is a good place to begin.

Otto Bradfisch was the head of Einsatzkommando 8, a mobile killing unit that followed in the wake of the German army as it pressed eastward across Poland and Belarus toward the ultimate prize of Moscow during World War II. Like the other Einsatzkommando units, it was tasked with rounding up and killing Jews and Communist Party members. The standard procedure was to line up men, women, and children at the edge of a large pit or ditch, and then shoot them either in machine gun salvos or by a single bullet to the back of the head. Those who were still alive among the mass of blood-soaked corpses were finished off with another shot.

The eighty or so men of Bradfisch's unit were experienced killers who executed thousands of people in this manner. In 1942, in his capacity as head of the Gestapo in the Polish city of Lodz, Bradfisch was also responsible for deporting more than 20,000 Jews from the Lodz ghetto to the Chelmno extermination camp. Here is how holocaust scholar Guenter Lewy describes testimony from Bradfisch's 1961 trial in Munich: "The court noted that Bradfisch was known as a reliable and efficient officer who showed initiative in finding his victims. In at least two instances, he personally participated in the shooting by providing the coup de grâce to Jews lying wounded in the pit. There was no evidence, the court noted, that Bradfisch had made any attempt to escape this assignment. 'His conduct was that of a faithful follower of Hitler. The will of the Führer for him was law irrespective of its content.' At an execution in Minsk, a member of his unit testified, Bradfisch had pointed out that '*the Jews were not to be regarded as human*'" (emphasis added).[1]

Now, picture the men of Einsatzkommando 8 looking at a row of men, women, and children lined up along the edge of a pit—Jews whom they will, in a few moments, exterminate. According to Nazi ideology, Jews are *Untermenschen* ("subhumans")—beings that are more like vermin than they are like human beings. So, insofar as they accepted the doctrine of Jewish subhumanity, the men of Einsatzkommando 8 would not experience these weeping, trembling, and terrified people as human beings. Instead, they would be gazing at disgusting, evil, subhuman creatures—creatures that ought to be exterminated.

If you think about it, this is perplexing. The ostensibly less-than-human beings lined up along the edge of the killing had the bodily form of human beings. They were bipedal and had two arms. They could speak. They took the streetcar to work, wore clothes, shielded themselves with umbrellas from the rain, tucked their children in bed at night, and read the daily newspaper. They looked and behaved exactly like real human beings look and behave, and yet, in Bradfisch's men's eyes, they were not human beings.

Episodes like this occurred often during the Holocaust. Under the impact of political propaganda, Jews came to be seen not only as dangerous human aliens, but also, at the extreme, as subhuman monsters, in spite of their human appearance and behavior.

The example of Einsatzkommando 8 teaches us something important about the phenomenology of dehumanization. Dehumanization is not about how people look. Dehumanized people are often physically indistinguishable from those who dehumanize them, and even in cases where there are striking physical differences, such as the dehumanization of Black people by Whites, the target population is not thought of as less than human *because* of their outward appearance. Rather, their appearance is imagined to conceal something deeper about them, something that is located "inside" them.

If you are well acquainted with the history of racism, you might protest that when White Americans dehumanized Blacks they sometimes cited what they considered to be anatomical evidence such as the size and shape of the cranium, or the form of the heel, as evidence that Blacks belong to an alien species. But this alleged anatomical evidence was not the *foundation* for the dehumanization of Black people. It couldn't be. Minor phenotypic variations, whether imagined or real, do not have any bearing on whether two beings belong to the same species. The role of such "scientific" studies was to provide post hoc justifications for a preexisting commitment to the view that Black people are less than human.

This is why appeals to observable similarity to counteract dehumanization virtually always fall on deaf ears. When one Dr. Grant, who seriously proposed that Black people were apes, disrupted an 1850 meeting of the American Anti-Slavery Society with a supposedly scientific explanation of Negro subhumanity, Frederick Douglass responded, "We have heard all that can be said against the humanity of the negro, from one who deals with the matter scientifically . . . but look at me, look at the negro in the face, examine his wooly head, his entire physical conformation; I invite you to the examination, and ask this audience to judge. . . . Am I a man?"[2]

In a similar vein, in 1868 Henry McNeal Turner addressed the Georgia state legislature after it had expelled all of its Black elected officials with the question "Am I a man? If I am such, I claim the rights of a man." He continued,

> A certain gentleman has argued that the Negro was a mere development similar to the orangoutang or chimpanzee, but it so happens that, when a Negro is examined, physiologically, phrenologically and anatomically, and I may say, physiognomically, he is found to be the same as persons of different color. I would like to ask any gentleman on this floor, where is the analogy? Do you find me a quadruped, or do you find me a man? Do you find three bones less in my back than in that of the White man? Do you find fewer organs in the brain? If you know nothing of this, I do; for I have helped to dissect fifty men, black and White, and I assert that by the time you take off the mucous pigment—the color of the skin—you cannot, to save your life, distinguish between the black man and the White. Am I a man? Have I a soul to save, as you have?[3]

Arguments of this sort were unpersuasive because the people that Douglass and Turner were addressing were not in the grip of a perceptual illusion. They were hostage to a conceptual one. They were married to the view that in spite of appearances, Black people are subhuman animals.

The phenomenon toward which I am gesturing—the idea that when people dehumanize others they think of them as subhuman on the "inside," notwithstanding their human appearance—is not something that is entirely alien to everyday experience. The basis of this way of thinking is the idea that appearances can be misleading, and that what a thing seems to be does not always correspond to what it really is. And this comes very easily to us.

Consider the fate of the protagonist of Franz Kafka's story "The Metamorphosis": "One morning, as Gregor Samsa was waking up from anxious dreams, he discovered that in bed he had been changed into a monstrous verminous bug. He lay on his armour-hard back and saw, as he lifted his head up a little, his brown, arched abdomen divided up into rigid bow-like sections. From this height the blanket, just about ready to slide off completely, could hardly stay in place. His numerous legs, pitifully thin in comparison to the rest of his circumference, flickered helplessly before his eyes." Gregor Samsa's outward appearance has morphed into the form of a "monstrous verminous bug." But in spite of his metamorphosis, he is still Gregor Samsa, a human being trapped in an insect body. The juxtaposition of what the protagonist is with what he seems to be is immediately understandable, and is what gives the story much of its heartbreaking poignancy. Kafka's story presents us with the inverse of dehumanization. When we dehumanize others, we conceive of them as having a human appearance that hides a subhuman essence, but in the story, Samsa's human essence is concealed behind a subhuman appearance.

Imagine a coffeemaker that is designed to look just like an ordinary food processor.[4] If you were to enter a kitchen that is equipped with such a coffeemaker, you would mistake it for a food processor. The reason is obvious, but it is nevertheless worth spelling out. We very often categorize things on the basis of evidence provided by our senses. Put crudely, we assign things to categories on the basis of what they look like. You think that the machine is a food processor because it looks like a food processor, because things that look like food processors almost always really are food processors.

But sometimes we are not content to classify things based on their appearance. Sometimes, we feel moved to dig deeper. Suppose that, for some reason or other, you decide to inspect the faux food processor more carefully, so you strip it down and compare its insides with the insides of a genuine food processor. If you did this, you would discover that the insides of the real food processor are configured very differently from the insides of the phony one. And if you then went on to compare the insides of the mock food processor with the insides of a more conventional looking coffeemaker, you would discover them to be very similar.[5] Confronted with this sort of evidence, you would reclassify the thing that looks like a food processor as a coffeemaker.

This coffeemaker example can help us to understand the pattern of thinking that made it possible for the men of Einsatzkommando 8 to conceive of their victims as subhumans. These men regarded Jews' ostensible humanity as merely cosmetic—a façade that deceptively masked their inner subhumanity—just like the outward appearance of the simulated food processor concealed the fact that it was really a coffeemaker.

As it stands, this analogy takes us only so far, because if you were to perform an autopsy on the body of the Jewish man and compare his internal anatomy to that of a German you would find that the two are virtually indiscernible, unlike the internal "anatomy" of food processors and coffeemakers. So, if Jews were supposed to be subhuman on the "inside," what was meant by this had to have been far subtler and more elusive than any anatomical dissection could reveal. Whatever it was that was supposed to distinguish Jewish subhumans from Aryan humans, and Black subhumans from White humans, had to be something that cannot be observed by the naked eye. To those who dehumanized Jews and Blacks, the mere fact of their racial identity—the mere fact that they were Jewish or Black—was enough to make them subhuman.

This points to a crucial connection between dehumanization and race, and raises two very important questions. The first is the question of what is it to think of a group of people as belonging to a race.

In everyday life, we tend to take the notion of race for granted without examining what it really means. Interrogating ordinary notions of race will help us understand why racism and dehumanization are so closely tied together. Once the first question has been settled, we can move on to the second one, the question of what is it about the psychological form of racial thinking that makes it so easy to transition from racializing others to dehumanizing them. I will take up the first question in the remainder of this chapter and move on to the second question in Chapter 4.

Juice of Very Special Kind

We can begin with Nazi anti-Semitism. The quest for a reliable, internal marker of Jewishness greatly preoccupied race experts in Nazi Germany. German scientists believed that there was such a thing as a typical Jewish physiognomy, and they tried to diagnose Jewishness on the basis of such supposedly typically Jewish traits. But they were also aware that Jews come in all shapes and sizes, and many could not be distinguished from Aryans by looks alone. Because there was no reliable method for distinguishing Jews from Germans on the basis of their appearance, it was possible to mistake them for one another. Jews could falsely present themselves as members of the master race, and Aryans could be wrongly persecuted and killed as Jews.[6] Here is how Ernst Heimer, a writer for the virulently racist newspaper *Der Stürmer*, expressed the problem in one of the children's books that he authored: "Just as it is often hard to perceive bacteria, so, too, it is often impossible to recognize the Jew. Not every Jew has the same racial characteristics! Not every Jew has a crooked nose or protruding ears! Not every Jew has a protruding lower lip or black, curly hair! Not every Jew has the typical Jewish eyes and flat feet! No! It is often hard to recognize a Jew. One must look very carefully to avoid being fooled. The variety in the Jew's appearance is a great danger for other peoples."[7]

Nazis solved the problem by looking at people's pedigrees. Initially, they looked to racist American laws for inspiration, but concluded that the American "one-drop rule" was too extreme.[8] An individual's racial status was determined on the basis of the racial status of his or her grandparents. According to the 1935 Nuremberg Laws, a person is Jewish if at least three of their grandparents were Jews. If only one or two grandparents were Jews, they were considered as *Mischlingen*, or racially mixed persons, although other sectors of the Nazi state, such as Heinrich Himmler's SS, demanded that candidates meet far more exacting genealogical standards of racial purity.[9]

This "ancestral proof" of racial identity was underpinned by certain assumptions that are easily taken for granted but which should be laid out explicitly. Why should ancestry matter for determining race? Why should it be that a short, dark-haired, olive-skinned, full-lipped woman—that is, a woman who had what the Nazis regarded as a typically Jewish appearance—could have been classified as German while a tall, blond, blue-eyed woman, whom the Nazis regarded as having a paradigmatically German appearance, could have been classified as a Jew solely on the basis of their grandparents' racial status? Like the naïve questions that children ask, these questions force us to notice something that is easily overlooked. The idea that a person's race depends on their appearance is false.

The fact that European Jews were not, for the most part, physically discernible from non-Jews made idea that Jews disguise themselves as gentiles a fixture of European anti-Semitic mindset long before the Nazis came upon the scene. The belief that Jews have innate capacity to mimic the culture, behavior, and appearance of Aryans, and thereby conceal their true identity, was an important aspect of the anti-Semitic stereotype. As historian Steven E. Ascheim argues, Jews were thought to possess "a crafty, histrionic ability to camouflage their essence. . . . This is most strikingly elaborated in . . . the writings of Hans Blüher. . . . Every people, he declared in classical *völkisch* fashion, has its own built-in being and aptitude (*Geschick*). Jewish *Geschick*—radically incompatible with the deeply historical nature of *Deutschtum*—consisted in the dissimulatory mastery of appearances. The faculty of disguise was built into their sick substance. 'The Jews,' he declared, 'are the only Volk [people] that operate through mimicry. Mimicry of the blood, the name, and the form.'"[10]

Nazi ideologues rejected the idea that a person's race is fixed by their appearance. They thought that one's race is located in one's blood—blood that is transmitted down the so-called bloodline from parents to their offspring. The idea that race is carried in the blood explains the logic of diagnosing race by descent. Anyone who is descended from Jews is tainted with the Jewish blood and is therefore a Jew, no matter whether they look Jewish or not, and whether they observe the Jewish religion or not. And of course, if Jews were subhuman, it follows that their subhumanity (and the humanity of Aryans) is located in their blood as well.

This general conception of the nature of race was already established in Europe long before the rise of National Socialism. During the Middle Ages, the hereditary distinction between nobility and commoners was justified by the idea that the former are of royal blood and the latter are not.[11] In fifteenth-century Spain, Jews and Muslims who had been forcibly converted to Catholicism were excluded from public life by *limpiesa de sangre* ("purity of blood") laws. By the seventeenth century, when European physicians were beginning to experiment with transfusions, some were intrigued by the possibility of cross-species transfusions, and speculated that if such transfusions were made, the characteristics of the donor would modify the appearance and behavior recipient. As historian Rachel Boaz notes, "The idea that blood contained the attributes of the creature [that it] came from (human or animal) became most apparent when clinical experiments with transfusing blood became more common. Robert Boyle, a British chemist and physicist of the seventeenth century, wondered whether a recipient dog would recognize his master, whether a dog transfused with sheep's blood would grow horns or wool, whether a small dog would change in stature if transfused with blood from a larger animal, and even whether marital discord could be treated by reciprocal transfusions of husband and wife."[12]

Others extended this general idea to theories about race. Seventeenth-century scientists adopted the notion that there is something in the blood that is responsible for observable racial characteristics. The conviction that race is, in some mysterious sense, carried in the blood had such a powerful grip on the European imagination that it could lead observers to dismiss what their own eyes told them. For example, an English physician living in Barbados wrote to a colleague, "It will not be unwelcome to you, perhaps, if I tell you that the blood of Negroes is almost as black as their skin. I have seen the blood of at least 20 both sick & in health, drawn forth, and the superficies of it all is as dark as the bottome of any European blood, after standing a while in a dish; soe that the blackness of Negroes is likely to be inherent in them."[13]

Similarly, colonists of European descent instituted what was (and is) called the "blood quantum" criterion for determining who is and who is not a Native American. In its most general version, of this principle defines Indians as persons having at least 50 percent Indian blood, while the more delimited versions define tribal membership in terms of the proportion of a person's blood that is blood from a particular tribe. The general principle was enshrined in law—complete with the scientifically absurd reference to blood—in the

1934 Indian Reorganization Act.[14] Native American groups have retained this rule. Among these, there are variations in the "amount" of tribal blood that an individual must have in order to qualify as a tribal member.[15]

In Germany during the Weimar period, folk conceptions of race and blood became yoked to the new science of serology to produce a potent, blood-centered racist cocktail.[16] Weimar seroanthropologists thought that it might be possible to use blood typing to objectively distinguish one race from another.[17] And as the twentieth century wore on, the race-obsessed intelligentsia of the Nazi movement—and later those of the Third Reich—took up this project with alacrity. Their aim, of course, was to use the analysis of blood to distinguish "true" Germans from Jews, so that they wouldn't have to rely on imprecise physiognomic criteria or cumbersome ancestral pedigrees.

Even though these scientific efforts eventually proved to be fruitless, the Nazi regime continued to produce the belief that race is located in the blood, as is evident in the 1935 Law for the Protection of German Blood and German Honor, which forbade marriage or sexual relations between Jews and Aryans. And the rhetoric of Nazi propaganda was replete with references to *Bluteinheit* ("unity of blood"), *Blut und Boden* ("blood and soil"), *Blutbewusstein* ("blood consciousness"), and *Blutsgemeinschaft* ("blood community").

In all of these examples of Nazi lingo, "blood" is a proxy for "race." The association between blood and race was starkly explicit in many Nazi publications. For example, one text from the Ministry of Propaganda stated, "We know that blood is not simply a red fluid that flows through our veins. Rather, it is our very being—which carries our ancestry and represents the lineage to which we will return. The same physical and spiritual predispositions are only found among men who are of the same blood. We are related to those who have carried the same blood. These carriers of the same blood—the different races—are different from one another."[18]

It is important to grasp that, bizarre though this may seem, the Nazis' use of blood imagery wasn't merely figurative. When they spoke about race being carried in the blood, they were expressing the idea that a person's race is *literally* located in the fluid flowing through their veins and arteries—the substance that Goethe's Mephistopheles called "juice of very special kind."[19] In 1935, just a few weeks after Germany instituted the Nuremberg race laws, a German-Jewish physician named Hans Serelman donated his own blood to save the life of a seriously injured Nazi storm trooper. German physicians loyal to the Reich reported Serelman to the Gestapo, and despite the fact that he had saved a Nazi's life, he was convicted of the crime of *Rassenschande* ("race defilement," the pollution of Aryan blood by Jewish blood) and was sent to Sachsenburg concentration camp for *Schutzhaft* ("protective custody").[20] That same year, a Nazi storm trooper who was seriously injured in an automobile accident was rushed to a nearby hospital and given a life-saving blood transfusion. The blood that he received was Jewish blood, and a German court subsequently convicted him of race defilement (the court allowed him to remain in the Sturmabteilung because the donor was a World War I veteran). Wounded German soldiers died on the Eastern front because transfusions of "Jewish blood" were banned.[21]

A Folk Theory of Race

The pattern of racial thinking that I have just described should sound familiar to anyone who's even minimally versed in the history of North American racism. The idea that a person's race is fixed by their genealogy was the basis for the one-drop rule of the American

South, which remained in legal force well into the twentieth century. In its most extreme version, the one-drop rule (also called the rule of "hypodescent") specified that having even a single black ancestor made it the case that one was black (or, at least, non-White).[22] For example, Homer Plessy—the plaintiff in the famous case of *Plessy v. Ferguson* was visually indistinguishable from a White person, but was nonetheless considered Black because one of his great-grandparents was born in Africa. In spite of his appearance and his predominantly European ancestry, it was illegal for Plessy to ride in railway carriages reserved for Whites.

American racists took the idea of racial blood every bit as literally as the Nazis did, which is unsurprising give the fact that the Nazis looked to the United States for guidance. This is why in 1942, after relaxing a ban on Black blood donors, the American Red Cross segregated White and Black blood supplies, a move that "reflected ambivalence and uncertainty in the minds of White Americans who believed in the dominant racial mythology of the 1940s."[23] This mythology led them to believe that there was a fundamental difference between the blood of different races, that it was possible to transmit the traits and characteristics of one race to a member of another race by means of a blood transfusion, and that it was possible for blood transfusions to implant potentialities in an individual of another race that would show up in succeeding generations.

The core assumptions of both German and North American racial thinking were in essence identical. According to legal scholar Judy Scales-Trent, "Both societies, thus, use the language of descent in an effort to transform the sociolegal categories they are creating into biological categories. In the ideology of both cultures, there is a very real genetic taint that can be transmitted from grandparent to parent to child through 'blood.' As a reflection of the value both societies placed on the biological necessity of maintaining the 'purity' of 'Aryan' or 'White' blood, both societies separated their blood supplies—Aryan from Jewish, White from colored."[24]

Versions of the notion that race is located in the blood, or sometimes that it is located in bodily fluids such as milk or semen, are widespread, and are aspects of a prevalent folk theory of race. For instance, some Nazis believed that the racial essence could be transmitted by sexual intercourse, through semen, like a sexually transmitted disease. A 1935 article in *German People's Health through Blood and Soil!*, a medical journal edited by Julius Streicher, stated that "'alien albumin' is the semen of a man of another race. As a result of intercourse, the male semen is partially or totally absorbed by the female body. A single incident of intercourse is sufficient to poison her blood. She has taken in the alien soul along with the 'alien albumin.' Even if she marries an Aryan man, she can no longer bear pure Aryan children, but only bastards in whose breasts dwell two souls, and who physically look like members of a mixed race."[25] This essentialist conception of race is vital for understanding the nature of dehumanization because the way that we think about race conforms to the same pattern as the way that we think about dehumanization, and because racializing a population is very often the first step toward dehumanizing them.

Folk theories are commonsensical views about the nature of things. They often consist of implicit, unarticulated background assumptions that remain unquestioned. We absorb these folk theories from the culture in which we are embedded, without the need for any formal instruction. Unlike scientific theories, which are explicitly articulated and subject to testing and revision in light of disconfirming evidence, folk theories are often implicit and impervious to contrary evidence.

Although this is an important difference, there are other respects in which folk theories and scientific theories are quite similar. In both cases, theories are tools for explaining observable things by citing unobservable things—things that are *assumed* to exist because of the role that they play in making sense of our experiences. We observe patterns of phenomena in the world, look for ways to make sense of them, and suppose that their explanation lies in something deeper than meets the eye—something that is hidden behind the curtain that separates the aspects of the world that are accessible to our sense organs from those that are not. It is these unobservable things (called "theoretical entities" in the philosophical jargon) that do the explanatory and predictive work in any theory. For example, human beings have known for thousands of years that characteristics of domesticated plants and animals can be engineered by selective breeding. Apple trees are bred to bear more fruit, cattle to yield more milk, dogs to run faster, and so on. The practice of selective breeding was based on the everyday observation that offspring more often than not resemble their parents. Around the middle of the nineteenth century, Gregor Mendel undertook a painstaking series of experiments on nearly thirty thousand pea plants to figure out how to account for the similarities between parents and their offspring. First, he bred pure strains of pea plants—plants that "breed true." Then, he crossbred them and carefully noted the resulting patterns of resemblance in subsequent generations. This experiment revealed some peculiar facts. For example, Mendel found that when he crossed pure strains of tall pea plants with pure strains of short ones, all of their offspring were tall, but when he bred two of this tall offspring together, three-quarters of their offspring were tall and one-quarter of them were short.

Mendel was not content simply to observe these patterns. He wanted to explain them. To do that, he had to posit theoretical entities that he called hereditary "elements" or "factors." These, he supposed, combined with one another in accord with three rules later known as "Mendel's Laws" to produce these particular tall/short ratios among offspring. Mendel's theoretical entities, later renamed "genes," together with his combinatorial laws, are the foundation for the science of genetics.

Another good example, this time from the world of physics, is Einstein's explanation of Brownian motion. Brownian motion is the erratic movement of tiny particles suspended in a liquid or a gas. To picture it, think of motes of dust dancing in the sunlight. In 1905, Einstein elegantly demonstrated that this phenomenon can be explained by atoms and molecules colliding with the particles. Atoms and molecules had not been observed in 1905. At the time, they were theoretical entities that were only conjectured by some to exist. But Einstein argued that in this case what is observable (Brownian motion) is best explained by these unobservable theoretical entities.

This conception of what theories are applies just as much to folk theories as it does to scientific ones. So, to start to unpack any folk theory of race, we need to ask two questions about it. First, we need to ask what observations the theory purports to explain, and second, we need to ask what theoretical entities the theory posits to do the explaining.

With respect to folk theories of race, the answer to the first question is that these theories are supposed to explain observable patterns of human diversity. Go to sub-Saharan Africa and you will find that most people have dark skin and tightly curled hair. Go to Finland and you will find that most people have pale skin and relatively straight hair. Folk theories of race try to explain differences like these by proposing that humanity is composed of a small number of fundamentally different kinds of people, and that every human being is either a "pure" member of one of these kinds or a mixture of two or more of them. These kinds of people are what we call "races."

The principle that there are pure types of people as well mixtures of these pure types is so deeply entrenched in everyday patterns of thinking that it can be difficult to notice it is a theoretical rather than an empirical proposition. We observe similarities and differences between people, and we can group people together on the basis of their observable similarities and differences, but we do not observe that there are a few pure *kinds* of people. The notion of human races is an interpretive grid that is superimposed upon the dappled landscape of human diversity. That is the first theoretical component of the notion of race.

You might rightly object that it is not enough to say that the folk theory of race is the idea that human beings come packaged in discrete kinds, because there are plenty of kinds of people nobody would be inclined to think of as races. Men and women are different kinds, and so are babies and adults, as well as college professors and people who sell shoes. So, we need to be more specific about the kind of kind that races are supposed to be. Races are supposed to be what philosophers call "natural kinds." These are the kinds that are part of the objective structure of the world, and are not human inventions. Carbon atoms and quarks are natural kinds, but Tuesdays and dollars are not. Pets are not a natural kind, because they do not have any biological properties that set them apart from animals that are not pets (there are not any biological features that set dogs, cats, canaries, and goldfish apart from all other creatures). Some kinds of animals are considered pets and others are not only by dint of human practices and conventions.

The claim that races are natural human kinds still does not fully capture the folk conception, however, because not all natural human kinds are thought of as races. The human race includes males and females. These are (unlike professors and shoe salespeople) human natural kinds, but we do not regard females and males as distinct races. So, it must be that the folk theory of race is focused on a particular kind of putative natural kinds.

Descent is a hugely important component. Some natural kinds are descent-based. For example, for something to be a porcupine it is sufficient for its parents to be porcupines (or, to flip it, the off-spring of any two porcupines will, of necessity, be porcupines).[26] Like porcupinehood, race is supposed to be transmitted by descent. This is a mainstay of systems of racial assignment. As I earlier ex-plained, when Nazi race experts were confronted with the problem of who counts as a Jew and who does not, they settled on the crite-rion of descent. They determined a person's racial status by their pedigree rather than how they looked, the language they spoke, or the religion they practiced (although all of these could be consid-ered in ambiguous cases).[27] Similarly, the rule of hypodescent is what fixed one's racial status in a large swath of the United States. Contrast this element of racial thinking with how we think about sex and gender. It would obviously be ridiculous to say that children inherit their sex or gender from their parents, because every human child is the offspring of a man and a woman. In contrast to sex and gender, then, the idea of race is the idea of a *human natural kind, the membership in which is transmitted by descent.*

To more fully understand the folk theory, we need to probe more deeply still. We need to look into what it is about a person that is supposed to make them a member of a certain race—what it is that is supposed to be transmitted from parent to child that determines the child's racial identity. This is the topic of Chapter 4.

CHAPTER FOUR

Essential Differences

There may well be several folk theories of race, but many scholars (including me) believe that one of them is far more prevalent, fundamental, and destructive than the others. Scholars call it *racial essentialism*. Racial essentialism is a particular manifestation of the broader psychological tendency known as psychological essentialism, which is also a large part of the psychological foundation for dehumanization. So, before delving more deeply into the essentialistic folk theory of race, and its connection to dehumanization, it is important to be clear about exactly what psychological essentialism is.[1]

Psychologists Douglas Medin and Andrew Ortony introduced the term "psychological essentialism" in 1989 as a name for the psychological tendency to attribute essences to certain kinds of things.[2] Saying that the word "essence" is ambiguous is an understatement. It has a wide range of meanings, from the quotidian to the esoteric. In everyday speech, something that is described as "essential" is central, important, or indispensable (as in "essential reading" or "essential amino acids"). In the more technical, scholarly arena, philosophers have been thinking about the notion of essence for at least two thousand years. Traditionally, they contrast essential properties with accidental ones. Accidental properties are attributes that a thing could lack while remaining the thing it is. For example, at this moment, your body consists of a specific number of cells, but you could have more or fewer while still remaining the person that you are. Suppose that right now your body consists of thirty-seven trillion cells, and that in the next fifteen seconds sixty-nine of them will die off. The fact that you will then have only 36,999,999,999,931 cells wouldn't make you any less you. You would retain your essential properties and lose an accidental one. In contrast, essential properties are those that a thing cannot lack and still retain its identity. For example, being a mammal is one of your essential properties. You couldn't be an oyster, or my left thumb, or the Brooklyn Bridge, and still be you. If a sorcerer were to wave a magic wand and turn you into the Brooklyn Bridge, you would immediately go out of existence.

Beyond this point, the philosophical hairsplitting takes over. There are very many more fine-grained conceptions of essences floating around in the philososphere which need not concern us here. Instead, I want to leave the esoterica behind and concentrate on the distinction between two quite different notions of essences that, if not differentiated, can lead to enormous confusion. One is the notion of "sortal essences." Sortal essences are the defining properties of a thing—all of those features that make a thing the kind of thing it is. When Plato defined human beings as "featherless bipeds" (and Diogenes the Cynic crashed his seminar brandishing a plucked chicken and blurting out "There is Plato's man!"), he was trying to specify the sortal essence of being human. Anything can have a sortal essence—even socially constructed things. For example, part of the sortal essence for Thursday is "the day after Wednesday."

But only members of natural kinds have causal essences. They are supposed to be "deep," fundamental properties that all and only members of the kind possess. The possession of a causal essence is supposed to be what makes an individual a member of a natural kind. These essences are imagined to permeate the *insides* of things that have them, mark off sharp boundaries between kinds, and remain constant in the face of superficial changes. Causal essences are theoretical entities. They are supposed to be unobservable but at the same time causally responsible for observable properties that are typical of members of the kind. In particular, essentialistic thinking is associated with the realm of living things, including human beings.[3]

According to psychologists who have studied our essentialist proclivities, we cannot help being drawn to thinking of the world as populated by sharply demarcated natural kinds, and we cannot help thinking of members of these natural kinds as having essences. This might seem questionable to you. You might sincerely say that you do not believe that species of organisms are natural kinds, or deny that animals have hidden essences that make them the kinds of animals that they are. This is an understandable response, but it does not comport with the usually tacit nature of essentialistic cognition. As the philosopher Sarah-Jane Leslie emphasizes, the essentialist mindset can be suppressed, but it probably cannot be overcome.[4] Scientific education can block the tendency to explicitly think of the human genome as a hidden essence or to imagine that species are neatly demarcated kinds of living things. However, these tendencies do not vanish with education. They just go underground.

Causal essentialism might sound scientifically respectable, because theoretical science traffics in the "deep" properties of things that determine their outward form and behavior. Causal essentialism does make sense in the domains of physics and chemistry. Chemical elements have causal essences. The causal essence of oxygen is located in its microstructure. Everything that is oxygen possesses this kind of microstructure, and everything that possesses this kind of microstructure is oxygen. And oxygen's microstructure accounts for its observable properties—its solubility in water, the temperature at which it condenses, its role in combustion, and so on. Essentialism is somewhat plausible in the chemical and physical domains, but it does not play out so nicely in biology.[5]

It is worthwhile to pause to consider just why it is that essentialism about species is inconsistent with what biological science tells us, because essentialistic biases have such a powerful and pervasive influence on how we view the world of living things. The essentialistic mindset is so difficult to resist that even those of us who are aware that it is a psychological bias that has no scientific support are likely to slip into it unless we are vigilant. The philosopher Paul Griffiths is one of a number of scholars who have explained why an essentialist picture of species is incompatible with the scientific perspective. He points out that the essentialist picture

> is precisely the . . . perspective on species that Darwin had to displace in order to establish the gradual transformation of one species into another. Species are not types to which individual organisms more or less imperfectly conform, but abstractions from the pools of overlapping variations that constitute the actual populations of that species. . . . The limitations of folk taxonomy become apparent when working on larger geographical and temporal scales. Many species grade into one another spatially, and all do temporally. When individuals exist who are intermediate between two species due to hybridization or incomplete speciation it is senseless to ask whether these individuals are "really" of one species or the other. That question presumes that the species is more than an abstraction from the varied individuals that compose it.[6]

To illustrate: from an essentialist perspective, what makes an animal a North American porcupine is its possession of the porcupine essence. That essence is supposed to be something that all porcupines possess and no nonporcupines possess. Furthermore, the porcupine essence is supposed to be causally responsible for the observable features that are typical of porcupines, such as their greyish color, having four legs, being covered in sharp quills. The idea that there are sharply demarcated species, each with a unique essence, is supposed to explain why there are many different kinds of living things: porcupines are different from bluebirds because porcupines have the porcupine essence and bluebirds have the bluebird essence.

On the face of it, if the observable traits of members of a biological species are caused by their essence, and if every member of a species shares the same essence, shouldn't every member of the species be exactly the same as all the others? How can the essentialism account for the fact that no two porcupines are exactly alike, and that some (for example, albino porcupines) depart dramatically from the species norm? It is here that a second component of the folk theory kicks in—one that is not much emphasized in the psychological literature but which is nevertheless very important for understanding both racial cognition and dehumanization. It is the notion of *development*. According to the essentialist folk theory, the development of any individual is internally driven. Development is just the gradual unfolding of an individual's essence over time. From this perspective, if development always proceeded perfectly, without obstruction or deviation, then every member of a biological kind would fully embody all of attributes that are typical for members of that kind. If this were the case, then every porcupine would be a paradigmatic porcupine, possessing only and all of the attributes that porcupines ought to have. The point can be put this way: an individual is *true to its kind* to the extent that its development is unimpeded, and within-species deviations from the ideal developmental trajectory produce within-species variation.[7] In very deviant cases, the appearance of an individual may depart so dramatically from what is characteristic of its kind that it is unrecognizable as a member of that kind. The folk theory allows that an animal might look and behave in ways that are unlike the appearance and behavior that is characteristic of porcupines generally, and yet still be a porcupine by virtue of possessing a porcupine essence.

There are three important additional aspects of the folk biological mindset that should be noted before we move on.[8] The first is that essences press forward to express themselves, so even if an essence is not manifest, it will become manifest if the obstacles to its expression are weakened or removed. Cognitive anthropologist Dan Sperber aptly captures the idea as follows: "If an animal does not actually possess a feature ascribed to it by its definition, then it possesses it virtually: not in its appearance but in its nature."[9] The second concerns the normative dimension of essentialist assumptions: the belief that it is "natural" for individuals to embody their essence, because the essence fixes how an individual *should* be, and thus that "individuals who deviate from their natural state are malformed."[10] And third, possessing the essence of a certain natural kind is supposed to be absolute rather than incremental. To possess an essence is to possesses it fully. As psychologists Gil Diesendruck and Susan Gelman put the point,

> All members of a category are believed to possess the category's essential properties to the same degree and are therefore considered members of the category to the same extent. Members of a category may differ, however, in the typicality of their nonessential features (e.g., physical appearance) and therefore may vary in how good an example of the category they are. The essentialist account, then, attempts to capture the intuition that, for instance, although a Chihuahua and a German shepherd differ in how representative they are of the category dog, the former is as much a dog as the latter. More generally, the essentialist account argues that categorization is all-or-none: Items are judged absolutely as either members of their category or not members of their category.[11]

So, according to the folk theory, kind membership is *absolute*. An animal cannot be more or less of a porcupine: it must be wholly a porcupine or not a porcupine at all. Later on, in Chapter 12, I will show why this feature of essentialist thinking is crucial for explaining the distinctive phenomenology of dehumanization.

From Soul to Genome and from Genome to Race

In past centuries, the essence of a being was often identified with its "soul." The type of soul that a being has was supposed to determine the kind of being that it is. According to the Aristotelian framework, which was a dominant influence on Christian, Muslim, and Jewish philosophical and scientific thought, even plants and animals were thought to be ensouled. Plants have "vegetative" souls insofar as they grow and reproduce, and animals have this plus a "sensitive" soul that allows them to have sense perceptions. Human beings were distinguished by having a "rational" soul that plants and animals lack. Aristotelians believed that it is this that sets us apart from "lower" organisms and therefore is what makes us human. It is important to bear in mind that the Aristotelian conception of soul is not some sort of metaphysical organ—it is a form of life. From this perspective, saying that a being "has" a rational soul is just to say that it has access to rationality.

Although the Aristotelian theory of the soul might seem to be little more than navel-gazing by a Greek aristocrat with too much time on his hands, it had vast and terrible ramifications. Aristotle used his theory to justify the institution of slavery. Some people, he argued, are "slaves by nature" (a category that included virtually everyone other than high-born Greek males) because they possessed the capacity for rationality to only a very imperfect degree. Aristotle did not go as far as to say that barbarians lack rationality entirely—which would have excluded them from the category of the human and ranked them with nonhuman animals. Barbarians were human because they had rationality, albeit a defective, third-rate grade of rationality. Unlike nonhuman animals, which are utterly incapable of rationality, the barbarian "shares in reason to the extent of understanding it, but does not have it himself."[12] In other words, these quasi-brutes have it in them to be responsive to reason, but they do not have the wherewithal to initiate it—they lack the "deliberative" component of rationality.[13] Aristotle also claimed that barbarians could participate, albeit indirectly, in a higher form of life by subordinating themselves to their Greek masters. As this is a good thing, it follows that Greeks should enslave barbarians, and that barbarians owe it to themselves to be enslaved by Greeks, because this allows them to participate in a higher form of life. As Malcolm Heath aptly puts it, Aristotle believed that the master is "a kind of cognitive prosthesis" for the slave.[14]

Aristotle distinguished natural slavery from slavery as a social institution. In his view, only those who are natural slaves should be enslaved. Similarly, he believed women are stunted, chronically underdeveloped human beings who should be subordinated to Greek men.[15]

It is clear from this summary that Aristotle viewed the social and biological world as having a hierarchical organization. Greek men were above Greek women, who were above barbarian men, who were (presumably) above barbarian women, who were above non-human animals.[16] Aristotle's opinions about natural slavery were hugely influential for more than two thousand years after his demise. The idea that whole groups of people are defective, and therefore benefit from being taken in hand by their superiors was very attractive to apologists for colonialism and slavery. Perhaps the best-known example is the exchange between the Dominican friar Bartolomé de las Casas and the jurist Juan Ginés de Sepúlveda in 1550, over the question of whether or not the indigenous peoples of the Spanish Empire in the New World were natural slaves, and therefore whether or not it was legitimate to enslave them. Echoing Aristotle but going one step further in excluding Indians from membership in the human family, Sepúlveda claimed that the "barbarians of the New World . . . are as inferior to the Spaniards as are children to adults and women to men. The difference between them is as great as . . . I am tempted to say, between men and monkeys."[17] North American apologists for slavery, such as South Carolina senator William Harper (1790–1847), also often cited Aristotle's thesis. Harper, who was but one of many who enlisted Aristotle's authority in support of this institution, wrote of Black people that "they approach nearer to the nature of the brute creation, than perhaps any other people on the face of the globe. Let me ask if this people do not furnish the very material out of which slaves ought to be made, and whether it be not an improving of their condition to make them the slaves of civilized masters?"[18]

For Aristotle, then, the soul was a form of life rather than a thing that people possess. But over time, the Aristotelian rational soul was replaced with the Christian conception of an immortal soul, an immaterial thing the presence or absence of which determined whether a being was human or not. Writings by seventeenth-century Anglican clergyman Morgan Godwyn make it clear that British colonists in the New World considered enslaved Africans to lack souls in this sense and therefore to be less than human. Godwyn wrote that he had been told "privately (and as it were in the dark) . . . That [sic] the Negros, though in their Figure they carry some resemblances of Manhood, yet are indeed no Men" and that they are "Unman'd and Unsoul'd; accounted and even ranked with Brutes"—"Creatures destitute of Souls, to be ranked among Brute Beasts, and treated accordingly."[19] Even during the nineteenth century, enslaved people in the United States were often told that they did not have souls. One former slave, interviewed in the late 1930s, recalled being told by a preacher that "only White people had souls and went to heaven" and that "niggers had no more soul than dogs."[20]

The possession of a soul is less often invoked as the criterion for humanness in today's secular societies. Instead, we have delegated this role to the genome, which has been charged with a pop-metaphysical significance that extends far beyond anything that science tells us about the biological role of DNA.[21] As sociologists Dorothy Nelkin and M. Susan Lindee observe,

> Spiritual imagery sets the tone for popular accounts of DNA, fueling narratives of genetic essentialism and giving mystical powers to a molecular structure. Indeed, DNA has assumed a cultural meaning similar to that of the Biblical soul. It has become a sacred entity, a way to explore fundamental questions about human life, to define the essence of human existence, and to imagine immortality. . . . Just as the Christian soul has provided an archetypal concept through which to understand the person and the continuity of self, so DNA appears in popular culture as a soul-like entity. . . . The genome appears as a "solid" and immutable structure that can mark the borders and police the boundaries between humans and animals, man and machine, self and other, "them" and "us."[22]

In light of its conceptual role as an essence-bearer, it is not surprising that DNA is often called upon to validate everyday notions of race. If genes are what make people members of one race or another, could it be that racial essentialism has been vindicated by science?

People who do not know the basic science, but who have the vague conviction that race must somehow reside in our DNA, tend to think that there are genes "for" race. This is the idea that there are sharp discontinuities in our genetic makeup that map perfectly or nearly perfectly onto the conventional racial partitions of the human family. To put the point as crudely as it deserves to be put, it is the notion that there are "White" genes, "Black" genes, "Asian" genes, and so on, that make it the case that one belongs to one or another of these races. This assumption, which simply transposes racial essentialism onto the genome, has zero scientific credibility.

Although the idea that racial divisions correspond to real, biological categories had begun to fade away earlier in the twentieth century, most notably in response to the horrors resulting from the Nazis' brand of scientific racism, the decisive event in its decline was work by Harvard geneticist Richard Lewontin. In his 1972 paper "The Apportionment of Human Diversity," Lewontin argued on empirical grounds that the genetic variation that exists between individual members of a given race far outstrips, on average, the genetic variation between members of different races. In other words, racial differences represent only a small proportion of the differences between people and are therefore not very significant biologically.

Let me flesh this argument out a bit. All human beings are practically identical at the genetic level. However, there are some places or "loci" on our genome that can be occupied by different "versions" of a gene. These variants are called "alleles." Variation among alleles accounts for many of our individual differences. For example, the fact that one person has straight hair and another person has curly hair results from the presence of different alleles at the loci that control hair texture. Obviously, some larger-scale differences between whole groups of people are likely to correspond to differences in allele distribution: alleles that produce curly hair will be far more frequent in populations where almost everyone has hair of that sort than in populations where few people have curly hair (this should not be taken to imply that variations in hair texture are always brought about by the same alleles, or that the relevant alleles do not depend on the presence of other alleles for producing this effect).

Lewontin's famous study considered allelic variation at only seventeen loci. However, with improved technology it has become possible to perform much more ambitious analyses of between-group genetic variation that consider much larger numbers of loci. When several alleles frequently occur together in a population, this is called a "cluster." Genetic researchers use a computer program called STRUCTURE (because it analyzes what biologists call "population structure") to discover such clusters in aggregated genetic data. This involves getting STRUCTURE to divide the data into the number of clusters specified beforehand by the researchers. STRUCTURE does not search for alleles that are unique to any group of people (as in the naïve essentialist picture of genes for race). Rather, it uses statistical facts about allele frequencies to distinguish between population clusters. You can think of clusters as defining the average genotype of the whole group rather than the actual genotype of individual members of the group.

Race apologists have been heartened by the fact that if you sample genetic data from all over the world and instruct STRUCTURE to segment the data into five clusters, it geographically groups individuals in a way that sort of matches the division of humankind into five races: Africa, the Americas, Oceania, East Asia, and Europe-Middle East-Central Asia. However, the claim that STRUCTURE scientifically vindicates the biological reality of race is questionable. Scientists and scholars have raised several telling objections to this interpretation of what STRUCTURE reveals about genetic diversity among human populations, and have argued against the view that population clusters are races.[23]

These arguments turn on empirical or methodological issues. But the claim that statistical facts about populations can underwrite the reality of race can also be faulted on conceptual grounds.

There are some characteristics that only individuals can have. An example is baldness. Individual people can be bald, but groups of people cannot be bald. To be bald, a thing has to have a head. Individuals have heads, but groups do not. Suppose that a bunch of bald people created a club called the Slaphead Club. Although it would be true to say that every member of the Slaphead Club is bald, it would be false to say that the Slaphead Club is bald. Because it does not have a head, a group that is composed entirely of bald people cannot itself be bald. Speaking loosely, one might refer to this group as "the bald club," but it is really the members of the club that are bald, not the club. To attribute the properties of the parts (baldness) to the whole (the club) is to commit what is known as the fallacy of composition: the fallacy of thinking that what is true of the parts of a thing must also be true of the thing that they are parts of.

There are also characteristics of groups that are not features of the individuals that constitute those groups. To attribute these sorts of properties to individual members is to commit what is called the fallacy of division—the mirror image of the fallacy of composition. Here is an example. According to the United States Census Bureau, the median age for American women in the year 2012 was 38.1 years. But it would be wrong to conclude from this that any individual woman has the median age of 38.1 years, because individual women do not have median ages. Constructs like "median age" give us information about aggregates of individuals, but they do not apply to the individuals that make up the aggregate.

To claim that a club is bald, or that an individual woman has a median age, is to commit a category mistake, as described in Chapter 1. Likewise, saying that measurements of allele frequencies vindicate folk conceptions of race rests on a category mistake, albeit a subtle one. To see why, the place to start is to consider whether people think of race as a property of individuals, a property of groups, or a property of both. Obviously, race is supposed to be a feature of individuals, otherwise it wouldn't make any sense to say that Barack Obama was the first Black president of the United States.[24] "Races," in the collective sense, are groups consisting of all and only those individual people who are of a certain race, but the races themselves—the aggregates of individuals that constitute the race—do not have racial properties (the White race is the sum of individuals with the property of being White, but the White *race* does not have the property of being White any more than the Slaphead Club has the property of being bald).

Allele frequencies are, like the median age of American women, statistical properties of whole populations rather than properties of individuals. So, although facts about different allele frequencies in different populations might provide the basis for a scientific conception of race (I say "might" because there are other reasons to doubt that this can be done), genetic clusters cannot be equated with ordinary conceptions of race, and racial essentialists cannot look to genetic studies of population structure for support.

Passing

Racial essentialism is a special case of psychological essentialism and conforms to the same general pattern as essentialism about species. To the extent that one is a racial essentialist, one believes that there is a hidden racial essence, the possession of which is what makes a person belong to a certain race and is also responsible for producing observable, race-related features of human beings. The racial essence imagined to be possessed by all and only Black people is supposed to be what makes such people Black, and is also supposed to cause such people to have the physical features that are typically used to identify members of the Black race—skin color, hair texture, facial morphology, and so on. However, according to essentialist thinking, it is possible for a person to be raced without ever manifesting the appearance or behavior that is associated with that race. Their racial essence is latent. They "have it in them" even though they do not express it, or express it fully. For example, Jews are supposed by anti-Semites to be essentially greedy, deceptive, and exploitative. Jews who do not behave in these ways are nevertheless imagined to be disposed to do so. It does not matter that a Jew behaves generously, honestly, and compassionately. This is merely a façade that conceals the Jewish person's true nature. From this perspective, the less a Jew conforms to anti-Semitic stereotypes, the more suspicious one should be of them, because this might lead you to falsely believe that he really is a decent human being. This way of thinking makes racist stereotypes irrefutable. Once person becomes entrenched in such beliefs, there is no possible evidence to convince them that Black people are not violent, Latinos are not feckless, and Roma are not thieves because any evidence that one might offer to show that these assumptions are false pertains only to their manifest behavior and not to their (by definition, unobservable and unalterable) essential nature.

CHAPTER FIVE

The Logic of Race

For historical reasons having to do with colonialism, both Americans and Western Europeans strongly associate race with skin color and other associated phenotypic traits, but the recurring nightmare of the dominant group in every racist regime is that members of the subordinate group will slip through the cracks in the wall of oppression and pass as members of their ostensibly superior kind. The term "passing" was already in use during the early nineteenth century. It appears in Richard Hildreth's 1836 novel *The Slave: or Memoir of Archie Moore* (the first American abolitionist novel) and is a central theme of many subsequent literary works.[1] The idea of racial passing is predicated on the essence/appearance distinction. If it is possible for a person not to appear to be of their race, then a person's race is fixed by their ancestry rather than their appearance. And race is regarded as being fixed by ancestry because of false, essentialist beliefs about the transmission of essences from one generation to the next.

Think back to the distinction that I made in Chapter 1 between having a cold and having the symptoms of a cold. Having a cold is not just having a bundle of cold symptoms. The cold is what *causes* the cold symptoms of stuffy nose, sore throat, and so on, but it is possible to have these symptoms without having a cold (you might have hay fever), and it is also possible to have a cold without having any of these symptoms (when you are first infected with a rhinovirus—which we can think of as something like the "essence" of a cold—you have a cold but the symptoms have not appeared yet). The relationship between having a cold and having cold symptoms is analogous to the relationship between having a race and appearing to be a member of that race. Physical characteristics that are associated with racial categories such as skin color, eye shape, and nose shape are taken to be generally reliable indicators of that person's race, but they are not diagnostically foolproof.

Changing one's race is ruled out by the logic of racial essentialism. If your race is essential to the person that you are, then it is impossible to change your race while remaining the person that you are. According to the folk theory, then, race is immutable and racial passing is a form of pretense or disguise. When a person passes as a member of another race they are *falsely* regarded as belonging to that race (they might even falsely regard themselves as belonging to that race). Their appearance contradicts their essence.

Because the idea of changing race flies in the face of essentialist assumptions, thought experiments with this theme are a rich source of insights into everyday beliefs about race. One such is Oskar Panizza's story "The Operated Jew," published in 1893. It has been described both as "one of the most repulsive and insightful narratives ever written about German anti-Semitism" and as a scathing parody of anti-Semitic beliefs.[2]

The narrative revolves around a medical student named Itzig Faitel Stern. He is an anti-Semitic caricature: physically grotesque, behaviorally eccentric, and speaks a mishmash dialect of Palatinate German and Yiddish. That Faitel is *racially* Jewish—rather than just culturally Jewish—is explicit in the narrator's description: "Now I no longer want to keep the reader in the dark as to how I became associated with this remarkable figure. There was certainly a great deal of medical or rather anthropological curiosity in this case. I was attracted to him in the same way I might be to a Negro whose goggle eyes, yellow connective optical membranes, crushed nose, mollusk lips and ivory teeth and smell one perceives altogether in wonderment and whose feelings and most secret anthropological actions one wants to get to know as well!"[3]

The narrator also remarks on Faitel's forlorn attempts to transcend his race. Faitel is a "monster" and an object of fascination, not just because of his own inherent grotesqueness, but importantly because of his efforts to ape the characteristics of superior Germans. "I observed with astonishment how this monster took terrible pains to adapt to our circumstances, our way of walking, thinking, our gesticulations, the expressions of our intellectual tradition, our manner of speech. . . . Consequently, he was beheld with ridicule and astonishment."[4]

Frustrated by his failure to assimilate, Faitel appeals to the distinguished surgeon Dr. Klotz, who agrees to perform a series of radical medical interventions to reconfigure his Jewish body into an imitation of an Aryan one. His bones are broken and reset to give him a Teutonic bearing, he wears a spiked belt ("as they do with dogs"[5]) to correct his Jewish slouch, his skin color is chemically lightened, his hair is straightened and made blond. And there are behavioral interventions too. His Yiddish patois is replaced by rasping Hanoverian High German, his Jewish blood is replaced by a transfusion of pure German Christian blood, and he changes his name to Siegfried Freudenstern. Finally, Faitel achieves the pinnacle of racial success. He becomes engaged to marry a blond, quintessentially Aryan woman.

But it is just at the point that Faitel's transmutation seems complete, and he has become a perfect counterfeit of a gentile German, that things go terribly wrong. He gets drunk at his wedding feast, and his sham Aryanness catastrophically unravels.

Now everyone's attention in the room was immediately drawn to him. Even the waiters carrying large piles of dishes came to a stop and stared at the middle of the rows of tables where a bloodthirsty, swelling, crimson visage spewed saliva from flabby, drooping lips, and gushing eyes stared at them. Even Klotz lost his composure and looked with horror at the Jew next to him. . . . At this moment Faitel jumped from the chair, began clicking his tongue, gurgling, and tottering back and forth while making disgusting, lascivious, and bestial movements with his rear end. . . . He jumped around the room. "I dun bought for me Chreesten blud! Waiererá vere iss mine copulated Chreesten bride? Mine briderá! Geeve me mine briderá! I vant you shood know dat I am jost a Chreesten human being like you all. Not von drop of Jewish blud!"[6]

Faitel's subhumanity is hinted at throughout the tale. As literary scholar Joela Jacobs observes, "By likening Faitel's appearance and behavior to that of animals, the text calls into question whether its alien protagonist is fully human. . . . Unrecognizable to his old acquaintances, the blond, tall, and upright Siegfried Freudenstern is now able to lead a different life . . . of someone who matches the normative description of a German man and a human being."[7] That Faitel was a human being in name only gets hammered home in the final sentence of the story: "Klotz's work of art lay before him crumpled and quivering, a convoluted Asiatic image in wedding dress, a counterfeit of human flesh, Itzig Faital Stern."[8] Even Faitel's straight faux-blond hair darkens and curls, reverting to its original Semitic condition.

"The Operated Jew" can be read either as blatantly racist propaganda or as a parody of racial essentialism. In either case, the explicit motif is obvious: transracialism is impossible. No matter what cosmetic changes are made, no matter how assiduously one masters the appearance, speech, and mannerisms of another race, no matter how effectively one passes for a member of that race, one's racial essence will win out in the end, precisely because although essences can be covered up, they cannot be changed.

In 1922, the German-Jewish philosopher and writer Salomo Friedlaender, using the pen name "Mynona," wrote a response to Panizza's fable. He named it "The Operated Goy." Friedlaender's story, which was written under the rise of fascism in Weimar Germany, is an inversion of Panizza's. And it exposes the madness of racial thinking. Friedlaender turned "The Operated Jew" on its head. Instead of a story about a grotesque Jew trying desperately and impossibly to change his race, we are treated to an account of an über-German man, Count Kreutzwendedich Rehsok, transforming himself into a Jew.[9] Rehsok ("kosher" spelled backward) belongs to a family that "was accustomed to boasting about the indisputable purity of a racial bloodline that had been documented for centuries." We are told that for the last two millennia every count in the Rehsok line had joined the "struggle against the Jewish plague," especially the struggle against those Jews who married noble Prussians and had thereby "poisoned the milieu of the king with the pestilential stench of their misbegotten blood."[10] Given this immaculate pedigree, it is not surprising that when Kreutzwendedich left home to visit his noble relatives in Bonn, "his parents, siblings, aunts and uncles . . . kept warning him: 'Keep your blood pure! There are now enormously rich Semitic daughters who are keen on our kind.'"[11]

On the face of it, this man was unlikely to fall for the seductive wiles of a Jewess. His anti-Semitic credentials were impeccable. An early supporter of the National Socialist movement, he strictly avoided purchasing any products produced by Jewish manufacturers, and he deleted all of the Jewish names from his copy of the Bible, replacing them with proper German ones (for example, "King Solomon" became "King Friedrich"). He cut a striking figure on his daily walks through Bonn, adorned with a bright red swastika armband and accompanied by a Great Dane, a pair of pet ravens, and his huge servant, who was responsible for choosing a route for him that steered clear of Jewish schools and synagogues. The count "strutted through the streets with the customary White student cap on his blond parted hair, his monocle on his eye, followed by his livery servant in a set distance." As soon as this entourage encountered anything or anyone Jewish, the manservant alerted them with a shrill blast on a silver whistle. The count's Great Dane was carefully trained to savage any Jew that came too close, and one of the ravens was trained to chirp the anti-Semitic "Borkumlied" ("Borkum Hymn").[12]

Kreutzwendedich's conspicuously anti-Semitic behavior delighted the gentile families of Bonn, but it aroused the ire of the beautiful Rebecka Gold-Isaac, a Jewess who vowed to bring this racist to his knees. "I am going to buy me this pompous turkey," she vowed, "even if I have to marry him out of revenge."

Donning a blond wig and assuming an aristocratic German name, Rebecka arranges to encounter Rehsok on one of his walks, and he immediately falls in love with her. Rebecka's first ploy is to arrange for the Count to travel to Vienna for an appointment with Sigmund Freud. Freud gets him to face the fact he is sexually attracted to Jewish women, and to admit to himself that the woman whom he desires is Jewish. Rebecka then tells him that she will not marry unless he transforms himself a Jew, one that is "completely Jewish, a Jew to the point of excess . . . You do not love me with all your heart unless you become Jewish deep in the marrow of your Aryan bones, a Jew and nothing but a Jew." Rehsok agrees, and he submits to a sequence of painful medical procedures at the hands of a physician named Dr. Friedlaender, who circumcises him, darkens his skin, flattens his feet, and performs cosmetic surgery to morph his nose into a Jewish-looking one. Rehsok's blond hair is removed and his bones are broken and reset so that his upright aristocratic posture morphs into a Jewish slouch. Finally, he is packed off to Romania to study Torah and learn to speak perfect

Yiddish and Hebrew, with all of the right inflections and gesticulations. The formerly ultragentile count emerges from this regimen
as a fully-fledged Jew, changes his name to Moishe Kosher, becomes
a Zionist, and emigrates to Palestine with his spouse. Friedlaender
concludes,

> Certain orthopedists are feared and resisted by people who are
> still proud of the purity of their race. Nevertheless, Professor
> Friedlaender has enjoyed an enormous increase in clientele. He
> has an institute that rents out masks, but it does not rent out
> mere costumes. Rather it produces skin and hair, bone and
> muscle as disguises. A former emperor from the West recently
> had himself transformed into a Negro in order to escape the
> Bolshevist rabble. Czar Nicholas, who had disappeared, is living
> today as a harmless Rabbi in Moishe Kosher's vicinity, and they
> are on familiar footing with each other. One no longer bases
> everything dogmatically on racial differences. Racial blood has
> stopped being considered a special kind of vital juice. Mean-
> while, Professor Friedlaender gathers it in bottles and continues
> to transfer it undauntedly from one vessel to another.[13]

Panizza and Friedlaender present us with opposed views of the
possibility of changing one's race, each of which is grounded in a different conception of what race is. For Panizza, a person's race is part
of their essence, and cannot be eliminated or exchanged for a different racial identity. Changes of appearance that make one resemble and therefore pass as a member of a different race are merely
cosmetic, and one's true racial essence—no matter how radical and
thorough the outward transformation is—will always reassert itself
and subvert the transracial pretense. Panizza's perspective thus accords with the popular, essentialist view of race as a permanent biological feature. Friedlaender presents us with an entirely different
conception. He denies that racial metamorphosis is possible, not
because race is fixed, but rather because it is an insubstantial social

contrivance. Joela Jacobs sums this up nicely: "In a world where one's skin color can be changed like one's hair color, categories such as race lose their power. Kreutzwendedich's total transformation results in a radical change in the way humankind conceives of identity. It is no longer understood as an unchangeable result of one's blood or physical properties, rather, it becomes mutable and mobile."[14]

Friedlaender presents us with a vision of a world in which the very notion of race has disappeared and been replaced by a humanistic perspective. As he wrote from Paris, where he had fled in 1933 to escape the Nazi menace, and where he died in poverty, "I shall defend the sublime, beautiful, good, pious, intelligent *human being*, that is just as much in the German as it is in the Negro and the Jew."[15]

George Schuyler's 1931 satirical novel *Black No More: Being an Account of the Strange and Wonderful Workings of Science in the Land of the Free, 1933–1940* is yet another literary treatment of the same thought experiment, this one in a distinctively American key. The plot revolves around the invention by a Black scientist named Junius Crookman of a process called "Black-No-More" that makes Black people visually indistinguishable from Whites. The novel's protagonist, Max Disher, decides to undergo the Black-No-More process after being rebuffed by a beautiful White woman in a Harlem nightclub who told him when he invited her to dance, "I never dance with niggers!" After his transformation, Disher changes his name to Fisher and moves to Atlanta, where, posing as an anthropologist, he becomes a senior member of the Knights of Nordica, a White supremacist order headed up by the father of the woman who had previously spurned him. Meanwhile, African Americans flock to Black-No-More sanitaria, and the nation is socially, politically, and economically convulsed by the evaporation of its racial underclass.

Black No More relentlessly undermines the concept of race. Schuyler skillfully plays on the essence/appearance distinction to make his point. Crookman denies that races are constituted either by their behavior or their appearance. When, early on in the novel, one of his associates worries that people who have undergone the treatment will retain "that darky dialect," Crookman replies, "There is no such thing as Negro dialect, except in literature and drama. It is a well-known fact among informed persons that a Negro from a given section speaks the same dialect as his White neighbors." And with regard to differences in facial appearance, Crookman delivers a mini-lecture on phenotypic variation that is worth quoting in full:

> Well, there are plenty of Caucasians who have lips quite as thick and noses quite as broad as any of us. As a matter of fact, there has been considerable exaggeration about the contrast between Caucasian and Negro features. The cartoonists and minstrel men have been responsible for it very largely. Some Negros like the Somalis, Filanis, Egyptians, Hausas and Abyssinians have very thin lips and nostrils. So have the Malagasys of Madagascar. Only in certain small sections of Africa do the Negros possess extremely pendulous lips and very broad nostrils. On the other hand, many so-called Caucasians, particularly the Latins, Jews and South Irish, and frequently the most Nordic peoples like the Swedes, show almost negroid lips and noses. Black up some White folks and they could deceive a resident of Benin.[16]

Crookman's understanding of the biologically insubstantial character of race—which is neither in the face nor in the blood—is effectively juxtaposed with the ignorance displayed by the White racists who, given the phenotypic changes wrought by Crookman's procedure, "couldn't tell who was who!"—that is, couldn't tell the difference between those who were *really* White and those who were merely indistinguishable from Whites. Schuyler's narrator repeatedly describes the Black-No-More process as "turning Negroes into Caucasians" while emphasizing that all that has changed about these people is their appearance. But he describes racists, whose world has been destabilized by racial ambiguity, as "always asking each other embarrassing questions about birth and blood" and worrying that the transformations wrought by Crookman will lead to ostensibly White couples producing phenotypically Black babies.[17] In a final ironic twist, it is discovered that the beneficiaries of Black-No-More—the "new Caucasians"[18]—are actually a lighter shade of pale than the old Caucasians are.

> To a society that had been taught to venerate Whiteness for over three hundred years, this announcement was rather staggering. What was the world coming to, if blacks were Whiter than Whites? Many people in the upper class began to look askance at their very pale complexions. If it were true that extreme Whiteness were evidence of the possession of Negro blood, of having once been a member of a pariah class, then surely it were well not to be so White! The upper class began to look around for ways to get darker. It became the fashion for them to spend hours at the seashore basking naked in the sunshine and then to dash back, heavily bronzed, to their homes, and, preening themselves in their dusky skins, lord it over their paler, and thus less fortunate, associates.[19]

In exploring the contours of racial thinking, Panizza, Friedlaender, and Schuyler all present a picture of folk racial thinking as essentialistic, as situating race "in the blood," and contrast this conception of race with the notion of race as appearance. In Panizza's story, transracialism is impossible, because one's race is fixed by one's biological essence. But it is also impossible for Friedlaender and Schuyler, not because race is essentialized, but rather because race is a tissue of illusion.

Panizza and Schuyler beautifully portray the essentialist presumptions of vernacular notions of race. In both works, a person's appearance belies what others regard as their true racial essence. And in both, the merely cosmetic racial transformation is disrupted by the racial essence reasserting itself—in the former by Faitel's unraveling at the wedding feast and in the latter by the birth of (phenotypically) Black babies to phenotypically White couples. However, unlike Schuyler and Friedlaender, who both express skepticism about the reality of race, Panizza vividly conveys the idea that a racialized person who pretends to be other—who does not know his social and metaphysical place—is grotesque.

The stories by these three authors might seem to be fables far removed from reality. But they are not. During the late nineteenth and early twentieth centuries, Jews in Germany dyed and straightened their hair, and even resorted to rhinoplastic surgery to help them conceal their Jewishness. Intellectual historian Sander Gilman states these procedures "were actually meant to 'cure' the disease of Jewishness, the anxiety of being seen as a Jew."[20] Likewise, Schuyler was influenced by early twentieth-century experiments in skin dyeing. For example, Major R. F. Shufeldt, MD, of the US Army wrote in his 1907 book *The Negro: A Menace to American Civilization*,

The Negro is not responsible for his animal nature any more than for the opportunities he takes to gratify the normal impulses which are a part of him. It is not a changing of the spots on the leopard, although some, indeed many, think this to be the case. For example, a writer in *The New York Evening Telegram* on January 28, 1904, claims to have discovered a treatment for the Negro which will have the effect of turning his skin White! Just as though all savagery, cannibalistic tendencies, thievish propensities, mendacity, and the rest were in the skin of the animal! Such an expedient might, if effective, prove to be of value politically; but it would be worse than useless biologically, for the danger sign—his color—would be removed, and the opportunity would be greater for this semimetamorphosed race to mix its cannibalistic blood with that of the unsuspecting Anglo-Saxon in the United States.[21]

Some Methodological Issues

I have been claiming that beliefs about race are often rooted in essentialist thinking: that thinking of someone as belonging to a certain race is often the same as thinking of them as a member of a discrete natural human kind, and that the person belongs to that kind by virtue of possessing an essence that is causally responsible for the surface characteristics that are taken to be typical of their race. But is it really true that whenever people use racial labels, they have some notion like this explicitly or implicitly in mind?

Sometimes, what seems like racial speech is nothing more than a way of using a person's appearance to distinguish them from others. For example, referring to a person as "Asian" is just a handy way of picking them out in a crowd. When I lived in an area with a large Afro-Caribbean population in London, England, I was sometimes the only beige-skinned person on the bus that took me home from work. One way I might have described this is that "I was the only White guy on the bus." In cases like this, the ostensibly racial term is more or less functionally equivalent to expressions like "I was the tallest guy on the bus today" or "I was the oldest guy on the bus today." I do not think that this way of talking should be considered as genuinely racial speech, because being a member of one or another race is not supposed to be a contingent matter like height and age are.

Anyone who wants to investigate folk theories of race has several strategies available to them.[22] One is to pour over the historical literature—to look into what ordinary people, as well as so-called

race experts, have said about race in days past. Another method—
beloved of philosophers—is to sit back in a comfortable armchair,
reflect on how you are inclined to think about race, and then gener-
alize this to others. Yet a third approach is to do empirical research
using instruments such as surveys or focus groups to investigate
people's beliefs about race.[23] The first two methods have obvious
drawbacks. Why assume that the writings of purported race experts reflected prevalent everyday views of their era? And even if
the historical sources allow us to build up a picture of how most
people thought about race in the past, why assume that people think
about race in the same way today? And with regard to the second,
the justification for thinking that the reflections of philosophers
from the solitary comfort of their armchairs are generalizable to
the general public seems wobbly at best. Philosophers are, after all,
notorious for departing from commonsense perspectives, sometimes
in outrageous ways, so it seems on the face of it unlikely that con-
sulting their own intuitions should give them access to other people's
views about race.

Ordinarily, if you want to find out what someone believes you
ask them, so it might seem obvious that just asking people about
their racial beliefs is the best way to discover the content of those
beliefs. However, I think that this seemingly obvious conclusion
is questionable, for several reasons. One is that people's explicit
responses to questions or vignettes about race, even if they are
entirely sincere, may coexist with other, unarticulated attitudes.
Whatever one makes of the research on implicit attitudes, it is
silly to deny that we often harbor attitudes toward members of
racialized groups—attitudes that are not conscious or only "sort of"
conscious—that conflict with the ones that we explicitly endorse.[24]
Putting this worry in a nutshell: it seems reasonable to suppose that
asking people about their beliefs about race may reveal their beliefs
about their beliefs about race, rather than their actual beliefs

about race. And these beliefs about their beliefs may fail to line up with reality.

Another cause for concern is that people's folk theories about race might be unstable. It seems reasonable to think that because these beliefs tend to be emotionally charged, they vary in response to the ebb and flow of experience, and with the context in which one is asked about them. What a person writes down on a questionnaire or tells a social scientist who's interviewing her might be very different from the way that she thinks about race when she is out on the street or chatting with a friend in a bar. Of course, there is also the problem of simple dishonesty. Because it is generally socially unacceptable to express derogatory attitudes about race, there is always the possibility that subjects will dissimulate, telling the researcher what they think they are supposed to believe rather than what they in fact do believe.

Finally, and I think very importantly, it is quite difficult to get the language right when designing research instruments for probing beliefs about race. One of the most interesting and sophisticated attempts to survey beliefs about race is a survey designed and implemented by the philosopher Joshua Glasgow, in collaboration with Julie Shulman and Enrique Covarrubias. Their method was to use racially themed vignettes, each of which was followed by a multiple-choice question.[25] For instance, question 5 (based on the plot of *Black No More*) begins with the following vignette: "George 'looks Black' to the average person, he has all Black ancestry, he identifies himself as Black, and he is accepted as Black by his local community. But George tires of being Black, so he invents a machine that can transform his entire physical appearance so that he 'looks White.' After using this machine, he steeps himself in White culture and moves to a new community where everyone identifies him as White."[26] Respondents are then asked whether, after George used his machine, he is (a) White, (b) Black, (c) Mixed, (d) Some-

THE LOGIC OF RACE ‡ 97

times White and sometimes Black, or (e) None of the above. Answers to these questions were taken to reveal respondents' beliefs about how the concept of race works. The authors report that only "51% of respondents determined that George was still Black after using the machine" and therefore that racial essentialism may be less common than many of the people who study race assume it to be.[27]

This percentage is certainly interesting, but there is a problem that may be skewing the result. As we have seen, words like "black" and "white" have more than one meaning. They can be used as names for colors (a black limousine, a white Christmas), or they can be used as names for races. When George, a *racially* Black man, emerges from the machine he "looks White." But what does this mean? It might mean that he looks like a typical racially White person, or that he is literally colored white, or that his skin is colored in way that is typical of people who are classified as racially White. So, the multiple-choice question can be interpreted in at least three distinct ways. A sophisticated reader *might* take the capitalization of "White" in the vignette to suggest that racial Whiteness is what is being talked about. But then again, she might not—or she might interpret the candidate answers as color terms. I emphasize this to show how difficult it is to design such studies in ways that are likely to yield reliably informative results.

Given all of the problems that plague attempts to use empirical methods to study racial concepts, we should be appropriately cautious about accepting their results. As Ann Morning, a sociologist who studies attitudes toward race, observes, claims about the pervasiveness or nonpervasiveness of racial essentialism "are based on a very thin layer of empirical research—often no more than one study, possibly conducted decades ago—and are often contradicted by another study's findings."[28]

We are not yet in a position to resolve questions about the folk metaphysics of race by turning to empirical, social-scientific studies.

The best that we can do at the moment and perhaps at any future moment is to triangulate: cautiously drawing on multiple sources of information, including, but not in principle limited to, historical research, philosophical reflection, naturalistic observation, and social science surveys, to discover areas of convergence and divergence. One thing that can be said with a high degree of confidence on the basis of this strategy is that although essentialism (as I have described it above) may not be a universal folk theory of race, it has been, and continues to be, a very pervasive one. And that is all that is necessary to take the next step of connecting the dots between racializing people and dehumanizing them.

Race, Dehumanization, and Psychological Essentialism

There are two reasons why understanding how we think about race is vital for understanding the phenomenon of dehumanization. One is that they are tied together causally. The dehumanization of a group of people is typically preceded and facilitated by their racialization. The examples that I have stressed in this chapter and in Chapter 4—the dehumanization of African Americans and Jews—illustrate this principle, and there are many more like these. The racialization and dehumanization by Europeans of indigenous people in the Americas, Australia, and Asia; the dehumanization of sub-Saharan Africans by Arabs; the dehumanization of the Japanese by allied forces during World War II (and vice versa); the dehumanization of Romani people; and the dehumanization of the Chinese by the Japanese during the 1930s are just a few examples. Most of the apparent exceptions—for example, the dehumanization of the Rwandan Tutsi by Hutus, the dehumanization of Armenians by Turks, and the dehumanization of the marginalized people of Sudan by the Khartoum regime and those loyal to it—are not really exceptions after all if one bears in mind the definition of race that

I have delineated earlier in this chapter. When we racialize people, we conceive of them as belonging to a separate and inferior natural human kind, transmitted by descent. The three seeming exceptions mentioned above, as well as very many others, all satisfy this general description.

The other reason why understanding the psychology of racial thinking is crucial to understanding dehumanization is because the two processes are structurally similar. Racialized people are seen as being categorically "other" while retaining their membership in the more encompassing category of the human. They may pass as members of the dominant group by virtue of having an appearance that departs from their supposed racial essence. However, when racialized people are dehumanized, they are seen as categorically "other" in a more extreme fashion. Even though they have a *human appearance* that leads the unwary to mistake them for human beings, they have a *subhuman essence*. The structural similarity between dehumanization and racialization—the conformance of these cognitive attitudes to the same pattern—is explained, in large measure, by the fact that both are rooted in psychological essentialism.

So far, I have been taking the notion of subhumanity for granted. But the time has come to unpack it. What exactly is meant by subhumanity? Where does the idea that some human beings are *less* than human come from? What role does this idea play in human life? An adequate theory of dehumanization has got to be able to answer questions such as these. I will address them next.

CHAPTER SIX

Hierarchy

In the last three chapters, I addressed the question of how it is possible to think of an entity that is outwardly indistinguishable from a human being as a nonhuman creature, and explored the relationship between dehumanization and racial essentialism. I argued that to conceive of people as less than human, one need only attribute a nonhuman essence to them. But this goes only part of the way toward explaining how dehumanization works, because although it tells us how it is possible to think of others as *non*human, it says nothing about what it is to think of others as *sub*human.

Many kinds of beings are labeled as "nonhuman." These include animals like snakes and rats, but also supernatural beings like God and angels. The former are thought of as subhuman, but the latter are not. To be subhuman, an entity has got to be in some sense *less than*—that is, inferior to human beings. The idea that there are subhuman organisms does not come from science. Although biological writings often refer to "lower" or even "subhuman" organisms, there no scientific warrant for this way of thinking. Biology does not give us any reason to think that organisms exist on a gradient from "lower" to "higher," with humans ensconced at the uppermost level.

Subhumanity is not an objective feature of the biosphere, so it must be a human invention. And this prompts questions about how it arose and what purpose it serves. In this chapter, I will explore where the idea of subhumanity comes from and why it has such a powerful grip on the human mind. I am going to unpack the notion of a hierarchy of nature, illuminate the role that it plays in the way that we think about the world of living things, explain how it adds another layer to the folk biology of race, and show how and why it allows us to think of other people as less than human. In doing this, I will introduce a number of ideas that will play a central role in the fuller explanation of dehumanization that I develop later in this book.

Higher and Lower

One thing that is so obvious that it can be confidently asserted right off the bat is that the idea of subhumanity presupposes a hierarchical framework. Social scientists use the term "hierarchy" for differences of status and power within human societies (for example, the relationship between an aristocrat and a commoner, or an employer and an employee) and biologists speak of dominance hierarchies in other, nonhuman species. Although these notions of hierarchy are not irrelevant to my subject matter, I reserve the term "hierarchy" herein for something that is much more inclusive and expansive: the idea that nature is structured as an ordered system of ranks, and that every natural kind permanently occupies a rank in that order: a position in an arrangement in which kinds of beings are higher or lower than others.

Most of us unquestioningly adopt the idea that the natural world has a hierarchical structure. It just seems obvious that human beings are inherently superior to goats, that goats are ranked above mosquitos, and that mosquitos are higher organisms than carrots. But on reflection, it is not clear *why* we think about organisms in this way. It is not obvious what is it about human beings that is supposed to elevate us above all of these others, and what is it about nonhuman organisms that is supposed to make them *less* than human. And yet, because dehumanized people are supposed to be subhuman, it is impossible to make sense of the phenomenon of dehumanization without addressing the question of why we think of other organisms as our inferiors.

Verticality

The language of verticality, of levels, ranks, and grades, is ubiquitous. A morally good person is *upright or upstanding*, and a bad one is *low-down*. People can be *degraded* (that is, reduced to a lower grade) or they can be *uplifted*. We *look down* on our *inferiors* and *look up* to our *superiors*. One's *subordinates* (from Latin *subordinatus*, "placed at an inferior rank") might be described as *underlings*, at the *bottom rung*. The verb "humiliate" means "to reduce to a lower position" and ultimately derives from Latin *humus*, meaning "ground." Transdisciplinary scholar Evelin Lindner observes,

> Whatever language, we always find a downward spatial orientation connected with words that signify humiliation. Consider the words *de-gradation*, *ned-verdigelse* in Norwegian, *Er-niedrigung* in German, or *a-baisse-ment* in French. The syllables *de, ned, niedrig,* and *bas* all mean *down from, low,* or *below.* To *put down, degrade, denigrate, debase, demean, derogate, lower, lessen,* or *belittle*—all these words are built on the same spatial, orientational metaphor, namely that something or somebody is pushed down and forcefully held there. . . . We apply such rankings to our evaluations of both the abiotic and the biotic worlds. Gold, worth much, is high up on the scale of worth and value, silver a little lower, and dirt is worth little and is somewhere far down. When we turn to the biotic world, we see divine powers usually being placed at the absolute top, somewhere in heaven, far above humans. The human scale begins just below gods and angels. At its "pinnacle" the human scale champions divinely ordained masters and continues downward until it reaches the lowest underlings, who are often seen as of little more value than animals.[1]

For many centuries, the way of thinking that Lindner describes was enshrined in a hugely influential model of the cosmos known as the "Great Chain of Being" or *scala naturae* ("the ladder of nature"). The Great Chain was an all-encompassing paradigm according to which every kind of being—plants, animals, human beings, and even God and his angels—occupied a fixed rank in a vast metaphysical structure. The rank of a natural kind (sometimes called its "dignity") was supposed to be determined by how "perfect" its members are—that is, how fully they embody God's perfection. God, who is by definition the supremely perfect being, was placed at the pinnacle, and because human beings were created in God's image and were therefore thought to possess a greater share of His perfection than any other creature, they were ranked higher than all of the other animals and placed just below the angels.[2] Plants were assigned a place below animals, and inanimate substances were ranked below plants. Furthermore, each tier of the Great Chain could also be split into more fine-grained levels. So, for instance, the realm of nonhuman animals had mammals at the top, followed by birds, reptiles and amphibia, fish, and invertebrates. And each of these divisions could be subdivided into mini-hierarchies consisting of species-like kinds. The loftiest rank of each of these categories was occupied by what was called its "primate" (Latin for "of the highest rank"). In early versions, the lion ("king of beasts") was designated as primate of the mammalian rank. But later on, monkeys and apes acquired primate status and replaced lions and elephants.

The reason that present-day scientists refer to monkeys, apes, and human beings as primates comes from the very first system of biological taxonomy, proposed by the Swedish naturalist Carl Linnaeus. In his great *System of Nature*, first published in 1735 and going through many revised editions in the decades to follow, Linnaeus grouped humans, apes, monkeys, and lemurs together in what he called—drawing on the earlier nomenclature—the "family of primates" (oddly, he also included bats in this grouping). His decision to place human beings in the same category as other "lower" animals appalled many his colleagues, and Linnaeus himself showed signs of ambivalence about it, stressing that although human beings anatomically resemble apes and monkeys, we have a spiritual nobility and a capacity for reason that sets us apart from and elevates us above all the other creatures belonging to this group.[3] Humans were, for Linnaeus, the prime primates.

Around the same time, when violent encounters with the indigenous people of the so-called New World became frequent and Europeans' enslavement of West Africans became big business, European thinkers began to speculate about a racial stratification within the human rank. Predictably, men of European descent unquestioningly regarded Whites as the highest grade of humanity, and relegated Africans and Native Americans to the lowest, most primitive stratum, just above the borderline dividing human beings from apes and monkeys.[4] The following passage from the nineteenth-century French naturalist Julien-Joseph Virey is typical of much of the scientific literature on race from this period: "From the orang-utan to the Hottentot bushman, through to the most intelligent negroes, and finally to White man, one passes indeed by almost imperceptible nuances. Whether all beings were created progressively, with the most perfected ones derived from the less noble and less accomplished ones, during the early eras of our planet, or every species was formed independently from the others with its actual degree of perfectness, in any case we observe a scale from White to negro to Hottentot, to orang-utan, and from the latter to other apes."[5]

During the nineteenth century the notion of the Great Chain of Being met its most formidable challenge. Just thirteen years after Virey's death, Charles Darwin's *On the Origin of Species* burst upon the scientific scene.[6] Darwin's book had momentous philosophical implications, not least of which was that it shattered the metaphysical foundations of the concept of a hierarchy of nature. Far from being a pyramid extending from less perfect organisms at the base to more perfect organisms at the pinnacle, Darwin presented a conception of the natural world according to which no successful denizens of the biosphere are any more or less perfect than any other. Evolution, he explained, is not progress toward a goal. All successful organisms are well adapted to their environments. The very idea that some are more "highly" evolved than others does not make sense within this scientific framework. So, with respect to the degree of their "perfection," human beings and earthworms are on a par. It is not for nothing that Freud described Darwin's theory as a massive blow to human narcissism.

Even though the theory of evolution theoretically dethroned the species *Homo sapiens* from its status as paragon of animals, the idea of human supremacism has had remarkable staying power. The presumption of human superiority is, if not strictly universal, at least ubiquitous. It is no surprise that many of the devout still cling to the idea that human beings have a standing above that of all other creatures on account of their being fashioned in God's image. "The human person holds a position superior to the whole of nature," wrote Pope John Paul II. "Our distinctiveness and superiority as human beings in relation to other creatures is constantly verified by each of us. . . . It is also verified by the whole of humanity." It is somewhat more surprising to find the view espoused by a political and ethical theorist such as George Kateb, who states, "The core idea of human dignity is that on earth, humanity is the greatest type of being—and that every member deserves to be treated in a manner consistent with the high worth of the species." And Kateb is but one of very many secular theorists who adopt this view.[7]

Belief in intrinsic human superiority, and the related notion of a hierarchy of natural kinds, is not limited to theologians, philosophers, and social scientists. It carries on a shadowy existence in the life sciences as well, as is apparent by the fact that even scientifically educated people, including professional biologists, very often speak of kinds of organisms as "higher" or "lower" than others. Biology has, to a very great extent, been unable to break off its romance with the Great Chain of Being, but this is not for want of trying. As early as the eighteenth century, biological taxonomists were increasingly dissatisfied with, and attempted to free themselves from, the linear and hierarchical way of classifying the profusion of forms of life. But, as intellectual historian Harriet Ritvo explains, "As it turned out, reports of the death, or even the displacement of the chain were greatly exaggerated. Although fewer and fewer naturalists explicitly endorsed it as a systematic model, it continued to shape the language of almost everyone who discussed relationships among animal groups. . . . [Thus] Robert Knox explained human distinctiveness in terms of the ostensibly discarded metaphor: 'The human family stands profoundly apart from all others, implying that in the great chain of being constituting nature's plan, some natural family filling up the link has disappeared.'"[8]

The intellectual bias described by Ritvo has not dissipated with the passage of time. In a search of more that sixty-seven thousand scientific articles published between 2005 and 2010 for references to "higher" and "lower" organisms, biologists Emanuele Rigato and Alessandro Minelli found that the *scala naturae* is alive and well in twenty-first-century biology: "Articles with *scala naturae* language were particularly frequent in *Molecular Biology and Evolution* (6.14%), *BioEssays* (5.6%) and *Annual Review of Ecology Evolution and Systematics* (4.82%). The fact that two of these three journals are in an area of evolutionary biology shows that the use of pre-evolutionary language can survive even in the most renowned professional journals."[9]

And consider what is revealed when we place diagrams of the biological Tree of Life—the paradigmatic graphic representation of the branching evolutionary trajectory of biological taxa—side by side with older illustrations of the Great Chain of Being. Sean Nee, an evolutionary biologist who laments the persistence of a hierarchical view in the life sciences, observes, "Common presentations of evolution mirror the Great Chain by viewing the process as progressive. . . . Illustrating this, when we represent the relationships between species, including ourselves, in a family tree, we automatically construct it so that the column of species' names forms a chain with us at the top."[10]

To see what is wrong with this way of thinking, consider the evolutionary relationship between chimpanzees (*Pan troglodytes*) and *Homo sapiens*. Chimpanzees and humans had a common ancestor around six million years ago, and it was only from that point onward the two lineages diverged. So, there is no scientifically reasonable sense in which human beings have blossomed more recently on the Tree of Life than chimpanzees have. But even so, it is incredibly easy to slip into thinking of chimpanzees as "lower" or more primitive than human beings, and even the most die-hard Darwinian realists are likely to hold that human lives matter more than chimpanzee lives do. This point applies as much to the relation between humans and other kinds of organisms—mushrooms, paramecia, bullfrogs, or whatever—as it does to the relation between humans and chimpanzees. To make matters worse for champions of human exceptionalism, there are plenty of "lower" organisms that have evolved much more recently than *Homo sapiens*. These include the flowering plant *Senecio eboracensis*, which was discovered growing next to a parking lot in the North of England in 1979.[11] And by the same token, many animals, including reptiles, birds, and even mammals, emerged tens of millions of years before flowering plants, but we are nevertheless inclined think of the latter as ranked lower than any of the former.

Alternatively, defenders of the human superiority thesis might try claiming that it is evolutionary *change* that underwrites human superiority. The argument goes like this: Human beings have changed a great deal since the human and chimpanzee lineages began to go their separate ways, but chimpanzees have not changed nearly as much, so (the story goes) we humans have climbed higher on the evolutionary tree than our more apish cousins have. The obvious problem with this line of argument is that it relies on the incorrect idea that evolution is progressive. The cyanobacteria (otherwise known as "pond scum") that first appeared on earth at least three and a half billion years ago are no more and no less evolved than *Homo sapiens* are. If chimps have departed less from our common ancestor than we have, that is because they have been excellently adapted to their environment for a very long time, rather than because they are retrograde. And if evolutionary change pure and simple is the yardstick by which to measure evolutionary progress, the viruses have us beaten hands down.

But what about the idea that change *in a certain direction* accounts for evolutionary progress? How about change toward greater complexity? Claims about greater or lesser complexity can only be evaluated if we are clear about what is meant by saying that one kind of organism is more complex than another. Is genetic complexity what counts? *Homo sapiens* do not have the most elaborate genomes by a long shot, and if complexity means behavioral complexity then we must accommodate the fact that the life cycles of some parasitic worms are far more complex than ours is. So what sort of complexity is supposed to be relevant and why? There does not seem to be an objective answer to this question, because none of these strategies for justifying human superiority (even if they succeeded) can justify *normative* claims about intrinsic human superiority. Sure, *Homo sapiens* are generally better at certain things than other organisms are. We're the only organisms that can do calculus or cook paella. But other organisms are adept at doing things that we cannot do. "Better at" does not entail "better than."

The Idea of a Natural Hierarchy

Perhaps the idea of a natural hierarchy is a cultural artifact—an accident of history. The locus classicus for this hypothesis is philosopher Arthur O. Lovejoy's 1936 monograph *The Great Chain of Being*. Lovejoy described the Great Chain as a formal model of the cosmos as a hierarchy, extending from inert matter at the bottom to God at the top and with everything else assigned a fixed rank somewhere in between. He argued that this conception of the universe was cobbled together by philosophers in antiquity using three components drawn from the thought of Plato and Aristotle. One of these is the Platonic "principle of plentitude," the peculiar idea that every kind of thing that can possibly exist really does exist. Another is the Aristotelian "principle of continuity," which has it that each natural kind merges with other kinds in any scheme of classification, and therefore that nature is a seamless continuum. And third is the "principle of gradation," which is the Aristotelian notion that natural kinds have a hierarchical relation to one another and can be ranked on the basis of their degree of "perfection."[12]

Instead of explaining the idea of a cosmic hierarchy in terms of degrees of perfection, which sounds rather odd to twenty-first-century ears, the principle can be explained using the more familiar framework of degrees of intrinsic value. As described in Chapter 1, the intrinsic value of a thing is the worth that it has in and of itself, in contrast to its instrumental value, which is its usefulness for getting us something else. Another way to put this is that the intrinsic value of a thing is the value that it has because of *what it is*, and the instrumental value of a thing is the value that it has because of *what it does*. Some kinds of things are accorded great instrumental value, but little if any intrinsic value. The purple blossoms produced by the *Crocus sativus* plant are not generally regarded as having great intrinsic value, but they have immense instrumental value as the source of saffron, one of the world's costliest spices. Likewise, American slave owners did not accord their slaves much intrinsic value, but they granted them a great deal of instrumental value. Black slaves' lives mattered only because of the profits that Whites accrued from their labor. On the other side, it is also possible to accord things high intrinsic value but low instrumental value. The impending extinction of the gharial—a crocodile-like reptile native to the Indian subcontinent—has virtually zero economic or other practical implications, but for many people (including me) gharials matter just because they are gharials, and the fact that they are teetering on the brink of oblivion is a tragedy.

Think of the Great Chain of Being as a hierarchy of natural kinds that is ordered on the basis of their intrinsic value. The higher a kind of entity is ranked, the greater intrinsic value members of that kind are believed to possess. The intrinsic value of the members of each of these kinds is supposed to be an objective feature of them, rather than a consequence of how we happen to value them. In ages past (and in many religious communities today), God was placed at the top of the hierarchy as a being of supreme and infinite value. And now, in the secular world, humans—or rather, those humans who deem themselves racially superior—enjoy the position that was once held by the deity. The hierarchical notion has important implications for beliefs about morality, because the greater the intrinsic value we accord a being, the less permissible it is for us to harm that being. It is because we rank mosquitos and other "lower" animals, not to mention plants and fungi, as very far down the scale that we routinely treat them in ways that it would be ut-terly impermissible for us to treat fellow human beings.

As I've already remarked, we need to understand the concept of a natural hierarchy to make sense of subhumanity. A being is subhuman—below human or less than human—if it is of a kind that occupies a lower rung of the ladder value than the one that humans occupy. It follows from this that when we dehumanize others, we regard them as being less intrinsically valuable, and thus as being less morally considerable, than ourselves. They can be killed or exploited in ways that it is allowable to kill and exploit nonhuman animals.

The belief the natural world is structured as a hierarchy also throws light on the distinction between dehumanization and racial-ization, as such. When we racialize others, we think of them as occupying inferior rank *within* the human community. But when we dehumanize others, we exclude them from the human commu-nity. In a nutshell, racialized people are *lesser humans*, while dehu-manized people are *less than human*. Racism so readily morphs into dehumanization because the two phenomena are nodes on a con-tinuum of denigration that conforms to a common template. Given that the category of the human lies just above that of nonhuman animals, and that the lowest division of the human is adjacent to the highest division of the subhuman, relegating a group of people to an inferior human rank pushes them closer to the realm of the subhuman.

The Moral Psychology of Hierarchy

Recall that Lovejoy proposed that the idea of a Great Chain of Being was a philosophical artifact that arose in a particular moment in European history, persisted for centuries, and then eventually faded away as a scientific conception of the natural order replaced the older metaphysical and theological one. As compelling as this account might seem, especially in light of Lovejoy's immense erudition, two key facts are against it. One has to do with the persistence of the idea of a natural hierarchy in a post-Darwinian age, and another concerns the pervasiveness of the hierarchical notion in non-Western cultures that were untouched, or touched only slightly, by Greco-Roman philosophical influences.

Even though the intellectual foundations for the idea of the Great Chain of Being have been superseded for well over a century and a half, we still tend to think of natural kinds as arranged in much the same way as our medieval forebears did. We still tend to think of ourselves as "higher" than the other forms of life, and all other creatures as situated somewhere beneath us. A number of psychological studies have shown this. Most are concerned with the degree to which we regard different kinds of nonhuman animals as worthy of moral consideration. The philosopher T. J. Kasperbauer summarizes and discusses some of these studies in his book *Subhuman: The Moral Psychology of Human Attitudes to Animals.* Kasperbauer explains that these studies show that when we attribute moral value to animals, we tend to do so from an anthropocentric perspective. All things being equal, we value nonhuman creatures to the degree that we regard them as resembling us.

> There are numerous . . . experiments that illustrate an anthropocentric bias in our treatment of non-humans. Westbury and Neumanns (2008), for instance, found that empathic emotional responses to animals in abusive situations increased according to phylogenetic similarity (as measured by survey as well as skin conductance responses). In a similar experiment Plaus (1993) showed participants pictures of a monkey, raccoon, pheasant, and bullfrog and told them that each animal had been abused in certain ways. Skin conductance measurements detected increased activity in response to the animals' similarity to humans.

In one experiment (Allen et al., 2002), people read about abuse of a goose, monkey, possum, or lizard. They were then asked how much punishment they would give the transgressor. Those who scored higher in empathy gave out higher punishments, which the results showed were further mediated by similarity to humans. Some people did indeed express moral concern for animals, but this was limited to species nearest to us, most notably the primates.[13]

One would expect the hierarchical theory to persist in fundamentalist and scientifically uneducated communities. It is more surprising to notice that secular humanists use the presumed superiority of human beings to ground political ideas about human rights by linking the presumed metaphysical status of human beings to their "human dignity." Thus, legal scholar Catherine Dupré writes,

> The legal system of human rights protection in Europe (and more generally in the West) rests on the assumption that, as human beings, we are born with the unique quality of dignity that distinguishes us from other beings (primarily animals), justifying and explaining the special protection of our rights. . . . We are here at the philosophical roots of the constitutional concept of human dignity as it is largely understood today, namely a concept that is exclusive to human beings, so that it can be used to distinguish them from other beings, which do not have dignity but a relative worth. . . . Dignity is used to define humanity not with reference to God, but by distinction from other beings which only have a 'relative worth', namely animals or things.[14]

The notion of a Great Chain of Being has proven to be more tenacious than many other ideas that have been long entrenched in Western culture. Its persistence cannot be explained simply by the fact that it saturated Western thought so thoroughly in the past that it has been difficult to dislodge. The idea that a Supreme Being created and sustains the cosmos permeated virtually every aspect of European life for many centuries. But the idea of a divine Creator has no place in today's scientific cosmology. Likewise, the long, influential history of alchemy does not tempt chemists to indulge in talk about the souls of metals, as the alchemists did, and medical science has consigned the time-honored notion of the four humors to the trash bin of history. The persistence of the vertical metaphor in biology and in the ordinary discourse of educated people, and the lack of anything similar in most other scientific disciplines, beg for an explanation.

With regard to the second key fact, the idea of a divinely ordained, value-infused natural hierarchy is and has been much more widespread, both geographically and historically, than Lovejoy's intellectual history allows. This point was made by the philosopher Paul Kuntz, who demonstrated that the theory of a cosmic hierarchy is not limited to the Christian West, but can be found in Jewish and Islamic, as well as in Indian and Chinese, philosophical traditions. Kuntz does not elaborate fully, but detailed and convincing examples are not difficult to come by. We can start close to home, with a familiar passage from the book of Genesis:

> Then God said, "Let us make mankind in our image, in our likeness, so that they may rule over the fish in the sea and the birds in the sky, over the livestock and all the wild animals, and over all the creatures that move along the ground." So God created mankind in his own image, in the image of God he created them; male and female he created them. God blessed them and said to them, "Be fruitful and increase in number; fill the earth and subdue it. Rule over the fish in the sea and the birds in the sky and over every living creature that moves on the ground."[15]

Genesis describes a hierarchical order with God at the top, humans in the middle, and all of the other animals at the bottom, but it would be implausible to suppose that this ancient Middle Eastern myth owes anything to Plato, Aristotle, or the Neoplatonists, as Lovejoy's thesis demands. We find similar beliefs in the ancient Indian canon. Wilhelm Halbfass, a scholar of Indian philosophy, points out that many Indian metaphysical writings assume that there is a "pervasive hierarchy of living beings, which 'extends from Brahma to the tufts of grass.'" Halbfass continues, "The Indian authors use a variety of terms to characterize this hierarchy of human, subhuman, and superhuman forms of life, such as *tāratamya* ('gradation'), *uccanīcabhāva* ('high and low status'), and *utkarṣāpakarṣa* ('superiority and inferiority')."[16]

Versions of the Great Chain of Being also prevail in African philosophy. According to Nigerian philosopher Francis E. Ekanem, "What force is to the Africans is what being is to the West. . . . Life forces are in hierarchical order. The highest of the force is God, followed by divinities, ancestors, spirits, man, animals, plants and minerals."[17] In ancient China, we come across a version of it in the writings of the philosopher Xunzi.[18] And in the Americas, ancient Aztec cosmology has it that "Gods, humans, and animals were ordered according to a chain of being in which each segment participated in a common essence and depended on other segments to survive. . . . The present version of mankind was . . . placed below the gods and above all other animals in the ladder of power, merit, and perfection. This ladder was revealed in the eating order. Lower orders of animals ate one another and plants, humans ate all of them, and the gods ate humans to subsist."[19] Anthropologist Eva Hunt adds, "This basic idea of an arrangement of the living orders of the universe as a phagohierarchy was the theological justification for human sacrifice."[20] Examples like these can easily be multiplied, but I think those that I have given are enough to show that the idea of a Great Chain of Being is not an exclusively European construct.

We need some other way to account for the near-universality of the idea of a natural hierarchy. The answer cannot be that it is because the world really is arranged that way, and it cannot be because the idea is encoded in our DNA. I think that the best explanation is that hierarchical conception persists because it is a feature of the human condition—a powerful solution to a universal problem of human life. If I am right about this, then the European scholars cited by Lovejoy and others, as well as the sages from China, Africa, India, Mexico, and elsewhere, developed their sophisticated accounts of the *scala naturae* to rationalize a gut-level, intuitive, folk-metaphysical representation of the natural order that is on a par with, and orthogonal to, our disposition to essentialize. The Great Chain of Being answers to a deep human need to justify the systems moral and political order upon which human societies depend.

CHAPTER SEVEN

The Order of Things

The hierarchical framework detailed in Chapter 6 is supposed to objectively represent the order of nature, rather than being merely a description of subjective perspectives and values. So, explicitly or implicitly buying into it, as virtually all of us cannot help doing, involves accepting that human beings really do have greater intrinsic value than mosquitos do—and not merely that we humans happen to be strongly prejudiced in favor of our own kind over mosquitos.

Given that the Great Chain of Being purports to describe the order of nature, it is important to be clear what is meant by the concepts "order" and "nature" to fully get the sense of it. The concept of the "order of nature" refers to the way that the universe is organized. In the hierarchical paradigm, this "order" can be mapped along two dimensions: a horizontal dimension and a vertical one. The horizontal dimension segments the world into an array of mutually exclusive natural kinds—plants, animals, humans, and so on. It is supposed to be complete, in that it encompasses—or is capable of encompassing—every existing natural kind. The vertical dimension intersects with it, and consists of the relations of superiority, equality, and inferiority that obtain between these horizontal categories. That the world includes humans and mosquitos has to do with its horizontal structure, while the idea that humans exist on a higher metaphysical plane than mosquitos do is an aspect of its vertical structure. In the passage from the book of Genesis I quoted in Chapter 6, God's creation of "the fish in the sea and the birds in the sky, over the livestock and all the wild animals, and over all the creatures that move along the ground" represents the horizontal aspect of the order of nature. And God's creation of humankind to "rule over the fish in the sea and the birds in the sky and over every living creature that moves on the ground" refers to its vertical aspect.

What about the concept of "nature"? I have heard scientists and quasi-scientists ridicule the benightedness of humanistic scholars who say that "nature" is a social construction. But they are wrong to do this. They incorrectly assume that in making this claim, humanists are claiming that world of living things is a human invention. But that is not the point. The point is that *nature is not a natural kind*. It is not on a par with things like species, organs, or patterns of interaction between organisms, which *are* natural kinds. Rather, "nature" is part of a conceptual, interpretive scheme that is *imposed* on the world (rather like lines of latitude and longitude are imposed on the globe). It is a term that gets put to a variety of uses to organize our large-scale conceptions of the world and the place of human beings and other organisms within it. And importantly for the theory of dehumanization, it is often an ideologically loaded concept that is used to justify racialized and gendered relations of dominance.

There is not just one concept of nature. There are several of them, and they are easy to conflate. John Stuart Mill wrote about this issue in a posthumously published essay entitled "On Nature," where he disentangled three distinct meanings of the term. Mill pointed out that sometimes "nature" is used as "a collective name for everything which is." In this sense, everything is natural—not just birds and bees and butterflies, but also social constructions such as dollars and Thursdays. But, he observed, the concept of nature is also often used in a more restricted sense to refer to only those things that are untouched by what he called "voluntary human intervention." In this sense, birds, bees, and butterflies are all natural, but dollars and Thursdays are not. Mill's final distinction is a normative one—one that is concerned with how things should be rather than how they are (of course, this leaves open the possibility that some things are as they should be—but it is the element of "should-ness" that is important here). In this sense, Mill remarks, "Nature does not stand for what is, but for what ought to be, or for the rule or standard of what ought to be."[1]

To appreciate what Mill was getting at, it is helpful to contrast each of these senses of what is natural with its corresponding conception of what is nonnatural. Starting with the first of Mill's meanings, if nature consists of all that exists, it excludes only those things that do not exist; a line is drawn between the natural world—the real, existing world—and fictional worlds. Unicorns are nonnatural in this sense. This way of thinking about the natural lures us into the notion of "spooky" entities. To say that unicorns are nonnatural entities might suggest that they are entities with the property of not existing. After all, saying "unicorns do not exist" seems to be saying something true about unicorns—but to say something true about unicorns seems to require that there are unicorns to say something about! So maybe unicorns *are* real in a strange way: maybe they "subsist" rather than exist, or maybe they exist "in your consciousness" or supernaturally, or maybe they graze in meadows on some possible worlds but not on the actual one. There is been a river of philosophical ink spilled over the centuries teasing out exactly what confusions are at work in these putative solutions to what turns out to be a semantic problem.

Mill's second meaning, that nature includes only those things that have not been created or modified by human hands, excludes all artifacts (using "artifacts" very broadly to include such things as dog breeds and anthropogenic climate change),[2] so in this case the contrast is between the natural things and artificial things, rather than between real and fictional things. There are positively and negatively valenced versions of this idea. We find it in the notion of "raw nature"—the idea of the natural as crude, primitive, or unrefined (think of Hobbes's "state of nature," and Tennyson's "Nature, red in tooth and claw"). Used in this sense, it has often been used to characterize marginalized or colonized groups (for example, women, Black people, and Native Americans) as "closer to nature" in the sense of being savage, primitive, or driven by their impulses, emotions, or appetites. More positively, it is used to refer to things (or people) in their primal, uncorrupted state (think organic food, Mother Nature, and the notion of the noble savage).[3]

Finally, Mill's third meaning is a normative conception that distinguishes between the natural and the *unnatural*. In this sense, the unnatural is *that which should not be*. This includes both things that should not be (the horizontal dimension of the natural order) and relations that should not obtain between existing things. The normative conception may at first be more difficult for readers to relate to than the other ones, because the very idea that there are ways that the world should be that are not dictated by human preferences and values is far removed from the picture of the world that is presented to us by science. But it is such an important component of the sort of hierarchical thinking that I am concerned with here that it will be useful to make sure that its meaning is clear.

One way to get a handle on the normative conception is to view it through a religious lens. Many religious people hold the view that a benevolent deity created the universe and therefore that the structure and workings of the cosmos manifest the Creator's intentions. Many of the same people believe that God endowed human beings with freedom of the will, which empowers them to perversely turn their back on God's intentions and to manage their lives and the world around them in ways that are contrary to His plan. From this perspective, such people are, in defying God's laws, living unnatural lives. The taboos itemized in the book of Leviticus and the homophobic and transphobic beliefs of some present-day religious fundamentalists are inspired by such a conception of nature.

Although the normative conception of nature is tied historically to an explicitly theological conception of natural law, it is detachable from a religious worldview. There are plenty of examples of thoroughly secular versions of it. Consider attitudes to genetically modified organisms. There are reasonable scientific concerns about the effects of creating genetically modified organisms, but popular opposition to genetic engineering is very often not based on these. People often have a gut reaction of horror at the prospect of transgenic organisms that is rooted in the idea that there is something profoundly wrong, in a deeply moral sense, with efforts to "tamper" with nature. In the case of genetic engineering, transgenic organisms seem to violate the natural order by transgressing the boundaries between natural kinds. For example,

> In a US survey, more than half of the respondents did not reject the idea that tomatoes of which the genome had been modified by insertion of catfish DNA would taste like fish. Apparently, people assumed that the fish's essence had been introduced into these tomatoes, including a fishy taste. That people systematically prefer cisgenic over transgenic organisms provides another indication of an essentialist bias. In their campaigns, opponents of GMOs explicitly appeal to these essentialist intuitions by distributing edited images of tomatoes with fish tails or by claiming that biotech companies insert scorpion DNA elements into corn (*Zea mays*) to produce crispy cornflakes. . . . Indeed, genetic engineering is considered to be the opposite of 'natural'. GMO opponents accuse scientists who produce transgenic plants of 'playing God' and condemn their acts as 'against nature'.[4]

Similarly, the prospect of growing meat in a laboratory for human consumption, or of producing human / nonhuman chimeras, often elicits intense repugnance—for which no real reason other than "because it is unnatural" can be adduced. The examples that I have just given pertain to unnatural *beings*, but certain sorts of *relations* between natural beings can also fall under the shadow of unnaturalness. For instance, in rigidly segregated societies, interracial sex and marriage are seen as unnatural, and therefore as profoundly abhorrent. Systems of oppression are typically predicated on the idea that different kinds of human beings have their preordained place in the natural hierarchy of human kinds. There is an immensely destructive and politically loaded version of the normative conception of the natural that asserts that there are natural kinds of human beings, each with a distinctive nature, and that in order to lead productive and fulfilling lives, we should each live in accordance with our nature. This general normative principle was laid out by Aristotle more than two thousand years ago when he claimed, "What is by nature proper to each thing will be at once the best and the most pleasant for it."[5] We can see this idea at work in Aristotle's theory of natural slavery, described in Chapter 4, as well as in the subordination of racialized groups, and in the belief that women's natural role is to be subordinate to men.

The conception of the natural order that undergirds the Great Chain of Being is a place where two of Mill's meanings intersect. The natural order is not a human creation and cannot be modified by human hands (Mill's second meaning of "natural"), and it is also a conception of how things should be (Mill's third meaning of "natural"). Very importantly, it allows for there being natural and unnatural social constructions and practices by the principle that humans should strive to create societies that mirror the order of nature—societies that reflect and enforce an unchanging, transcendent set of categories and relations. The idea underpinning this imperative is that social institutions depend for their authority on something that is deeper than mere human artifice.[6] As the anthropologist Mary Douglas points out, "Before it can perform its . . . work, the incipient institution needs some stabilizing principle to stop its premature demise. That stabilizing principle is the naturalization of social classifications. There needs to be an analogy by which the formal structure of a crucial set of social relations is found in the physical world, or in the supernatural world, or in eternity, anywhere, so long as it is not seen as a socially contrived arrangement."[7]

Consider gender hierarchy. The idea that women are naturally inferior to men not only legitimates the social subordination of women, but also makes their oppression obligatory. The ideology works like this: if it is natural for women to be subservient to men, and if human beings can live harmonious and fulfilling lives only if they live in the way that nature intended, it follows that men and women can lead harmonious and fulfilling lives only if women are subservient to men. Seen from this perspective, any woman who rejects patriarchy misunderstands her true nature and will be unable to lead a fulfilling female life unless and until she comes to accept her natural destiny. And any man who likewise rejects patriarchal norms is a deviant being who will be doomed to a life of unhappiness.

Of course, given that the whole idea of a normative natural order is false, the assumption that societies are structured to reflect that order inverts the direction of the causal arrow. Rather than social arrangements being fashioned to reflect the transcendent cosmic order, beliefs about a transcendent order are fashioned in such a way as to mirror and thereby justify social and political structures. We project ideological formations onto the world, and then use this to legitimate the relations of domination in the societies in which we live, or sometimes to justify changing those societies so as to bring them into closer alignment with that imagined order.

An easy and rather hackneyed riposte to the claim that the social order should embody the order of nature is to invoke Hume's law that how things are does not tell us how they should be. But this totally misses the mark, because the conceptions of the natural order that ground oppressive social arrangements are themselves normative. Those who, for example, try to justify the subordination of women by claiming that this is the natural state of affairs do not make the mistake of fallaciously deriving an "ought" from an "is." Rather, they take themselves to be deriving a social "ought" from a deeper and more authoritative metaphysical "ought." The real problem with this way of thinking is not the logical fallacy of thinking that "is" statements entail "ought" statements. The problem is that there is no justification for the claim that nonartificial hierarchies of the relevant sort exist, much less that such nonexistent hierarchies dictate how things should be.

The Human Prejudice

Having laid all this out, I can now address the difficult question of why the hierarchical conception is so robust, pervasive, and psychologically compelling. Because psychologists have neglected this topic, I do not have an extensive empirical research literature on which to draw, and my story will of necessity be somewhat speculative—but it is also quite plausible in light of what we know about ourselves.

I begin with what the philosopher Bernard Williams called "the human prejudice," which is a term that he used to describe our tendency to regard human beings as positively special and as inherently more valuable than other organisms. It is obvious that, were it not for the human prejudice, dehumanization could not get off the ground, because in that case conceiving of other human beings as rats or lice would not be conceiving of them as less than human.

Williams referred to this attitude as a "prejudice,"[8] but most people seem to think of human specialness as an unassailable fact and so obviously true that questioning it is more or less on the same intellectual footing as questioning that the earth is round. But of course, defenders of the view that it is *objectively* true that humans possess a special moral status must, if they are intellectually responsible, have some way of justifying their position. For centuries, this was done theologically: humans are special because God chose to make them special. But this theological story no longer carries as much weight in a secular age—which is why, ever since the Enlightenment, thinkers wanting to account for the specialness of human beings have tried to ground it in natural characteristics that all members of our kind possess, and that all other creatures lack or possess only to a lesser degree. Beginning in the ancient world, we find the idea that the special moral status of human beings is due to their unique moral sensibilities. Aristotle wrote in the *Politics* that "it is a characteristic of man that he alone has any sense of good and evil, just and unjust,"[9] and he also emphasized rationality as demarcating human beings from all the other forms of life. Two centuries later, Cicero developed the theme further:

> It is relevant to every aspect of obligation always to focus on the degree to which the nature of man transcends that of cattle and of other beasts. Whereas animals have no feeling except pleasure, and their every inclination is directed towards it, human minds are nurtured by learning and reflection; and enticed by delight in seeing and hearing, they are constantly investigating something or performing some action. . . . Moreover if we are willing to reflect on the high worth and dignity of our nature, we shall realise how degrading it is to wallow in decadence and to live a soft and effeminate life, and how honourable is a life of thrift, self-control, austerity and sobriety.[10]

Next, the torch passed to Medieval philosophers, who were saddled with the unenviable task of squaring classical Greek and Roman philosophy with Christian doctrine. They accounted for humans' superior status in much the same way that Aristotle and Cicero (and other classical thinkers) had, but with the crucial addendum that we possess the rational faculty by virtue of having been created in God's image. Thus, in the thirteenth century Thomas Aquinas wrote in his *Summa Theologicae*, "Since man is said to be the image of God by reason of his intellectual nature, he is the most perfectly like God according to that in which he can best imitate God in his intellectual nature."[11] The trend continued over the next four or five centuries. Then, during the Enlightenment, justifications for the elevated moral status of humans took a different turn. They were resecularized, and to this day rationality and freedom of the will—whether divinely implanted or not—have been the prime candidates for underwriting human exceptionalism.

Examined closely, all of these explanations sound like rationalizations for unwarranted convictions. It is true that humans are rational deliberators. We can use higher-order thought to weigh up the pros and cons of courses of action and decide which path to take, and we can evaluate the evidence for and against claims and decide what to believe on that basis. And it is also probably true that this ability is uniquely human, or at least possessed by other animals only to a very rudimentary degree. But there is a problem with arguing that a fancy kind of rationality is the sine qua non for human dignity, because of what philosophers call "the problem of marginal cases." Not all human beings are blessed with the capacity to reason. Infants and severely cognitively impaired individuals do not have access to it (in fact, there are some chimpanzees that are more adept at practical reasoning than some humans are). So, either these people get excluded from the category of the human, or the criterion of rationality needs to be exchanged for something more promising. The first option is a dehumanizing one, and therefore should not be on the table, and the problem with the second one is that no matter what distinguishing characteristic or characteristics one might choose, there are always going to be some humans who slip through the definitional net, as well as some nonhumans that are captured by it.[12] And it will not do to resort to grounding human exceptionalism in one's "intuitions" and assert that our special status is self-evident. "Intuition" is just philosophical jargon for cognitive bias, and relying on one's biases to lead one to the truth is a fool's errand.

It is worth reflecting on the fact that, even if something close to a watertight justification for human exceptionalism were to be found by some clever philosopher (and believe me, there are many clever philosophers working hard to do just that), this would not provide any explanation for our anthropocentric prejudice. Instead, it would be a post hoc excuse for it. Williams's characterization of our attitude as a "prejudice" is right on the money, and we need to turn to psychology, rather than philosophical speculation, to come to grips with it.

The Hierarchical Mentality

Why do we tend to think of human beings as superior to other organisms? The most obvious place to begin is with the suite of attitudes known as in-group/out-group biases. Psychological research confirms that people tend to be biased in favor of members of their in-group—the group that they identify with—and biased against members of out-groups. The idea of in-group/out-group bias goes back at least to the seventeenth-century writings of David Hume and was first applied to relations between ethnic groups by the Yale political scientist (and social Darwinist) William Graham Sumner. It was Sumner who popularized the term "ethnocentrism," which he defined as "the technical name for the view of things in which one's own group is the center of everything, and all others are scaled and rated with reference to it."[13] The tendency toward in-group favoritism certainly seems to be a robust component of human nature. It is found in many other social animals, too. Chimpanzees, for example, are notorious for attacking and killing members of neighboring groups that stray into their territory and sometimes conduct lethal incursions into the territory of other groups.[14]

However, in-group / out-group biases do not give us what we need for understanding the human prejudice, because citing these biases does not explain our tendency to place *human beings* in general high up on the natural hierarchy. The biases that are studied by social psychologists concern attitudes toward other human beings, rather than toward other kinds of organisms. In-groups and out-groups are human groups. So, although there is a tendency to think of in-group members as having greater intrinsic value than their out-group counterparts, this does not have any direct bearing on our evaluation of other creatures.

Ultrasociality

To grasp the nature of the human prejudice, we must turn to some facts about human sociality and their psychological ramifications. We humans are ultrasocial animals. No other mammal comes anywhere near to our extraordinary degree of sociality. *Homo sapiens* live in nested and interlocking social groups and depend upon high levels of mutual trust and cooperation to survive and flourish. And these bonds of cooperation are not just with members of immediate communities, but also with members of vastly wider networks, including, remarkably, complete strangers. Brian Hare and Vanessa Wood point out that our sociality does not only exceed that of other primates in degree. It is also different in kind.

What allowed us to thrive while other humans went extinct was a kind of cognitive superpower: a particular type of friendliness called cooperative communication. We are experts at working together with other people, even strangers. We can communicate with someone we've never met about a shared goal and work together to accomplish it. As you would expect, chimpanzees are cognitively sophisticated in many of the ways humans are. But despite our many similarities, they struggle to understand when communication is intended to help them accomplish a shared goal. This means that as smart as chimpanzees are, they have little ability to synchronize their behavior, coordinate different roles, pass on their innovations, or even communicate beyond a few rudimentary requests. We develop all of these skills before we can walk or talk, and they are the gateway to a sophisticated social and cultural world. They allow us to plug our minds into the minds of others and inherit the knowledge of generations. *Homo sapiens* were able to flourish where other smart human species didn't because we excel at a particular kind of collaboration.[15]

Of all the great thinkers of the past, it was perhaps Thomas Hobbes who most effectively put a finger on the overwhelming significance of sociality in human life. In his 1651 masterpiece *Leviathan*, Hobbes presented an origin myth, the fable of a primal "state of nature" in which brutish human beings lived solitary lives and were unable to trust and cooperate with one another. He described this condition as one of perpetual conflict and danger, a "warre of all against all," and famously conjectured: "In such condition there is no place for industry, because the fruit thereof is uncertain: and consequently no culture of the earth; no navigation, nor use of the commodities that may be imported by sea; no commodious building; no instruments of moving and removing such things as require much force; no knowledge of the face of the earth; no account of time; no arts; no letters; no society; and which is worst of all, continual fear, and danger of violent death; and the life of man, solitary, poore, nasty, brutish, and short."[16]

Hobbes offered this thought experiment to motivate and underpin his political philosophy. He used it to argue that any rational being would want to leave the state of nature behind, and would be prepared to sacrifice a portion of their liberty to escape from it. They would, he reasoned, willingly subordinate themselves to "a Common Power to keep them in awe, and to direct their actions to the Common Benefit" in exchange for security and the many benefits made possible by collective action.[17]

Whatever its virtues as a thought experiment for political philosophers, Hobbes's fable does not work as an account of the origins of human social organization. We now know that this primeval state of nature never existed, and that prehistoric humans did not sign on to a social contract to leave it behind. Our remote ancestors were group-living primates since well before our species came into being. Bands of *Homo erectus* were already cooperatively hunting big game, crafting tools, and transmitting cultural knowledge across the generations two million years before *Homo sapiens* appeared, and they were descended from a long line of earlier, group-living primate species. But even though it is a fiction, Hobbes's invitation to imagine a dystopian world where human beings do not cooperate is helpful because it highlights something that we normally take for granted: the degree to which human ways of life are built upon, and are utterly dependent upon, a platform of thoroughgoing sociality.

Given our gregarious nature, and the fact that we are descended from a lineage of social primates spanning many millions of years, it is more than reasonable to think that our minds are endowed with built-in psychological mechanisms that have the function of fostering "ultrasociality." At a minimum, this entails that we are designed by evolution to regard other human beings as having a special status as compared to other creatures—a robust tendency to value other human beings *just because they are human beings.*

At this point, you might be wondering how this claim can be squared with the facts about in-group / out-group biases that I alluded to a few paragraphs ago. If other humans have a special value for us, how does this line up with our robust tendency to devalue outgroup members? How can it be reconciled with our ethnocentrism, our xenophobia, and the horrific episodes of mass atrocity that litter our species' journey through time? How does it comport with the Georgia mob's torture and execution of Sam Hose that I described in Chapter 1?

The answer to these questions is complex and goes to the heart of the dynamics of dehumanization. Consequently, I will have to defer answering them fully until I have laid down some more theoretical foundations. For now, simply bear two points in mind. First, I do not claim that the human prejudice explains the totality of our attitudes and behavior toward one another. That would be a ridiculous presumption. Second, our attitudes toward enemies and rivals involve recognition of their special status. Our attitudes toward them, however denigrating or antagonistic, are quite unlike our attitudes toward nonhuman animals. Their significance for us is both qualitatively distinct from and quantitatively greater than the significance that we grant to other kinds of living things.[18]

Morality

Human beings manage their social relations through systems of morality. Every human society creates and implements moral rules and norms that define what kinds of behaviors are good, bad, obligatory, permissible, impermissible, and so on. Although the details vary from one culture to the next, and from one historical epoch to another, and although it is not clear whether or not there are

fundamental moral principles that are universally shared, it is un-
deniable that all human beings are born into, and structure their
lives in the context of, moral frameworks.[19]

Morality is not just a matter of doing or failing to do the right
thing. Rather, it involves accepting a system of values and beliefs
about how one should or should not behave. This involves making
distinctions. These are not limited to distinctions between permissible and impermissible acts per se, because in any moral system it
is permissible to treat some kinds of entities and objects in ways
that it is impermissible to treat others. When I was growing up in
the Deep South, it was considered wrong to leave an American flag
to fly in the rain. This wasn't just because doing so violated the US
Flag Code, which states, "The flag should not be displayed on days
when the weather is inclement, except when an all-weather flag is
displayed." Leaving the flag out in the rain was considered to be an
act of disrespecting the flag and thus in violation of the rule that
one should respect the flag as a sacred object. In contrast, the shrimp
fishermen who lived in my neighborhood would regularly leave
their nets out in the rain. The nets were useful and instrumentally
valuable, and it was important to take good care of them, but they
were not items that merited veneration.

Now consider this. Often, when I am preparing dinner, I go out
to my herb garden to pluck some sprigs of thyme for seasoning. In
doing so, I tear apart a living thing, and I consider this act of dis-
memberment to be morally inconsequential. But if one of my neighbors were to catch and dismember a living chipmunk, I would be
appalled. Similarly, there are acts that I think are morally permissible, or even obligatory, with respect to chipmunks (for example,
culling them) that I would find deeply objectionable if they were
meted out to human beings, but—and this is crucially important—*I
do not think that there are any acts that are morally impermissible with
respect to nonhuman animals that it is permissible to perform on human*

beings. In my eyes, and I am pretty sure in the eyes of most other people, our greatest moral obligations are to members of our own species.[20]

The same act may be morally acceptable when performed on one kind of thing, but morally unacceptable when performed on another kind of thing. You might quibble with the details of my examples. For instance, you might disagree with my view that culling non-human animals is ever morally permissible. Fair enough, but it is the general point rather than the details that matter. Even if you disagree with me about chipmunks, you will likely agree with me that for any sort of realistic moral framework—any moral framework that is actually implemented, as opposed to the conceptual fantasies that philosophers are prone to indulge in—morally significant distinctions must be made between kinds of things.

Compare this human distinction between how different kinds of things *should* be treated with how other social animals regulate one another's behavior. Nonhuman organisms respond differentially to different kinds of things. Their survival depends on it. Animals must respond differently to predators and prey, to edible and inedible items, to members of their own species and members of other species, and so on. But for the vast majority of animals, it is implausible that they *conceptualize* these differentiations as falling under kinds (there is controversy about whether nonhuman primates and cetaceans, and perhaps other mammals, do this). When an owl treats a vole as prey, she does not classify it as prey. The fact that she treats voles differently than, say, rubber doorstoppers, has to do with her responsiveness to attributes that trigger her behavior rather than her determining that voles belong in the "prey" category.

If moral systems have got to involve conceptual distinctions between kinds of things, then only certain sorts of minds can operate within moral frameworks. For a person to believe that it is wrong to cull humans but that it is fine to cull chipmunks, they have got to have the concepts of "human" and "chipmunk." Most concepts that we use to make moral distinctions are natural-kind concepts—the horizontal dimension of the Great Chain of Being—and the differential value that we impart to members of these kinds (for example, the idea that human lives matter more than chipmunk lives) gives us it is vertical dimension. In short, hierarchical rankings of natural kinds fall out of moral systems, with those that we attribute the greatest intrinsic value to at the top and those that we consider to have the least intrinsic value at the bottom. It is because we are moral animals that we cannot manage to expunge the Great Chain of Being from our conception of the world. Once morality was invented, hierarchy came along for the ride.

The Politics of Metaphysics

I have argued that historians of ideas, unduly influenced by Arthur Lovejoy's work, have grossly underestimated the pervasiveness and intractability of the idea of natural hierarchy. But although the idea that nature is arranged as a hierarchy is very widespread across times and cultures, it is not universal. Looking carefully at which cultures endorse it and which ones do not reveals something important about the forces that shape the dehumanizing process.

Often, the members of hunter-gatherer societies regard other animals (and even plants) as beings that are very much like themselves. In such cultures, the human / animal difference is considered to be quite superficial, and the relationship between the hunter and the hunted is viewed as cooperative rather than adversarial.[21] Often hunter-gatherer groups believe that animals offer themselves to the hunter. On this view, game animals allow themselves to be killed because they *want* to be killed. This view is often linked to more complex spiritual beliefs—for instance, that animals renew themselves by dying and being reborn in new bodies, or that they seek to join others in the afterlife. For Cree hunters, for example, "there is no radical division of nature from culture or society. The animal world is a part of the same kind of social world that humans inhabit, and in much conversation a social metaphor serves to talk about the whole world. . . . When asking why an animal went into a trap, or allowed itself to be caught, the Cree answer with similar kinds of reasons for why a human gives food away to another person. That is, because it appreciates the need of the other."[22]

Anthropologist Helga Vierich notes, in an account of her field-work among the Kua of Botswana, that "a careful tracking, and quiet approach, followed by a swift stab to open an artery in the neck, was the preferred end to the hunt. A prayer of thanks followed, and I was always moved to tears at the quick ritual phrase that ended this tribute, biding the spirit of this creature to wait for the hunter in the unknown dimension where the two would dwell again as kinfolk."[23] This is in striking contrast to pastoral and ag-riculturally based societies, which tend to buy into the hierarchical ideology. Once plants are domesticated as food crops, and animals are domesticated as walking larders and beasts of burden, the rela-tionship with them changes, becoming less reciprocal and more hi-erarchical. And this development mirrors the emergence of social stratification. For the most part, foraging societies are egalitarian, and what stratification there exists is based on competence and is collectively endorsed rather than imposed on a subjugated popu-lace. Christopher Boehm explains in his fascinating book *Hierarchy in the Forest* that the egalitarian way of life is an upshot of a suite of political norms and practices that are aimed at keeping the propen-sity for despotism in check, but as societies become sedentary, and population pressure increases, there is a transition to hierarchical social arrangements in which the laboring many are subordinated to the rule of the few.[24]

It is tempting to conclude from this that the idea of a natural hi-erarchy is a way that stratified societies legitimate inequality. They project their own structure onto the cosmos and then propose that the hierarchical social order is underwritten by the hierarchical order of nature: societies ordered by rank—classes, castes, and other stable relations of domination—justify their existence by appealing to a cosmic framework in which natural kinds are similarly ranked. There is much to be said for this explanation, but it is not yet complete. I will return to it to supply what I believe to be the missing pieces.

———

We have covered a lot of territory so far, so, before concluding this chapter, I want to underscore six key points that are crucial to bear in mind as we drill down deeper into how dehumanization works the chapters to follow.

First, there are many different conceptions of what dehumanization is in the scholarly literature, and even more in popular, vernacular writings. To theorize dehumanization properly, it is vital not to conflate these various conceptions of it. "Dehumanization," as used in this book, specifically refers the attitude of conceiving of others as subhuman entities.

Second, although some scholars doubt that dehumanization, in this sense, ever occurs, there is good evidence that people have sometimes thought of other people as less than human. There are explicit claims about the subhumanity of other members of our species that are clearly meant to be taken literally. So, in any particular case of ostensible dehumanization, we should therefore be open to the possibility that it is an episode of real dehumanization.

Third, dehumanization is closely tied to ideas about race. To properly understand the connection between racialization and dehumanization, it is important to have a sufficiently broad notion of what the idea of race involves. In this book, I take the idea of race to be the idea that there are natural human kinds the membership of which is transmitted biologically by descent. Dehumanization is tied to racism, both because racialization typically precedes and facilitates dehumanization, and because dehumanizing thinking has the same form as racial thinking.

Fourth, both dehumanization and racism are informed by psychological essentialism, the tendency to carve the world up into natural kinds and to attribute a unique causal essence to each of these kinds. The idea of causal essences is the idea that there are "deep" properties that are unobservable, possessed by only and all members of a kind, and are causally responsible for observable characteristics that are typical of the kind. Psychological essentialism allows that the appearance of a being can belie its essence.

Fifth, when we dehumanize others, we conceive of them as having a human appearance but a subhuman essence. Dehumanized people are thought of a subhumans passing as humans.

And sixth, the idea of *sub*humanity presupposes a hierarchical conception of the biosphere, which more perfect beings as "higher" and less perfect beings as "lower." This idea is often referred to as the Great Chain of Being. Although most scholars think of the Great Chain of Being as an intellectual artefact that was fashioned by Western in late antiquity, evidence suggests that this is incorrect and that the hierarchical conception is an entrenched feature of human moral psychology. This hierarchical conception may be a consequence of morality. Any system of moral rules presupposes a value-infused hierarchical conception of the relation between natural kinds. When we dehumanize others, we conceive of them as having the essence of a biological kind that is ranked lower on the hierarchy than humans are.

CHAPTER EIGHT

Being Human

Although I have argued that human beings have assigned themselves to a lofty position in the hierarchy of nature, I have not explained what characteristics an entity must have in order to be regarded as human. I have been taking the category of the human for granted, but now we have got to find out what it means to say of some beings that they are human beings.

What Are Human Beings?

What are human beings? You might think that the answer to this question is obvious, because science has shown that to be human is to be a member of the species *Homo sapiens.* But the scientific literature is not so straightforward. It is reasonable to say that all *Homo sapiens* are human, but is it also right to say that all humans are *Homo sapiens?* Most paleoanthropologists equate being human with either being a member of a certain biological species—the species *Homo sapiens*—or with being a member of the genus *Homo.* But some prefer a very narrow definition of the human, restricting it to the subspecies *Homo sapiens sapiens*, and others think that all of the hominins that have existed since the moment our lineage parted ways with that of the chimpanzees should come under the human umbrella.[1] So we have at least four possible "scientific" answers to the question "What are human beings?" And that is not the end of it, because even if the scientists managed to settle on the notion that to be a human is to be a member of genus *Homo*, we would still be in the dark because it is unclear which species belong to that genus. As paleoanthropologist Ian Tattersall tells us,

> You might . . . be tempted to imagine that, in the century and a half since Charles Darwin pointed out that we are joined to the rest of nature by common ancestry, science might have begun to make some progress toward a biological definition of the human genus. But if so, you would be doomed to disappointment. Scientists are still arguing vehemently over which ancient fossil human relatives should be included in the genus *Homo*. And they are doing so in the absence of any coherent idea of what the genus that includes our species *Homo sapiens* might reasonably be presumed to contain.[2]

Why is there so much scientific confusion about what humans are? One might think that it is because the fossil record is too sketchy, and that science will be in a position to give us a definitive answer once enough remains are discovered. But it is a mistake to think that science can settle the question of what humans are. The problem would still be there even if we had a complete and detailed fossil record of our ancestral lineage, because the question "What is a human being?" is a philosophical question rather than a scientific one.

Natural and Invented Kinds

We humans are inveterate taxonomists who order our picture of the world by sorting organisms into typological boxes. Present-day scientific taxonomies—the ones presented in biology texts—were built on foundations laid by older, prescientific ones. And these prescientific frameworks for parsing the lifeworld were driven by the psychological biases that move us to carve up the messy profusion of life forms into discrete, essentialized, natural kinds.

Essentialism gives us a false picture of the natural world, but it can be useful. "If psychological essentialism is bad metaphysics," asked the psychologist Douglas Medin, "why should people act as if things had essences?" His answer was that "it may prove to be good epistemology." Essentialism is bad metaphysics because post-Darwinian science has shown us that organisms do not come neatly packaged as essentialized kinds. But it is good epistemology because it allowed our ancestors to make inferences about the world that could mean the difference between success and failure, life and death. Dividing organisms into kinds, and extrapolating from the known to the unknown, allowed our forebears to distinguish the plants that are edible and those that are toxic, figure out where and when certain kinds predators might be lurking, and make educated guesses about where to find game. This sort of knowledge is not so vital for those of us who do our hunting and gathering in supermarkets, but it is indispensable for those that depend on nature's wild bounty to survive.

The fact that our taxonomic instincts are rooted in psychological essentialism does not mean that folk taxonomies always depart from what science tells us about how nature is arranged. Sometimes the scientific classification of organisms into species mirrors folk classifications with breathtaking fidelity. For instance, when the evolutionary biologist Ernst Mayr visited the Arfak mountains of New Guinea in 1928 to study the wildlife there, he found that the indigenous New Guineans classified native birds into 136 species, and that these corresponded almost exactly to the 137 species identified by ornithologists. But folk taxonomies and scientific taxonomies do not always fit together so tidily. It is plain to see why people, impressed by certain similarities, might think that whales are fish, but it is far more perplexing that the Karam of New Guinea, the land that Mayr visited, classify the large, flightless Cassowary not as a bird.[3]

In recent decades, the ways that scientists carve up the biosphere into kinds of organisms has increasingly parted ways with everyday taxonomic intuitions. Biologists have become less and less concerned with readily observable morphological characteristics and more and more concerned with tracing evolutionary patterns of descent via the microscopic lens of molecular genetics. This shift has transformed the scientific image of biological taxa and their relationships to one another. Science now teaches us that the Nile crocodile—a massive, lumbering, predatory, semiaquatic beast—is more closely related to the miniscule bee hummingbird (which weighs in at less than a tenth of an ounce) than it is to the world's largest lizard, the fearsome Komodo dragon (locally referred to as a "land crocodile"), which can polish off a whole pig for dinner. In fact, the group of organisms formerly known as "reptiles" has, in effect, been taxonomized out of existence.

This is typical of how science proceeds. The more developed a science becomes, the more deeply scientific research explores the fundamental nature of things, the further it departs from ordinary, intuitive, commonsense conceptions of the world. That is why in biological taxonomy, as well in many other matters, we defer to science when we want to know what is really real. Science is in the business of representing the world in a way that lines up with its objective structure. In mapping the fundamental structure of the world, science focuses on natural kinds: physical kinds like quarks and photons, chemical kinds like oxygen and radium, and biological kinds like species and genera. Therefore, a large part of the role of science is correcting mistaken views about the kinds of things that populate the natural world.

One way that science accomplishes this is by distinguishing natural kinds from the products of human invention. There are various kinds of invented kinds. Some, such as unicorns and demons, are purely imaginary. They are nonnatural in Mill's first sense of "natural." They are *fictional kinds*. Others, such as chairs, highways, and expressionist paintings, are real artifacts that are fashioned out of natural (in Mill's second sense) stuff. These are *physically assembled kinds*. Still other *cognitively assembled kinds* are gerrymandered collections of items belonging to different natural kinds. They are things grouped together on the basis of the role that they play in human life rather than because of their natural properties.

The concept of cognitively assembled kinds is especially important for understanding what it means to be human, so I will dwell on it a bit longer to make sure what I am talking about is clear. The category "weed" is an example of a cognitively assembled kind. What makes a plant a weed has nothing to do with its biological properties. There is nothing, biologically speaking, that all weeds have in common but no other plants share. The category "weed" is assembled from a whole variety of plants that do not have any special botanical properties in common. They are grouped together only by our attitude toward them. What makes a plant a weed is that it is a wild variety growing in a place that is reserved for cultivation. Consequently, the very same plant that is a weed if it is growing in a flower bed may not be a weed if it is growing in a meadow. Although the plants that we call "weeds" would still be around in the absence of the human practice of horticulture, the category "weed" would vanish. Or, to put the same point differently, if human beings were to disappear, the plants that are weeds would no longer be weeds.

To understand what weeds are, you have got to understand human social practices. Superintelligent alien biologists who did not know that Earthlings cultivate plants would be perplexed by the concept "weed." Presented with a collection of plant specimens, and told that these are all weeds, the aliens would be at a loss to understand what on earth these plants have in common. The same principle is true of many other categories that are important to human beings, such as pets, vegetables, and creepy crawlies. These are all cognitively assembled kinds.

Cognitively assembled kinds are not always recognized as such. Sometimes they are mistaken for natural kinds. Racial groupings are examples. Most people seem to think that races are biologically meaningful groupings of human beings, and that every member of a race has some important biological property that sets them apart from everyone who does not share their common racial identity. However, as I explained in Chapter 3, there is a scholarly near-consensus that human races are inventions rather than biologically meaningful categories. Racial categories are like weeds in that they consist of biologically and culturally diverse groups of people that are united by a name ("Black," "White," "Asian," or whatever) but not by shared, underlying, natural properties that would consolidate them as a natural kind.

The category "human" is also widely assumed to be a natural kind. But is "human" really a natural kind, or is it an invented kind? This question has important implications for understanding the phenomenon of dehumanization. When people dehumanize others, they deny those others' humanity. So, unless we are able to decide what it means to think of others as human beings, we will never be able to form a clear idea of what is going on when we dehumanize them.

What Kind of a Kind Is Humankind?

Whatever its ultimate metaphysical status, "human" is a folk category. Unlike *homo*, the Latin word from which it is derived, it is not part of any strictly scientific vocabulary. Of course, scientists use the word "human" in scientific contexts, just as they use many other vernacular terms. But that does not make "human" a scientific term any more than their using the term "weed" makes "weed" a scientific term. Getting clear about the fact that "human" is a folk category helps us to see what is really going on when a scientist says that being human is the same thing as belonging to the species *Homo sapiens.*

When scientists claim that humans are *Homo sapiens* (and vice versa), they are making a claim about the relationship between terms taken from two separate vocabularies. They are making the claim that the vernacular term "human beings" and scientific term "*Homo sapiens*" name exactly the same kind of animal—the kind of animal that you and I are. As I explained at the start of this chapter, there is no scientific consensus about which biological taxon maps on to the folk category "human." Given this, we can now ask a deeper question: Is there any possible empirical evidence that would establish that the category "human" corresponds to one biological taxon rather than another? Are there any observations that scientists could make that would establish that being human equals being a member of the species *Homo sapiens?* The answer to this question is "no." There is not and cannot be any such evidence because questions about the relation between folk categories like "human" and scientific categories like "*Homo sapiens*" are philosophical ones, and part of what makes a question a philosophical question is precisely that it cannot be settled by observing facts about the world. We could know all of the facts about the anatomy, physiology, and behavior of members of the hominin species *Homo ergaster,* for example, and still not know whether these ancestors of ours were human beings.

Philosophical Humanness

Perhaps, then, philosophers are better equipped than scientists to answer the question of what it means to be human. For the most part, philosophers regard the concept of the human as unproblematic. For example, the burgeoning literature on human nature rarely if ever addresses the question of what sorts of beings count as human beings. And "transhumanist" writings, which talk about how the use of technological enhancements may catapult us into a post-human condition, are not explicit about what the humanity that we are supposedly leaving behind really is. Often, rather than concerning themselves with the question of what humans are, philosophers pursue questions about how we should treat other human beings—questions about the basis for human rights and human dignity, and whether we have moral special obligations to one another that we do not have to other animals. In these cases, philosophers often take the concept of the human for granted, perhaps assuming that it has already been settled by science.

In centuries past, the question of what humans are had a lot more traction. In the Aristotelian tradition, to be human was to be rationally ensouled—that is, to be equipped participate in a rational form of life. Over time, the Aristotelian conception of the rational soul morphed into the more otherworldly Christian conception of the rational soul—a nonmaterial *part* of the person. Consequently, being human was equated with possessing a such a soul.[4] Souls are invisible and undetectable, and therefore readily deniable. This fact gave European and American slaveholders an easy way to claim that the Africans whom they enslaved, and the indigenous people whom they oppressed, were not really human. Spanish intellectuals claimed that the native people of the Americas lacked fully rational souls, and were therefore barbarians who could legitimately be enslaved. But some English colonists (and later, some Americans) extended this line of thinking further, by claiming that enslaved Africans did not have souls at all, and therefore were not human beings.

The writings of the seventeenth-century Anglican cleric Morgan Godwyn, whom I mentioned in Chapter 4, are an important source of information on this topic. Godwyn, who had been John Locke's student at Oxford University, traveled to Virginia in 1666, and aroused the hostility of planters there by baptizing Black slaves and Indians. Next, he sailed to Barbados, where he continued advocating for admitting Black people to the Anglican Church, against the wishes of those who enslaved them. He also fiercely condemned the dehumanization of Africans and atrocities that White colonists inflicted on these people.[5] Godwyn testified that English colonists held a "disingenuous position" that "the Negros, though in their Figure they carry some resemblances of Manhood, yet are indeed no men," and that they advocated "Hellish Principles . . . that Negros are Creatures Destitute of Souls, to be ranked among Brute Beasts and treated accordingly."[6] In that time and place, to be human meant having an immaterial soul, and conceiving of others as sub-human beings entailed denying that they possessed souls.

Few philosophers nowadays give any credence to the idea that human beings possess immaterial souls. Contemporary philosophers mostly believe that human beings are, like all other organisms, purely physical beings. Even though they do not pay much attention to the concept of humanness, philosophers pay a great deal of attention to the nearby notion of "personhood." Although the term "person" is an ancient one (as far as anyone knows, it was the Roman philosopher Epictetus who introduced it), the idea of person-hood as a distinctive metaphysical status did not come into its own until the seventeenth century, and by the twentieth century it had eclipsed the notion of humanness in the philosophical literature.

Present-day ideas about personhood are mostly indebted to the work of John Locke, who defined a person as "a thinking, intelligent being that has reason and reflection and can consider itself as itself, the same thinking thing, in different times and places." The philosopher Charles Taylor gives a good general summary of the received view of personhood as it is understood today. "To be a person in the full sense," he writes, "you have to be an agent, a being that can thus make plans for your life, one who also holds values in virtue of which different such plans seem better or worse, and who is capable of choosing between them." Although there is a lot quibbling about the details of the concept of personhood, especially by those who want to extend personhood to include other animals, the general point on which they virtually all agree is that "to regard an entity as a person is to attribute a special kind of value to that entity."[7]

What is the difference, if any, between being human and being a person? Generally speaking, philosophers think of humanness as an unproblematically biological property (they assume that human equals *Homo sapiens*), but they conceive of personhood as carrying a special moral status. With this in mind, it is easy to see why many philosophers want to distinguish biological humanness from moral personhood. For a being to have a special kind of intrinsic value, it is reasonable to suppose that there is something about that being— some attribute or set of attributes—that accounts for their specialness. After all, when we say that someone is beautiful, or talented, or malevolent there is got to be something *about* them—something about how they appear or behave—that makes them beautiful, or talented, or malevolent. Imagine someone sincerely claiming that a certain person is beautiful, but also denying that there is anything about that person that makes them beautiful. This would be so incoherent as to be incomprehensible. Likewise, those who think that to be a person is to have a special moral value need to say what it is about being a person that underwrites that value. But it is difficult to see how the mere fact that an entity belongs to a particular evolutionary lineage can do this moral job.

And that is where the trouble starts.

If being a member of a certain species or genus is not enough to make an entity a person, then what is? Fans of the concept of personhood tend to believe that some extra, nonbiological ingredient needs to be added. And as soon as you specify characteristics that persons have and nonpersons do not, you inevitably exclude some members of our species from that group.

This conclusion is not always unwelcome. Consider abortion. Human fetuses are, by definition, human (in the sense of being *Homo sapiens*), but it is easy to make the case that they do not have characteristics that would make them persons, and therefore that they do not merit the moral consideration that we accord fully-formed humans. However, the claim that some humans are not persons, and for that reason do not merit the degree of moral respect that persons merit, was also the foundation for Hitler's euthanasia program and various other atrocities. So, anyone who distinguishes biological humanness from moral personhood is faced with the difficult problem of setting out criteria for personhood that do not exclude the "right" individuals. To avoid such exclusionary consequences, some philosophers embrace one or another version of a very abstract notion of personhood. Typically, the claim is that personhood resides in rationality, autonomy, infinite worth, or some such attribute. However, in such cases, the meanings of these words float away from their everyday usage in a way that renders them vacuous or absurd. A person who is imprisoned, enslaved, or who lives in a totalitarian state is still said to be autonomous; one who habitually behaves with irrational abandon is nevertheless said to be rational, and one whose society deems them to be unworthy of life is still said to have ultimate worth. The idea is that the deep attributes that make us persons transcend the merely contingent facts about our psychology and circumstances. This is supposed to ensure that, at a minimum, all human beings count as persons. As Taylor put it, "We believe that it would be utterly wrong and unfounded to draw the boundaries any narrower than around the whole human race." He continues, "Should anyone propose to do so, we should immediately ask what distinguished those left in from those left out. And we should seize on this distinguishing characteristic in order to show that it has nothing to do with commanding respect."[8]

But this takes us right back to square one. If all and only humans are persons, the category of the "human" turns out to be a moral category after all.[9] As Peter Singer astutely points out,

> Faced with a situation in which they saw a need for some basis for the moral gulf that is still commonly thought to separate human beings and animals, but unable to find any concrete difference between human beings and animals that would do this without undermining the equality of human beings, philosophers tended to waffle. They resorted to high-sounding phrases like "the intrinsic dignity of the human individual." They talked of "the intrinsic worth of all men" . . . as if all men (humans?) had some unspecified worth that other beings do not have. Or they would say that human beings, and only human beings, are "ends in themselves" while "everything other than a person can only have value for a person." . . . To introduce ideas of dignity and worth as a substitute for other reasons for distinguishing humans and animals is not good enough. Fine phrases are the last resource of those who have run out of arguments.[10]

If bare humanness has moral heft, and if being human is nothing more than belonging to a certain biological category, then the problem arises of explaining how belonging to a biological category can endow the members of it with a special moral status.

Psychological Humanness

To dehumanize others is *conceive* of them as less than human, and to humanize them is to *conceive* of them as human. It follows that the question of what it is for an individual to be human is less important for understanding dehumanization than the question of what it is to attribute humanness to that person. So, understanding dehumanization requires us to take a psychological stance toward claims about humanness.

Psychologist Nick Haslam, whose work I discussed briefly in Chapter 2, has an influential thesis about attributions of humanness. He proposes that we think of others as human to the extent that they are thought to possess certain psychological characteristics. *Uniquely human traits* are, as the name suggests, characteristics that only humans have. These are supposed to distinguish human beings from all other animals. Haslam lists civility, refinement, moral sensibility, rationality, and maturity as prime examples of uniquely human traits. *Human nature traits* are "features that are typically, fundamentally, or essentially human, representing those attributes that form the core of the concept 'human.'" Human nature traits do not have to be restricted to humans—they can be shared with nonhuman animals, but they are traits that we strongly associate with being human. Haslam lists emotionality, warmth, openness, agency, individuality, and depth as examples of human nature traits.[11]

Haslam and his coworkers gave subjects a list of eighty psychological traits and asked them whether each trait is an aspect of human nature or whether it is exclusively human. They were also interested in finding out whether psychological essentialism plays a role in how we think about humanness, so they asked participants some additional questions to determine whether subjects "essentialized" these traits. They predicted that "traits would be judged to be aspects of human nature to the extent that they were judged to be expressed consistently across situations, immutable, deeply rooted (inherent), and highly informative (inductively potent) about people who have them."[12] It turned out that there was a good deal of agreement that the more refined and sophisticated traits were classified uniquely human and that the other, cruder or more basic traits were classified as aspects of human nature. It also turned out that, according to the research protocol, human nature traits tended to be essentialized,[13]

Haslam draws on the distinction between causal essences and sortal essences in his account. As I have explained, causal essences are supposed to be hidden properties that only and all members of a natural kind possess, and which are causally responsible for the manifest, observable features that we associate with members of that kind. They are supposed to be concretely real, and located "inside" the objects that "have" them.

In contrast, sortal essences are "the set of defining characteristics that all and only members of a category share."[14] Sortal essences are the sum of the observable features that define category membership. They are not limited to natural kinds. Sortal essences are not *possessed* by individual things; they are not in any sense "inside" of those things but are rather the set of necessary and sufficient conditions that need to be satisfied in order for a thing to be assigned to a category. To say that anything that quacks, walks, and swims like a duck is *therefore* a duck is to specify the sortal essence of the category "duck," whereas to say that there is something unobservable that all and only ducks possess, and which is normally responsible for these forms of quacking, walking, and swimming, is to specify its causal essence.

Haslam claims human nature traits are "highly essentialized" in the causal sense, but "uniquely human characteristics may embody a different sense of essence than human nature." He goes on to say that "arguably they may be captured by Gelman and Hirschfeld's (1999) concept of sortal essence. . . . Plato's definition of human as 'featherless biped' exemplifies this sense of sortal essence: It distinguishes humans from other animals without any implication that featherlessness and bipedalism are core features of human nature.

We therefore argue that uniquely human characteristics may represent the human essence in a sortal sense, consistent with infrahumanization theory, and human nature characteristics represent the essence in a natural kind sense."[15]

There are multiple problems with this suggestion. First, the notion that traits can be causally essentialized is a category mistake. Recall that causal essences are supposed to be unobservable properties *cause* and *explain* traits. As such, they should not be conflated with the traits that they supposedly cause and explain. Second, Haslam's proposal that only human nature traits—that is, traits that we share with other animals—are thought of as having a causal essence implies that we do not think of human beings as possessing a distinctively human causal essence. This is inconsistent both with the historical evidence that I have presented in earlier chapters (for example, the idea of the soul as a human essence) and with work on essentialistic misunderstandings of genetics—some of which Haslam has elsewhere endorsed.[16] Third, if it is true that uniquely human traits constitute the sortal essence of the human—that is, if having such traits *defines* what it is to be human—then any being lacking those traits should be considered non- or subhuman. But human babies do not have these traits. They lack civility, refinement, moral sensibility, rationality, and maturity. And yet, human babies are considered to be human beings. Finally, Haslam's account of humanness does not comport well with facts about dehumanization (or, in his terminology, facts about the animalistic form of dehumanization). His theory predicts that people who animalistically dehumanize others conceive of these others as lacking uniquely human traits but possessing human nature traits. However, in many examples of exterminationist dehumanization, such as the Holocaust and the Rwanda genocide, dehumanized victims are conceived of as creatures akin to insects, lice, or reptiles, but these creatures lack paradigmatic "human nature" traits of emotionality, warmth, openness, agency, individuality, and depth that Haslam's theory states should be attributed to them.

Political Humanness

Claims that to be human is to belong to a certain biological grouping, or to be rational, or to possess a soul, or to have certain psychological characteristics all take it for granted that humanness can be boiled down to one or more objective properties. It is the idea that there are certain facts about others that make it the case that they are human beings. Political scientist Anne Phillips calls such approaches "substantive."[17] They are substantive because they assume that there is some fact of the matter about whether any given being is a human being. Phillips argues that substantive approaches are unsatisfactory because they either leave some people out of the circle of the human or so are rarified that they are devoid of content. She proposes that humanity is never *discovered* in others. Instead, it is given or taken—granted, claimed, withdrawn, or withheld. "People," she says, "assert, rather than prove, their claims to be regarded as human."[18] She holds that to accept another being as human is to grant them a certain status, and to refer to oneself as human is to stake a claim to that status. Philosopher Michael Hauskeller writes in a similar vein:

> It shouldn't matter how we classify, what we call human and what not, but to many people it obviously does. Why is that so? Why do we care whether we are human or not, or someone else is? And why do we care what makes us human, that is, why do we care for the reason we call ourselves human? I think the answer to the first question (and thus, as we will see, also to the second) is that 'human', to us, is usually more than just a descriptive predicate. It more often than not has a very strong prescriptive dimension. It is, just as the word 'person' according to

St Thomas Aquinas, a *nomen dignitatis*, that is a title of honour, or a dignity-conferring name.[19]

Phillips and Hauskeller are on the right track. Interpreting humanness as an assigned status avoids the problems that plague efforts to equate humanness with objective properties such as "rationality." But their story needs filling out more. We need to know more about what is involved in the act of claiming human status for oneself, and admitting or denying it to others.

We can start with self-reference. People generally take their own humanity, and the humanity of members of their immediate community, for granted. "I" and "we" are human, but "they" may not be human. As the anthropologist Claude Lévi-Strauss observed, "Humanity is confined to the borders of the tribe, the linguistic group, or even, in some instances, to the village, so that many so-called primitive peoples describe themselves as 'the men' (or sometimes—though hardly more discreetly—as 'the good', 'the excellent', 'the well- achieved'), thus implying that the other tribes, groups or villages have no part in the human virtues or even in human nature."[20] Tribal names are often "not formal designations, but merely equivalents of the pronoun 'we.'"[21] Let us suppose as a point of departure that the concept of the human is roughly equivalent to the concept of "us." If this is right, then "human" functions as what theorists of language call an *indexical* term. Indexical terms are expressions whose referents radically depend on the contexts in which they are used. The word "here" is an indexical term, because it names wherever the speaker is located when they say "here." "Now" is another indexical term—one that names the time at which the word is uttered. There are many more.

Even though indexicals can name totally different things depending on the contexts of their use, there is also a sense in which their meaning remains constant from one context to the next. "Here" always means "the place where I am" no matter where that place may be. And some of them can be construed in more or less fine-grained or coarse-grained ways: if I say "I'm here" I might be talking about a particular spot in my house, or I might be referring to the particular town, state, or country where my house is located. The word "human" is similarly elastic. As Lévi-Strauss pointed out, it can designate "the tribe, the linguistic group, or even . . . the village," and of course, at larger scales, it can designate the species, the genus, or some other extended biotaxonomic category.

The idea that "human" functions as an indexical term provides a good alternative to the predominant substantive accounts. But a problem remains that needs surmounting. The proposal that "human" just means "we" or "us" is not specific enough. Although when we use these words, we are normally referring to other human beings, it is usually some subset of the beings we think of as human beings that we are talking about. A person who phones a friend and says "We'll arrive in half an hour" is not equating himself and his partner—the "we"—with the whole of humanity. So, if being human is being one of "us," we need to look more carefully at the how these notions work. Recall the category "human" is supposed to be a natural kind. This suggests a refinement of the indexical theory of humanness. "Human" means "us" in the restricted sense of *my (natural) kind*. To think of other beings as human, then, is to regard them as members of the same natural kind as oneself, and as sharing the same essence as oneself.

This way of looking at the matter accommodates the fact that there are so many different substantive conceptions of what it means to be human. A person with a self-conception of being a member of a certain biological taxon—say, the genus *Homo*—will conceive of only and all members of that genus as a human. And a person who identifies primarily with the Aryan race (conceived of as an essentialized kind) will limit humanness to members of that group.[22] The content of "human" is whatever the speaker or thinker takes their natural kind to be—whatever population of beings they take to share their essence.

There are three more points that need to be made about how attributions of humanness work before I conclude this chapter. First, regarding others as members of one's own kind has a normative character—it elevates them (recall Hauskeller's observation that "human" is a dignity-conferring name). This is because we think of natural kinds as being ranked on a hierarchy of value, and are disposed to value our own kind above the others. To accord others human status is therefore to give them a *privileged* status. The idea that humans are simply those that are the same kind of being as oneself, and therefore that all others are, by default, nonhuman or subhuman, should not be confused with the in-group / out-group biases that I discussed in Chapter 7. The indexical analysis does not restrict humanness to the in-group. In-groups are constituted by those whom we consider to be members of our social kind—and in some cases by individuals whom we believe to be members of our natural kind, such as racial groups. But the in-group / out-group boundary does not have to demarcate the category of the human from that of the subhuman. In fact, the in-group / out-group dichotomy generally presupposes that both groups share a common humanity. It would be very odd to think of a nonhuman animal (say, a rat) as an out-group member. Rats are not the kinds of things that can fit into the in-group / out-group framework. Likewise, binaries like "friend" and "enemy," "ally" and "rival," all presuppose a shared humanity. It is perfectly true that out-group members become dehumanized, but their dehumanization is neither constituted by, nor a necessary consequence of, their out-group status. Second, although I have described the dignity-conferring act in individualistic terms, the boundaries of the human are almost always collectively legislated and usually entrenched in shared social ideologies that are handed down from one generation to the next. So, instead of thinking of "human" as meaning "*my* basic natural kind," it is more accurate to understand it as "*our* basic natural kind." This shows us that "human" is almost always a politically significant status.[23]

If this analysis is correct, then the human/subhuman dichotomy is an ideological construction. So, to understand dehumanization we have to understand the nature of ideology—a topic to which I now turn.

CHAPTER NINE

Ideology

The scholarly literature on ideology is very extensive. As philosophers Charles Mills and Dan Goldstick remark, "If there were a list of subjects about which it seems that there is definitely no more to be said—or that even if there were, nobody would want to hear it anyway—then surely the topics of ideology, in general, and ideology in Marxist theory, in particular, would have to rank very near the top."[1] But this literature is riddled with disagreements about fundamental issues—including disagreements about exactly what ideology is. The word "ideology" is used as a name for so many different phenomena, and these phenomena are explained in so many different ways, that talking about ideology without further qualification is useless or worse than useless. As John Gerring writes at the beginning of a paper aimed at extracting some order from the semantic chaos, "Few concepts in the social science lexicon have occasioned so much discussion, so much disagreement, and so much self-conscious discussion of the disagreement as 'ideology.' Condemned time and again for its semantic excesses, for its bulbous unclarity, the concept of ideology remains, against all odds, a central term of social science discourse."[2]

Trying to critically examine all of these conceptions of ideology would be a fool's errand. Instead, I will focus on the "functional" view of ideology, which is the view that ideologies are beliefs or belief-like states that have the function of producing, perpetuating, or otherwise augmenting oppression. It is this view of ideology that is most helpful for understanding the political dimension of dehumanization.

Functional Conceptions of Ideology

Most current theories of ideology grew out of the thinking of Karl Marx, beginning with the tantalizingly brief discussion in Marx and Engels's 1846 manuscript *The German Ideology*.[3] In the Marxist tradition, material power relations are thought to govern social and intellectual life. From the beginning, Marx and Engels stressed that, far from being a matter of individual psychology, ideologies result from, and are embedded in, social structures and processes. "In the social production of their existence," as Marx later put it, "men inevitably enter into definite relations, which are independent of their will, namely relations of production appropriate to a given stage in the development of their material forces of production." He went on to explain that "the totality of these relations of production constitutes the economic structure of society, the real foundation, on which arises a legal and political superstructure and to which correspond definite forms of consciousness. The mode of production of material life conditions the general process of social, political and intellectual life. It is not the consciousness of men that determines their existence, but their social existence that determines their consciousness."[4]

Marx and Engels proposed that insofar as we are enmeshed in ideology, we *misrepresent* social reality by giving the realm of ideas causal priority over material power relations. "If in all ideology (*in der ganzen Ideologie*[5]) men and their circumstances appear upside-down as in a camera obscura," they wrote, "this phenomenon arises just as much from their historical life-process as the inversion of objects on the retina does from their physical life-process."

Looked at closely, these two optical analogies reveal an important feature of Marx and Engels's conception of ideology. The camera obscura is likely to be something that most present-day readers are unacquainted with. It is a closed box with a small hole or lens in one side. When light from outside the box shines through the lens, it projects an inverted image on the opposite interior wall. Something similar occurs in the human eye. When light passes through the pupil, an inverted image is projected on the retina. The eye is, in effect, an anatomical camera obscura. The camera obscura was not designed to invert the image, and the "designer" of the eye—the process of natural selection—did not design the eye to do that either. In both cases, the explanation of why the image is turned upside down appeals only to the structure of the device and to the laws of optics. Image inversion is a purely accidental consequence of structural features of these devices. It is not part of their functional design, and additional equipment is required (both in the box and in the brain) to rectify the image.

If we take these optical metaphors as seriously as I think we should, in likening inverted representations of the social world to inverted visual images, Marx and Engels imply that ideological beliefs are accidental consequences of structural features of social systems. Put a little differently, Marx and Engels seem to be implicitly denying that ideologies have the purpose of representing social reality in a distorted fashion. Misrepresenting reality is not what ideologies are for, because in their view ideologies are not *for* anything at all. They are reflections of the relations of domination that already infuse a society. They are misleading, but it is not their function to mislead. According to Marx and Engels,

> The ideas of the ruling class are in every epoch the ruling ideas, i.e. the class which is the ruling material force of society, is at the same time its ruling intellectual force. The class which has

the means of material production at its disposal, has control at the same time over the means of mental production, so that thereby, generally speaking, the ideas of those who lack the means of mental production are subject to it. The ruling ideas are nothing more than the ideal expression of the dominant material relationships, the dominant material relationships grasped as ideas.[6]

Later writings, both by Marxists and by others, describe ideologies as purposeful. And those social theorists who see ideologies as purposeful often embrace what is known as a "functional" conception of ideology. According this conception, ideologies are beliefs (and associated values, practices, institutions, and so on) that have the function of promoting oppression. Philosophers Tommy Shelby and Sally Haslanger both describe ideology in this way. Shelby writes that ideologies "function . . . to bring about or perpetuate unjust social relations" and Haslanger similarly writes that "very broadly, ideology is best understood functionally: ideology functions to stabilize or perpetuate power and domination."[7]

To form a clear idea of the functional thesis, we first need to unpack the notion of oppression. Oppression is a relation of inequality in which one party secures or sustains advantages by exploiting others. It is normally used to describe relations between whole groups of people rather than between individuals. The philosopher Marilyn Frye provides a succinct description. "Oppression," she writes, "is a system of interrelated barriers and forces which reduce, immobilize and mold people who belong to a certain group, and effect their subordination to another group (individually to individuals of the other group, and as a group, to that group)."[8] Oppression need not be deliberate. In fact, it is often "embedded in unquestioned norms, habits, and symbols, in the assumptions underlying institutions and rules, and the collective consequences of following those rules. It refers to the vast and

deep injustices some groups suffer as a consequence of often uncon-
scious assumptions and reactions of well-meaning people in ordinary
interactions that are supported by the media and cultural stereotypes as well as by the structural features of bureaucratic hierarchies
and market mechanisms."[9]

There are at least two different conceptions of what functions
are. One is the causal role that a thing plays in a complex system.
I call these *causal functions*.[10] The procedure for identifying the causal
function of a thing is to take a complex system (for example, a
washing machine) and identify something that the whole system
can do (in this case, washing laundry). Then, select some part of
the system that you are interested in identifying the function of (for
example, the agitator), and determine its contribution to what the
whole system does (in this example, it enables the washing machine
to wash laundry by churning the laundry around in the tub). The
other notion of function is that the function of a thing is what it
is for doing. Understood in this way, the function of a thing is its
purpose—its *teleological function*. The procedure for identifying the
teleological function of a thing is to make inferences about what
that thing was designed to do. Going back to the washing-machine
example, the engineers that designed the machine included an agitator for the purpose of churning laundry around in the tub. That
explains why this is its teleological function.

When a washing machine functions properly, the causal and teleological functions of its agitator coincide. But they can come
apart when the machine is not working properly. Suppose that a mechanical fault prevents an agitator from moving as it should.
Rather than rotating back and forth it remains stationary and just
vibrates. In this case, the agitator has lost its causal function, because
it no longer contributes to the washing machine's capacity to wash
laundry, but it still has its original teleological function, because its
purpose is still to move laundry around in the tub, even though it
cannot fulfill this purpose.

Parts of systems can fail to do their job for two sorts of reasons. Sometimes this happens because there is something about the part that prevents it from doing its job. In this case we say that the part is "broken" or "defective" or "malformed." But it can also happen because there is something *external* to the part—some aspect of its "environment" that prevents it from doing its job. For example, the agitator might not be working because the washing machine is not plugged in, or not switched on, or perhaps because some other part of the machine has broken down.

The fact that "function" has two meanings implies that there are two functional conceptions of ideology, so it is misleading to speak of *the* functional analysis of ideology without qualification. Saying that ideology has the function of producing oppression might mean either that producing oppression is its causal function or that producing oppression is its teleological function. On the causal-functional interpretation, beliefs about the social world are ideological only if they actually produce oppression, and on the teleological interpretation beliefs about the social world are ideological only if they have the purpose of producing oppression. According to the causal approach, beliefs that produce oppression are ideological even if producing oppression is not what they are for, and according to the teleological approach, beliefs that are for producing oppression are ideological even if they do not actually produce oppression. The distinction between causal and teleological versions of the functional thesis is quite sharp and consequential for how we conceive of ideology.

Success-Aptness

One major difference between them has to do with what I call "success-aptness." A thing is success-apt if it is the sort of thing that can succeed or fail to meet a standard of performance. Ideological belief systems often produce oppression, but do they also *succeed* at producing it? And if ideologies sometimes fail to produce oppression, do they fail at producing it, or do they merely not produce it?

How to answer these questions will depend on which of the two perspectives on ideology is on offer. On the causal account, ideologies are not success-apt, because if ideology is what ideology does, as the causal conception demands, then any system of belief that does not result in oppression is therefore not ideological. The causal-functional thesis also implies that beliefs that once produced oppression, but have ceased to do so, have ceased to be ideological beliefs.

This is where doubts start to creep in about utility of the causal-functional approach to ideology. It is peculiar to say that beliefs that are explicitly *aimed* at producing oppression, but which no longer do so, are not ideological beliefs. Picture a world in which there are people who hold White supremacist views, but who are prevented from oppressing Black people. On the causal account, these White supremacist beliefs do not qualify as ideological because they do not have oppressive effects. Of course, there are ways that a person who's committed to the causal approach can finesse this. They might claim that beliefs that do not produce oppression are nevertheless ideological if they *tend* toward producing oppression—that is, if they would have resulted in the oppression of Black people under different circumstances. This is not helpful, because the causal approach is not concerned with merely possible effects of beliefs. It is concerned only with the real, occurrent consequences of those beliefs.

In contrast, the teleological approach allows that ideologies are success-apt. They can succeed at producing oppression, or they can fail at producing oppression, and ideologies that produced oppression at one time, but do not do so any longer, retain their oppressive function, even though that function is no longer being executed. Consequently, if one accepts that it is possible for ideologies to fail, and if one is also inclined to accept a broadly functional notion of ideology, then one should adopt the teleological conception of ideology.

Accidental Ideologies?

Although the causal approach does not *require* that ideologies are accidental effects of social structures, as Marx and Engels seem to have suggested, it allows for the existence of accidental ideologies. This is because whether or not a belief is ideological depends on whether that belief plays an oppressive causal role. From this perspective, even beliefs that are not aimed at producing oppression—or indeed even beliefs that are aimed at ameliorating oppression—can produce oppression, and therefore can count as ideologies. Consider the racialization of Africans during the colonial period of US history. The Enlightenment ideals of liberty and equality—the notion that all men are created equal and are endowed with God-given rights—arguably contributed to the oppression of Africans by bringing about their racialization, denigration, and dehumanization. As historian Barbara Jeanne Fields points out,

> Race is not an idea but an ideology. It came into existence at a discernible historical moment for rationally understandable historical reasons and is subject to change for similar reasons. The revolutionary bicentennials that Americans have celebrated with such unction—of independence in 1976 and of the Constitution in 1989—can as well serve as the bicentennial of racial ideology, since the birthdays are not far apart. During the revolutionary era, people who favored slavery and people who opposed it collaborated in identifying the racial incapacity of Afro-Americans as the explanation for enslavement. American racial ideology is as original an invention of the Founders as is the United States itself. Those holding liberty to be inalienable and holding Afro-Americans as slaves were bound to end by holding race to be a self-evident truth.[11]

It is a stretch to think that the founders of the United States endorsed the doctrine of liberty and equality *in order to* oppress Africans. Nevertheless, this doctrine contributed to their oppression.

Hence, on the causal account, the ideals of liberty and equality constitute an oppressive ideology. And if Washington, Jefferson, and the rest had embraced these political ideals as a *means* to oppress Africans, this wouldn't have made a bit of difference, because, on the causal account, the purpose of a belief, or the purpose for which a belief is held (a distinction that I will shortly explain), is irrelevant to its ideological status. In contrast, the teleological conception does not countenance accidental ideologies. Ideological beliefs are, by definition, aimed at producing oppression, even if they do not have this effect. On the teleological account, the ideals of liberty and equality might still be ideological, but for a very different reason, which I will now move on to explain.

Against Intentionalism

Terry Eagleton points out that the notion that ideologies are systems of belief that have the purpose of promoting the interests of socially dominant groups at the expense of others "is probably the single most widely accepted definition of ideology," and he lists six "strategies" by means of which this purpose gets implemented: "A dominant power may legitimate itself by *producing* beliefs and values congenial to it; *naturalizing* and *universalizing* such beliefs so as to render them self-evident and apparently inevitable; *denigrating* ideas which might challenge it; *excluding* rival forms of thought, perhaps by some unspoken but systematic logic; and *obscuring* social reality in ways convenient to itself."[12]

The term "strategies" makes it easy to suppose that groups of people who endorse ideologies deliberately and self-servingly misrepresent the social world. But this conspiratorial interpretation is inconsistent with a key feature of ideology. It is true that those holding the reins of power sometimes lie, manipulate, and deceive others to maintain their dominant status. But lies, manipulations, and deceptions are not the same as ideologies. People who are truly immersed in an ideology do not espouse their beliefs in order to achieve some goal. They regard their beliefs as true—usually as *self-evidently* true. Consider again the ideology of White supremacism. White supremacism emerged and proliferated alongside the expansion and consolidation of the transatlantic slave trade. The practice of chattel slavery was an economic powerhouse that generated immense wealth not only for the plantation owners, but to many others who benefited less directly: the insurers, shipbuilders, sugar importers, insurance companies, and many, many others. This made it attractive for Europeans to believe themselves to be inherently superior to Africans, and also to believe that, because of their inherent inferiority, Africans themselves benefited from being enslaved to their White overlords. Beliefs like these legitimated the brutal business of slavery in the eyes of the many of those who profited from it. These White supremacists did not *pretend* to believe that people of color are inferior to Whites, as a strategy for oppressing them. They *sincerely* believed in the essential inferiority of Black people. There were those who did *not* believe that Black people were really the inferiors of Whites, but who nevertheless cynically espoused and promoted this view in order to benefit from their enslavement. But these people weren't enmeshed in the White supremacist ideology. If they had been so enmeshed, the thought that Black people are their equals would have seemed ludicrous to them.

It follows that a satisfactory teleological theory of ideology needs to square the principle that ideological beliefs have the purpose of oppression with the fact that those who adhere to the ideology do not hold those beliefs in order to oppress others.[13] They hold these beliefs because they sincerely regard them as true.

How does this work? It cannot be true that a person believes something *because* they think it is true and also believe it *in order* to reap certain benefits. It might be tempting to suppose that if people do not consciously adopt ideologies for purposes of domination, then they must do so unconsciously and are self-deceived about why they believe what they do. They falsely think that they embrace ideological beliefs because they deem them true, but they *really* embrace them because of the rewards that these beliefs seem to offer. There is a better alternative to this speculative and unsubstantiated assumption. We do not have to assume that people who adopt ideological positions do not really believe them, because philosophical work on how purposes arise in nature can give a compelling account of how it is possible for a belief to have a certain purpose and not yet be held for that purpose.

How Ideologies Get Their Purposes

Advocates of a functional account of ideology face a dilemma. Either ideology has the causal function of producing oppression or it has the teleological function of producing oppression. Looked at through the lens of causal functions, ideologies cannot fail and belief systems count as ideologies even if they produce their oppressive effects accidentally. Alternatively, from the teleological perspective, it looks like ideological belief systems get their function from oppressive intentions of their adherents, but this is inconsistent with the principle that those who embrace ideological beliefs do so because they consider these beliefs to be true, rather than because they promote oppression.

Both alternatives seem unacceptable. There is a way to get beyond this dilemma—a way to explain how ideologies get their teleological functions without these functions springing from people's oppressive intentions. To do this, we need to consider how functions are understood in evolutionary biology.

When people suffer from heart failure, their heart stops beating. When this happens, does their heart *fail?* Or is it just the case that their heart simply ceases beating? A knee-jerk response might be "no," their heart does not literally fail, because failure presupposes that there is some *goal* that the heart has not achieved, and hearts, unlike the people who house them, do not have goals. It is only whole people, and not their parts, that can succeed or fail.

This knee-jerk answer is incorrect. Even though hearts do not have purposes in the sense that people do, there is a standard of performance that is intrinsic to human hearts, which hearts can fail to achieve. Hearts do not have intentional purposes, but they have a biological purpose, and that is what makes it possible for them to fail (or, on the other side of the coin, to succeed). The purpose of the heart is to pump blood through the circulatory system. This is not some sort of subjective interpretation that we foist on purposeless biology. It is an objective property that distinguishes healthy hearts from diseased ones, hearts that are intact from those that are damaged or deformed.

The notion that parts of organisms have purposes is indispensable for understanding them. Just as hearts have the purpose of pumping blood; eyes have the purpose of gathering visual information; wings have the purpose of flight; teeth have the purpose of biting, tearing, or chewing; and threat displays have the purpose of driving others away. None of these purposes are purposes *of the organisms themselves.* The fact that eyes are for seeing has nothing to do with our states of mind. It is a purpose that was fixed long ago by the process of evolution.

The purposes of parts of organisms are real purposes, but they are not intentional ones. The philosopher Ruth Garrett Millikan, who pioneered the analysis of nonintentional, biological purposes, draws on biological principles to explain how such purposes come into being. She refers to such purposes as "proper functions" or "teleofunctions," a term that I will use from here on.[14]

Millikan has a theory of how things get their teleofunctions. She argues that for a thing to have a teleofunction, it must satisfy two conditions. First, the thing must be a reproduction, or a reproduction of a reproduction, of an ancestral prototype. Here the term "reproduction" refers to any process of copying, including biological forms of reproduction, but also extends far beyond the biological realm to include imitation, repetition, retweeting, and so on. Second, for a thing to have a teleofunction there must have been something about earlier members of its reproductive lineage that caused it to be reproduced enough of the time. There must have been some effect that the thing had, in that ancestral environment, that enhanced its reproduction. The phrase "enough of the time" is important, because the effect does not have occur invariably or even commonly. Millikan uses the example of the sperm cell to get this point across.[15] The biological purpose of sperm cells is to fertilize ova. There is no dispute about that. But of the many millions of sperm that are produced by male animals (men can produce a billion in a single ejaculation), hardly any of them fertilize an ovum. The fact that *some* of them have fertilized ova, and thereby ensured their continued reproduction, is sufficient to give them the teleofunction of fertilizing ova.

Anything that satisfies Millikan's two conditions has a teleofunction. And its teleofunction is whatever effect its predecessors had that accounted for their proliferation. So—to continue with the example—eyes have the teleofunction of seeing because (a) all eyes are part of a lineage of eyes, and (b) ancestral eyes were reproduced because they enhanced the reproduction of eye-bearing animals by enabling those animals to see.

Teleofunctions are often described as "backward-looking" because they are fixed by the effects that were responsible for the success of a thing's ancestors. What a thing does now is often the same as what kept its ancestors going. Hearts pump blood when they are working as they should, just as ancestral hearts did. This is why we are often able to make good inferences about teleofunctions on the basis of present-day effects (understanding the teleofunction of hearts did not have to wait for scientists to uncover their evolutionary history). Very often, the design of a part in relation to the design of the whole does not admit of any other plausible inference—especially when the performance of the function for which the part been designed is necessary for the survival of the organism. However, there are cases that are not so transparent. This is often because the organism's environment has not remained stable, and the trait consequently cannot perform the function that its precursors performed in the past. John Byers's classic study of the American pronghorn antelope, evocatively subtitled *Social Adaptations and the Ghosts of Predators Past*, presents a great example. Pronghorns are extremely fast runners. They are built for speed, and this requires an evolutionary explanation. The obvious one is that pronghorns are fast so that they can evade fast-running predators. Those ancestral pronghorn antelope who were the speediest were more likely to survive long enough to reproduce than their herd-mates were, and this athletic ability was handed down genetically to their offspring. The problem is, these "truly Olympian runners" live "in a world of less-than-Olympian predators." None of the predators that kill pronghorns today are particularly fast. Byers recalls being asked,

> "Why are pronghorn so *over built?*" Why indeed? In my opinion there is only one convincing answer—pronghorn evolved their running ability during a time when Olympian predators pursued them. . . . These predators included a long-legged hyena, a large lion, a huge long-legged bear, and at least two species of cheetahs. These predators, along with many other mammalian

species, became extinct in North America about 10,000 years ago at the end-Pleistocene extinction event that decimated mammals on several continents. Although selection for running ability has been relaxed since the extinctions, limb proportions, and thus apparently running speed, have not changed.[16]

The pronghorn physique has the teleofunction of evading predators. That is what natural selection designed pronghorn bodies to do, even though there are no longer any fast-moving predators to prey on them.

Millikan's analysis is not just a restatement of Darwin's principle of natural selection. It applies beyond the biological sphere, because it allows that *anything* that is copied because of its effects has a teleofunction. Ideologies have all the ingredients that are required for this recipe. Ideologies are beliefs that have been reproduced again and again, over historical rather than evolutionary time, because they benefited one group of people at the expense of another, and this is what gives them the purpose of promoting oppression. Because of this, ideologies can have the teleological function of promoting oppression without it being the case that those who embrace the ideology do so in order to promote oppression.

False Consciousness

People adopt ideological beliefs because they regard them as true. There are many reasons why one might regard an ideological belief as true, depending on the content of the ideology and the particular circumstances that allowed it to gain traction. Often ideologies are believable to those who benefit most from them because these people's judgments are biased in favor of the ideology. And because the people who benefit are often those that control the apparatuses of cultural reproduction, the views that benefit them are also likely to spread through a society. Also, ideological beliefs often get popular traction when they are endorsed by people whose opinions are taken to carry epistemic weight. These include scientific authorities, religious leaders, politicians, and even celebrities and talk show hosts. And sometimes people cling to ideologies because we are led to believe that rejecting them exposes them to grave dangers, and this sense of threat lowers the evidential bar for accepting them as true. Whatever the reason for its proliferation, once an ideology becomes sedimented in a community it is treated as self-evidently true. As Shelby rightly points out,

> Moreover, the truth or objective warrant of such beliefs is more or less taken for granted, treated as common knowledge. Thus within a society where racist ideology holds sway, nothing could be more "obvious" than that there are different races with corresponding mental traits and behavioral tendencies. The beliefs of racists, moreover, seem to them to be of immense social importance, as they define the boundaries of Self and Other, of in-group and out-group, of who deserves respect and who contempt. And these beliefs are so firmly held that they often fail to yield to criticism and counter-evidence.[17]

Scholars who write about ideology almost always claim that the oppressive purposes of ideologies are concealed, and that by their very nature they *misrepresent* the social world. Examples of this view are legion. Raymond Geuss remarks that "agents . . . are deluded about themselves, their position, their society, or their interests" and consequently that "an ideological critique criticizes ideological forms of consciousness."[18] For Allen Wood, ideological beliefs are illusions that "exist . . . because societies and individuals need them." He continues, "People are subject to them because social relations of production require for their survival and smooth functioning that the people that are subject to them be unable to see them for what they are. . . . Oppression is one reason why societies need illusions, because oppression works best when it is hidden—not only from the oppressed but also from the oppressors, who would not be as effective in maintaining the relations from which they benefit if they saw them as oppressive."[19]

In a similar vein, Haslanger writes that ideology perpetuates power and domination "through some form of masking or illusion."[20] And Shelby tells us that ideological beliefs and judgments "misrepresent significant social realities and . . . function, through this distortion, to bring about or perpetuate unjust social relations."[21] Elsewhere he spells out that "in short, ideologies perform their nefarious social operations by way of illusion and misrepresentation. What this means practically is that were the cognitive failings of an ideology to become widely recognized and acknowledged, the relations of domination and exploitation that it serves to reinforce would, other things being equal, become less stable and perhaps even amenable to reform."[22]

In sharp contrast to these views, the teleofunctional theory does not require that ideologies be false. Ideological beliefs can, in principle, accurately portray the social world. What is crucial for their status as ideologies is not their truth value. It is the reasons for their proliferation. To count as ideological, a belief's spread must be explained by its oppressive power, *enough of the time*, rather than its truthfulness. Relatedly, the teleofunctional theory does not require that ideologies conceal their true, oppressive purposes. Ideologies do not wear their oppressive purposes on their sleeve, but this does not mean that they are hidden away. The idea that ideologies must conceal the oppressive agenda of a dominant group is based on a misunderstanding of how ideologies get their functions. The purposes of ideologies are just the effects that accounted for their proliferation. Ideological agendas are neither hidden nor manifest, neither implicit nor explicit, because their oppressive functions are a consequence of their epidemiology rather than the motives of those who embrace them.[23]

The idea that ideologies must be false or misleading is historically tied to an inaccurate interpretation of the notion of false consciousness. The term "false consciousness" is often attributed to Marx. However, its real source is a letter written by Engels to Franz Mehring a decade after Marx's death, in which Engels stated,

> Ideology is a process accomplished by the so-called thinker consciously, indeed, but with a false consciousness. The real driving forces (*Triebkräfte*) impelling him remain unknown to him, otherwise it would not be an ideological process at all. Hence he imagines false or apparent driving forces. . . . . He works with mere thought material which he accepts without examination as the product of thought, he does not investigate further for a more remote process independent of thought; indeed its origin seems obvious to him, because as all action is produced through the medium of thought it also appears to him to be ultimately (*in letzter Instanz*) based upon thought.[24]

"False consciousness" is often interpreted as false beliefs about the social order. But Engels did not claim that ideological beliefs must be false, only that people holding such beliefs misapprehend their real source. They are unaware that ideological beliefs originate in "remote" social forces (false consciousness is actually false *self*-consciousness).[25] Engels's concept of false consciousness is entirely consistent with the teleofunctional approach to ideology. In common with it, Engels did not require these beliefs to be false. He only requires that those who adopt ideologies believe them to be true, and that these beliefs spread because they benefit oppressors.

Ultimate Explanation

Beliefs are psychological states, and the psychological process of belief-acquisition is the medium through which ideologies spread. But this psychological process is not what Engels called their "ultimate" source.

Engels's use of the term "ultimate" dovetails with what biologists call "ultimate explanations."[26] Ultimate explanations of biological traits are historical explanations. They tell us why a trait has proliferated through a population by citing how the trait produced effects that contributed to its own reproduction. In contrast, what biologists call "proximate" explanations address the causes of traits in individual organisms, but not the effects that accounted for their continued reproduction.

Teleofunctional explanations of ideology mirror biologically ultimate explanations, but in the social rather than the biological sphere. What it is that makes a belief an *ideological* belief is not a proximate psychological cause, such as the desire to oppress others, and there is nothing that *psychologically* distinguishes an ideological belief from a nonideological one. What sets ideological beliefs apart from their nonideological counterparts is their social history. It follows that when ideological beliefs succeed in producing oppression, this is not *because* they are ideological, for nonideological beliefs can bring about oppression just as effectively as ideological ones do. It is because of their proximate causal power—their power to influence human behavior.

Systems, Practices, and Social Ecologies

I have been talking about ideologies as systems of belief, but this is a simplified—in fact, an oversimplified—picture. There are several reasons for this. First, individual beliefs or mere aggregates of beliefs are not ideologies. Ideologies are whole systems of belief. They are organized, self-sustaining, cohering networks of belief. Because of this, ideologies often have tremendous inertia. They are able to remain intact over hundreds, or even thousands, of years. Second, systems of belief cannot have oppressive effects all on their own. They produce these effects by being tied to oppressive practices. Describing ideologies as systems of belief is shorthand for a more complex description of a causal nexus. Third, systems of belief can only have oppressive effects in social environments that are hospitable to them—environments to which they are adapted or that actualize their causal powers. Ideologies that give rise to oppressive practices in one social environment may produce quite different effects, or no politically significant effects at all, in a different social environment. Fourth, as social and political circumstances change over time, hibernating ideologies can reawaken. And fifth, political propaganda is often the spark that ignites latent ideologies—but only when other political and economic circumstances are hospitable to their reawakening.

Notions of race, humanity, and subhumanity function as ideological structures. The psychological dynamics of dehumanization—psychological essentialism and hierarchical thinking—need to be understood against the background of the ideological function of dehumanizing tropes, which can only be properly addressed by attending to forms of social organization and historical contingencies that account for them. That is why the study of dehumanization necessarily has one foot in the political-historical-economic sphere and the other in the psychological sphere. The former is its ultimate dimension and the latter its proximate one. A theory of dehumanization that ignores its ideological context is bound to be impoverished. It is like trying to explain the movements of a pair of tennis players without any reference to the trajectory of the ball or the rules of the game. And emphasizing ideology at the expense of dehumanization's psychological dynamics is equally inadequate, because it cannot explain how political forces gain a foothold in human minds, and how they structure human behavior. To theorize dehumanization accurately, we must work at the interface between these two spheres, with an understanding that although we can *conceptually* separate ideology from psychology, they are inextricably entangled in reality.

CHAPTER TEN

Dehumanization as Ideology

In this chapter I will explore the ideological character of dehumanization with the help of a single, extended example—the racialization and dehumanization of European Jews from the late Middle Ages to the present. This sordid history provides an illustration of the growth of an ideology from oppression, through racialization, to dehumanization in response to shifting social and political forces, as well as illustrating the extraordinary inertia of entrenched ideological structures.

There is a massive scholarly literature on the history of European Jewry. It is complex, full of regional variation, and often subject to conflicting interpretations. Here I address only certain episodes of that history to illustrate the theory of ideology that I set out in Chapter 9. In particular, I will use the episodes to illustrate the relationship between racialization and dehumanization; how, once established, ideologies persist; how they adapt to shifting social ecologies; and how shifts in the social and political environment can ignite latent dehumanizing beliefs, granting them new life and catastrophic power.

Teaching Contempt

The teaching of contempt for Jews goes back to some of the earliest Christian writings, such as the Gospel of John.[1] The Gospel includes an account of Jesus ranting to Jews who refuse to recognize him as the messiah. He says, "You are from your father the devil, and you choose to do your father's desires. He was a murderer from the beginning and does not stand in the truth, because there is no truth in him. When he lies, he speaks according to his own nature, for he is a liar and the father of lies."[2] The reference to Satan is no pale metaphor. He was a terrifyingly real entity in the minds of Christians—the concrete personification of all malevolence, deception, and depravity—and this Christian text purporting to be the words of the Son of God charged that the Jewish people, being Satan's progeny, inherited these vile traits from their father. As literary scholar Moshe Lazar comments, this portrait of the Jews set the stage for much of the horror that was to follow. "Branded the son of the Devil, the latter being the most absolute incarnation of Evil and destined to become the most dreaded monstrous creature, the Jew was thus cast in a mythical image from which all the other negative attributes were to be genealogically derived: liar, deceiver, agent of corruption and debauchery, treacherous, poisoner and killer, horned beast, etc. Any new verbal or visual characterization of the Devil in the following centuries is then automatically applied to the Jews."[3]

Early derogatory characterizations of Jews may have been driven by Christians' desire to differentiate themselves from the parent religion. But as Christianity swelled in power, numbers, and influence, Christian propaganda became more intense and violent. As early as the fourth century, when Christianity became the state religion of the Roman Empire, Saint John Chrysostom, the "golden mouthed" bishop of Constantinople, wrote in an eerie anticipation of Nazi rhetoric that "although such beasts [untamed calves] are unfit for work, they are fit for killing. And this is what happened to the Jews; while they were making themselves unfit for work, they grew fit for slaughter."[4]

Augustine of Hippo, who was the most influential Christian philosopher of late antiquity, promoted the anti-Jewish stereotypes of his predecessors and fatefully added a new one. He identified Judas, the betrayer of Christ, with the Jewish people as a whole. This image of the venal, selfish, disloyal Jew who sacrificed the savior in exchange for thirty pieces of silver was to haunt the gentile imagination for many centuries to come. However, Augustine also urged that Jews should be permitted to practice their religion and not be persecuted for it.[5] This was not because of moral rectitude or compassion for the Jewish people, or because he was committed to an ethic of tolerance. It was because the Jews' continued existence would be useful grist for the Christian propaganda mill, and would help for converting pagans. Judaism was, in Augustine's estimation, a living fossil—an anachronistic testimony to the religion from which Christianity sprang and which Christianity was destined to replace. And the oppression and degradation of the Jewish people would serve as a warning to those who might be tempted to turn their backs on the Christ.[6]

Augustine's ambivalent doctrine that the Jews should be allowed to exist, but in a condition of wretchedness and subjugation, was immensely influential. It set the stage for the anti-Semitic ideology of the later Middle Ages. It was echoed in the words of Peter the Venerable, abbot of Cluny, more than half a millennium later. "God does not wish them to be entirely killed and altogether wiped out," he wrote, "but to be preserved for greater torment and reproach . . . in a life worse than death."[7] By the time Peter wrote these words, the fragile balance between religiously motivated hatred and bare toleration was beginning to tip precariously toward atrocity.

The Turning Point

Despite the toxic religious rhetoric and occasional acts of violence, relations between Jews and Christians remained relatively stable and peaceful for centuries. The figure of the evil Jew was a theological conceit that had relatively little impact on the everyday lives of Jews and Christians.[8] However, by the late eleventh century shifting social and political circumstances weaponized the image of the Jew in Christian society, with catastrophic results. In 1095 Pope Urban II called for a crusade to wrest the Holy Land from the Saracens. Urban's call was a bid for Catholic supremacy, both within a Europe that was riven by contending political factions, and in the further reaches of the Byzantine and Muslim East. The text of Urban's speech has not survived, but we have several later accounts of it, one of which was written twenty-five years later by a man named Robert the Monk, who may have been present at the event. As Robert presented it, Urban's speech is a piece of propaganda, packed with graphic detail that would have done Dr. Goebbels proud. According to Robert, it was a call to arms against "an accursed race, a race utterly alienated from God."

> They destroy the altars, after having defiled them with their uncleanness. They circumcise the Christians, and the blood of the circumcision they either spread upon the altars or pour into the vases of the baptismal font. When they wish to torture people by a base death, they perforate their navels, and dragging forth the extremity of the intestines, bind it to a stake; then with flogging they lead the victim around until the viscera having gushed forth the victim falls prostrate upon the ground. Others they bind to a post and pierce with arrows. Others they compel to extend their necks and then, attacking them with naked swords, attempt to cut through the neck with a single blow. What shall I say of the abominable rape of the women? To speak of it is worse than to be silent.[9]

Urban's call to arms was catastrophic for Jewish communities that lay in the crusaders' path. Three kinds of crusaders marched East. One was an organized army of nobles—a formidable fighting force that eventually conquered Jerusalem. Another was a ragtag army under the leadership of a charismatic itinerant preacher named Peter the Hermit. And a third consisted of radicalized bands of northern Europeans. It was the third group that rampaged through the thriving Jewish communities of the Rhineland. Assisted by gentile townspeople, Christian militias massacred the residents of these communities or forced them to choose between conversion or death. As many as one-third of the Jewish inhabitants of the region—perhaps as many as ten thousand souls—perished. Many were killed by the crusaders. Others preferred to take their own lives, and the lives of their family members, rather than be forced to betray their faith or be murdered by the Christian mob.[10] The Jewish prayer "Av Harachamim" ("Merciful Father"), which was composed in the aftermath of this medieval holocaust to commemorate those who lost their lives, is recited in synagogues to this day.

Why did this happen? The call for Christians to wage war against the Saracen infidel suggested that this war should also be waged against the enemies of God in their midst. Some of the images in Urban's speech—references to an accursed, unclean race; to circumcision; bloodletting; and the defilement of Christian holy places—either were then or would soon become features of Christian representation of the vile, demonic Jew. There was also another important factor that contributed to the mass murder of Jews during the First Crusade. It had to do with the emergence of a novel political and legal status for Jews that had been taking shape in the medieval world. Jews were defined as the *servi* ("slaves" or "servants") of the monarch—they were explicitly described as the ruler's *property*. As Holy Roman Emperor Louis IV of Bavaria proclaimed, "You, the Jews, your bodies—as well as your property—belong to us and to the empire, and we can do to you, treat you, and handle you the way we want and consider proper."[11] Jews were granted special protections in virtue of this status, because killing or harming Jews was damaging or destroying royal property. But it also reduced them to the status of chattel. Historian David Nirenberg explains,

The special relationship between Jews and rulers proved to be tremendously useful to European monarchs and magnates trying to establish and expand their power. . . . The most notorious way in which control of the Jews served to extend sovereign power was through money lending. Any number of European princes channeled Jewish economic activity toward lending at interest to Christians, so that they could then expropriate a considerable share of the proceeds from the Jews. . . . At a time when the power of princes was sharply constrained by custom and competing jurisdictions, exactions on interest collected by Jews from Christians gave lords new access to the wealth of their Christian subjects.[12]

Poised precariously between exploitation by the rulers and resentment by the ruled, this situation was a perfect storm for the racialization of Jews and the proliferation of anti-Semitic ideology. As race scholar Geraldine Heng describes,

Jews constituted targets with the ability to draw the resentment of virtually all groups in society needing financing of any kind: peasants and townsfolk, knights of the shire, monastic houses, and great magnates. Systematic dependence on Jews at every level of . . . society, in tandem with the distinctiveness of Jews as a minority population, bred fertile ground for generating racialized modes of group redress against Jews. Redress took a variety of forms. Popular correctives included periodic slaughter in organized or spontaneous mob attacks. State engineered correctives included sweeping anti-Jewish legislation. . . . The economic superiority of Jews, as successful bankers and agents of capital, jostled uneasily against their subordinate status as social and ideological subjects. . . . But when economic rationality collides with ideological constrictions that define the minority population managing capital as inferior, morally suspect, and theologically condemned, identification with capital renders the association with wealth, under such circumstances, monstrous and troubling.[13]

During the eleventh century, a changing social and political ecology caused the centuries-old anti-Jewish ideology to turn lethal. And as the next two centuries rolled on, there was much worse to come. During the twelfth and thirteenth centuries, European Jews were systematically oppressed to an unprecedented degree. No longer merely the inferiors of Christians, they were quasi-slaves of the ruling elites. State-sponsored networks of systematic oppression, implemented by discriminatory laws, came into being. Heng explains,

> Monitored by the state through an array of administrative apparatuses, and ruled upon by statutes, ordinances, and decrees, they were required to document their economic activity at special registries that tracked Jewish assets across a network of cities. No business could be lawfully transacted except at these registries, which came to determine where Jews could live and practice a livelihood. Jews needed official permission and licenses to establish or to change residence. . . . Subjected to a range of fiscal extortions and special, extraordinary taxations (tallages) which milked them to the edge of penury, Jews were barred from marriage with Christians, from holding public office, from eating with Christians or lingering in Christian homes, or even from praying too loudly in synagogues. They were required to wear large, identifying badges on their outer garments, and denied the freedom of walking publicly on city streets during Holy Week and of emigration, as a community, without permission.[14]

Racialization

In my view, it was at this point that European Jews began to be racialized. But it is worth mentioning that others disagree. For example, Hannah Arendt, drawing on the work of Jacob Katz, remarked in *The Origins of Totalitarianism* that it was only after the fifteenth century that "Jews, without any outside interference, began to think 'that the difference between Jewry and the nations was fundamentally not one of creed and faith, but one of inner nature' and that the ancient dichotomy between Jews and Gentiles was 'more likely to be racial in origin than a matter of doctrinal dissension.' This shift in evaluating the alien character of the Jewish people, which became common among non-Jews only much later in the Age of Enlightenment, is clearly the condition *sine qua non* for the birth of antisemitism."[15]

Another commonly held view is that the concept of race originated in Spain during the fifteenth century, because it was there and then that Jews who had converted to Christianity were deemed to possess "impure" blood. Proponents of this thesis readily admit that Jews were oppressed prior to this cultural-historical moment, but they hold that earlier forms of oppression had a purely religious basis ("anti-Judaism") rather than a truly racial one ("anti-Semitism").[16]

I do not think that the distinction between religious and racial Jewishness is as clear-cut many scholars assume.[17] It is based on a sharp distinction between culture and biology that was probably foreign to the medieval mind. And it is also predicated on a very limited notion of how the concept of race works. According to the account of race that I have presented earlier in this book, people are racialized when they are thought to possess an innate causal essence—one that renders them morally inferior, that is automatically passed down from parents to their offspring. Twelfth- or thirteenth-century German Christians certainly thought of Jews as fitting this description. And as early as the twelfth century, we find references in Jewish writings to the effect that Jews are biologically distinct from gentiles.[18]

Those who argue that race began in fifteenth-century Spain typically stress that the element of blood is crucial for racialization. I explained in Chapter 3 that folk biological theories often locate people's racial essence in their blood. But this is not a *necessary* component of the concept of race. To properly assess the significance of blood in folk metaphysical theories of race, it is necessary to turn to the difference between a causal role and its realizer. Causal roles are job descriptions. They are characterizations of what a thing is supposed to do. Going back to the example of the agitator of a washing machine that I discussed in Chapter 9, the causal role of the agitator is to churn laundry through the water in the tub. The realizer of a causal role is the kind of thing that performs the role. In this case, it is the post-like structure in the center of the tub of top-loading washing machines. Philosophers say that causal roles are *multiply realizable*. That means that in principle and often in practice *many* different things can realize a given causal role. To illustrate, before the invention of electrically powered washing machine, clothes were churned around in a tub by people using a muscle-powered paddle. At that time, wooden paddles realized the agitator role.

Washing machines are material artifacts, but the role / realizer distinction also applies to theories. Consider again Gregor Mendel's account of heredity discussed in Chapter 3. Mendel inferred that there are physical hereditary "factors" that are passed on from parents to offspring in accord with three laws that he described. This is a causal role description. Mendel did not know what it was that realized this role—what physical objects did the job. True, he used the term "factors," but this was merely a placeholder for the unknown. This blank spot only began to be filled decades later with the discovery of chromosomes. Folk theories also often rely on the role / realizer binary. According to the folk theory of race that I articulate in this book, there is something—a racial essence—that accounts for race and that is transmitted from parents to offspring. This describes a causal role. Often it is blood that is imagined to realize that causal role (or, in more fine-grained versions, something carried in the blood). That is why Douglas Medin and Andrew Ortony, the psychologists who coined the term "psychological essentialism" (see Chapter 4) call the notion of essence a "placeholder" concept—one that specifies a causal role without necessarily any definite commitment to what it is that occupies that role.[19] It might be blood that occupies the role, or it might be something else (historically, maternal milk or semen have sometimes played that role[20]), or it might be entirely unspecified. So, the fact that thirteenth-century European Christians didn't identify Jewishness with a blood-borne essence shouldn't be taken to imply that they didn't racialize Jews.

Finally, there is the objection that Jews were not racialized during the High Middle Ages because race is a strictly biological concept and therefore a full-blown conception of race could only come into being after biological science emerged in the eighteenth and nineteenth centuries. Even though the idea of race may have had precursors in earlier centuries, it only reached maturity with the development of scientific racism.

I agree with those who say that the concept of race is essentially biological, but I reject their conclusion that the concept of race depends on *scientific* biology. Not all biological concepts are scientific biological concepts. Folk biology is biology too. Broadly speaking, biological theories are theories purporting to explain similarities among and differences between organisms—including human organisms. Historically, such theories have very often relied on notions of sharply bounded natural kinds demarcated by hidden essences, and involve notions of development and intergenerational transmission. The idea of purity of blood was certainly a biological conception in this sense, even though it was far removed from biological science. Likewise, the medieval theory of spontaneous generation—the notion that living organisms can emerge directly from nonliving matter—was a biological theory, and the theological doctrine of traducianism—the belief that children inherit their souls from their parents—was a prescientific biological theory. Geraldine Heng argues that the concept of race was born in the European Middle Ages, when Jews were first demarcated as essentially other. She argues that the racialization of Jews even then had irreducibly biological components. "Jews," she writes, "were systematically defined and set apart via biomarkers such as the possession of horns, a male menstrual flux or the generationally inherited New Testament curse of visceral-hemorrhoidal bleeding, an identifying stink (the infamous *fetor judaicus*), [and] facial and somatic phenotypes."[21]

Another, more serious objection to the claim that Jews were racialized during the Middle Ages concerns the idea that race is a permanent condition. As I illustrated in Chapter 5, the idea that one cannot change one's race is central to the logic of racial ascription. However, in seeming contradiction to this, converting Jews to Christianity was an important part of the Christian project from the early period onward. The fact that conversion was conceivable, and medieval Jews were sometimes presented with the choice between conversion or death, seems to suggest that Christians did not think of Jews as a race distinct from themselves. I believe that this contradiction is more apparent than real. Strange as it may sound to the twenty-first-century ear, it was possible for the medieval mind to racialize Jews while at the same time holding that Jews can be transformed into Christians. It is possible to accept that a person *cannot* change their race—or even more broadly, that a person's race cannot be changed by any natural means—while also accepting that a person's race *can* be changed. To see this, it is crucial to leave a scientific worldview behind and exchange it for the medieval metaphysical paradigm. Medieval Christians lived in a world in which transubstantiation was taken for granted as a real phenomenon, but was not a natural phenomenon that could be accomplished by merely human agency. The transformation of the wafer and wine into the body and blood of Christ was a miraculous act, performed by God through priestly mediation. And just as God is capable of transmuting the sacramental host, he was also capable of transubstantiating Jews into Christians. As Moshe Lazar puts it, conversion was seen as "the miraculous cure which metamorphoses wolves into sheep, demonized Jews into baptized human creatures."[22] Steven Kruger notes that the miraculous transformative power of conversion could even transform racialized bodies:

> Depictions of "Saracens" as "dogs," or the distant "monstrous races" as only partly human, or Jews as having tails and horns, present ontological distinctions that would seem difficult to overcome through a process of conversion. Still, there are accounts that depict even such biological differences as disappearing with moral change. In the king of Tars romances, when a Saracen sultan who has married a Christian princess converts and is baptized, "he changes color from black to white." And in some Eastern versions of the Saint Christopher story, in which Christopher is depicted as originally from a "dogheaded" race, his conversion to Christianity also effects a transformation of physical form.[23]

That this was possible did not entail that it was always actual. Jews might merely appear to open their hearts to the grace of God, deceiving the Christians around them and stubbornly protecting their Jewish essence. In fifteenth-century Spain, the so-called new Christians were accused of retaining their Jewishness. This deception is pithily expressed in a fifteenth-century inscription at the cathedral at Freising, Bavaria: "As much as the mouse does not eat the cat, the Jew won't become a true Christian."[24] As Kruger goes on to confirm, "Such examples of striking racial conversion, however, are relatively rare, and Jews and Saracens, thought of as both religiously and racially different and as possessing bodies somehow essentially other than Christian bodies, are often depicted as strongly resistant to conversion, with Jewish 'stubbornness' becoming a platitude in medieval Christian depictions of Jews."[25]

Likewise, art historian Sara Lipton notes that it was not until the mid-thirteenth century that Christian art portrayed Jews as having a distinctive, stereotyped physical appearance, and wonders, without reaching a definite conclusion, "Does the development of the Jewish caricature reveal new thinking about Jewish bodies? Is the naturalistic 'Jew's face' in effect an assertion that substantial Jewish-Christian physical differences did exist, that Jewishness was indelibly rooted in the flesh, its traces visible in many if not all members of the tribe . . . and so not fully eradicable even with the cleansing waters of baptism?"[26]

The racialization of Jews is clearly evident in the anti-Jewish legislation of the Fourth Lateran Council held in 1215, which introduced a series of Jim Crow-like restrictions on Jewish and Muslim life. These included requiring Jews to wear distinctive clothing to make them easily identifiable, forbidding them to leave their homes during the three days before Easter, forbidding them to hold any position of authority over Christians, and urging secular authorities to punish Jews for disrespecting Christ. This hardening ecclesiastical attitude was amplified in the popular consciousness, as is evidenced by the massacres of European Jews in the late thirteenth and early fourteenth centuries. The Rintfleisch massacres of 1298 took the lives of a large proportion of an already small minority. The murderous mobs that fell upon Jewish communities were referred to as *Judenschächter* ("Jew butchers"). Thousands died. And the in Armleder massacres a few decades later, a peasant militia pledged to exterminate the Jews of Alsace. They marched from town to town, murdering over a thousand people.[27]

Then, starting in 1347, the bubonic plague raged across Europe. Its effects were catastrophic. Europe was decimated, losing up to half its population over the course of just a few years. Massive mortality led to critical labor shortages, which upset the traditional, hierarchical structure of medieval society in which Jews already occupied a precarious position. Grassroots anti-Semitic violence became much more virulent and intense in the pandemic's wake. Jews had long been associated with plague, but this became cemented into anti-Semitic ideology during the fourteenth century, when they were accused of deliberate spreading the Black Death to destroy Christendom.[28] It was rumored that they were in league with mythical "Red Jews"—an exceptionally vile, sinful, and warlike Jewish nation living beyond the Caucasus mountains who were thought to be allied with the Antichrist or Muslims in Spain—who gave them poison to contaminate Christian water supplies.[29] These accusations prompted violent persecutions, especially in Germany, where thousands were burned to death. Here is how historian Samuel Cohn describes the horror of this fourteenth-century holocaust:

> Most repeated the charges of Jews poisoning rivers and wells, noting them down as cold facts without casting any doubts on their veracity and without any outcry against the mass executions of men, women and children that ensued. . . . Still other chroniclers were more vehement in their condemnations of the Jews as plague spreaders. While they dispassionately tallied the numbers of Jews exterminated in one city after another, they reported the rumours and justified them as historical facts. Instead of recording the cries of women and children as they were thrown into the fires, chroniclers such as the "World Chronicler" of the monastery of Albert in Cologne stressed the "horrible means by which the Jews wished to extinguish all of Christendom, through their poisons of frogs and spiders mixed into oil and cheese." In two poems, Michael de Leone, a contemporary chronicler of Wurzburg and the protonotary of

the region's bishop, agreed with the accusations that the Jews had poisoned streams, and thus "the Jews deserved to be swallowed up in the flames."[30]

Some chose to kill their families and themselves. They shut themselves inside their homes and set them ablaze. Others, who were expelled rather than killed, or who were fortunate enough to escape, fled eastward into what is now Poland and the surrounding regions. But more than 70 percent of Jewish communities suffered mass executions, often by burning, and some were completely obliterated.[31] Much of Germany became what the Nazis would, seven hundred years later, called *Judenrein*—cleansed of Jews.

From Race to Subhumanity

"The most vivid impression to be gained from medieval allusions to the Jew," wrote Joshua Trachtenberg in *The Devil and the Jews,* "is of a hatred so vast and abysmal, so intense, that it leaves one gasping for comprehension."[32] From roughly the thirteenth century, the position of Jews worsened. They were increasingly seen as demonic predators—as cannibals, vampires, and child-murderers. The idea of an international Jewish conspiracy that had been set in motion at the time of the First Crusade emerged again in the fourteenth-century well-poisoning charge, as ever more grotesque and sinister elements were added to the picture. One was the belief that Jews ritually sacrificed, tortured, and cannibalized Christian children, a bizarre fantasy that morphed into the cannibalistic "blood libel"—the idea that Jews kidnapped Christian children and drained them of their blood, which they mixed with matzoh dough for the annual Passover meal. The ritual murder charge was a new edition of the ancient portrayal of Jews as the murderers of Christ. The murdered Christian boy in the blood-libel stories was a proxy

for the murdered savior (in fact, in some versions, the child is cru-
cified).[33] And in another variation of the same theme, Jews were accused of torturing or desecrating the sacramental host, often by
stabbing or boiling it.

The extreme gravity of this charge must be understood in the
context of late medieval beliefs about the eucharist. The Fourth
Lateran Council had written into canon law that the body and blood
of Jesus Christ "are truly contained in the sacrament of the altar
under the forms of bread and wine; the bread being changed by divine power into the body, and the wine into the blood." These sacred substances were to be protected from abuse by Jews by being
"kept in properly protected places provided with locks and keys, that
they may not be reached by rash and indiscreet persons and used
for impious and blasphemous purposes."[34] Because every crumb of
every wafer was said to contain the entire body of Christ, wafers
became objects of religious adoration. So, when Christians accused
Jews of harming this sacred object, they were accusing them of performing acts of physical violence against Christ himself.

Once racialized, Jews became dehumanized as subhuman beasts
and as diabolical monsters. We hear this in the words of Peter the
Venerable, who argued that the Jews' refusal to adopt the Christian religion shows that they are irrational, subhuman animals, and
we see it in the demonic representations of Jews in religious art.[35]
Lazar describes the fatal transition from the image of Jews as morally inferior human beings to subhuman animals as follows: "As
traitors and murderers, as money-changers and thieves, the Jews
still retained some semblance of human physionomy [sic]. . . . But
once identified with the Devil, the Jews not only enter the imaginary domain of the mythical monstrous races but become mythical beings themselves. The mythicization and diabolization of the
Jews led consequently to their dehumanization. They became now

serpents, vipers, aspics, basiliscs, goats, pigs, ravens, vultures, bats, scorpions, dogs, cormorants, hyaenas, jackals, vermine, to name only a few among the most frequent zoological qualifiers."

But representing Jews as animal-like beings was only a prelude to conceiving of them as monstrous predators. Lazar continues, "In the next phase. . . . the range of lexical dehumanization is further extended. Among the numerous mytho-zoological beasts, the *manticore* is described as a "beast born in the Indies. It has a three-fold row of teeth meeting alternately, the face of a man with gleaming, blood-red eyes, a lion's body, a tail like the sting of a scorpion, and a shrill voice. . . . It hankers after human flesh most ravenously.'"[36] Medieval Christians did not think that Jews really were manticores, but the representation of Jews as manticores was not just a metaphor for Jewish sinfulness. It was intended to convey a message about the moral and metaphysical standing of Jews, by expressing the idea that Jews are *something like* manticores—not quite human, but not quite subhuman either. They are monstrous fusions of humanity and subhumanity: wanton, degenerate, and terrifying.[37]

Apparatuses of Reproduction

The process that shapes and constitutes ideologies is similar to the process of natural selection. Ideologies are systems of belief that proliferate through a population because they promote the interests of one group at the expense of the interests of others. And just like the genes and phenotypic traits that proliferate and become established through natural selection, ideological beliefs become entrenched and are often highly resistant to change. The tendency of phenotypes to persist in a biological lineage, even when they no longer serve a function, is known as *phylogenetic inertia.* I refer to their social counterpart—the tendency of ideological beliefs to persist over long stretches of time—as *ideological inertia.*

In order for ideologies become entrenched, they must first become established. As I pointed out in Chapter 9, beliefs become ideologies only if they are reproduced (reproduced "enough of the time," as Millikan puts it).[38] And for this to happen, there must be some means by which they are produced, copied, distributed, consumed. This requires socially imbedded apparatuses of replication. The speed with which these representations spread, and the thoroughness with which they penetrate a society, depends in part on the means of replication that are available for their proliferation.

The history of the circulation of anti-Semitic ideology from the thirteenth century to the present provides insights into the relationship between ideology and the means of its reproduction. Illiteracy was widespread during the Middle Ages, and the availability of written materials was very limited even for those who could read. Johannes Gutenberg had not yet ushered in the era of mass communication with the invention of movable type printing, and books were expensive, scarce, mostly written in scholarly Latin rather than in the vernacular, and were accessible only to elites. Because of this, dehumanizing representations of Jews circulated only very slowly and inefficiently. One way that they spread was from mouth to ear, by ordinary speech or by religious instruction. Another was through dramatic performances such as the Passion Plays that depicted the agony and execution of Christ at the hands of a malevolent Jewish mob. A third, very potent way circulating anti-Semitic propaganda was through publicly accessible visual representations. With regard to the latter, historian Birgit Weidl notes, "The general importance of images for the inhabitants of medieval Europe cannot be underestimated: Bernhard Blumenkranz called the walls of medieval churches 'huge picture books,' while other scholars have pointed out the impact sermons had on the illiterate masses, which taught them how to read the paintings and sculptures they came across in and outside the church: 'a picture,' as (allegedly) Pope Gregory the Great put it in a letter, 'is like a lesson for the people.'"[39]

One such lesson for the people was the ubiquitous image of the *Judensau* ("Jew pig"), which adorned churches, public buildings, and even private homes.[40] These were carvings that depicted Jews gorging on milk that they are sucking from the teats of a sow. On some, there was also the image of a Jew copulating with the pig, eating its feces, drinking its urine, or gazing into or caressing its rectum. Sometimes, Satan is also in attendance. And occasionally the sow is a chimera having a pig's body and a Jew's head. The *Judensau* emerged during the thirteenth century and became a popular anti-Semitic meme. By the seventeenth century, it had become a popular topic in broadsheets and pamphlets, often accompanied by the caption "*sauff du die milch friß du den dreck, das ist doch euer bestes geschleck*" ("You guzzle down the milk and you devour the filth, this is after all your favorite dish").[41] These images were more than visual equivalents of verbal slurs. They were meant to conjure the familiar idea that Jews are not real human beings. Wiedl, a scholar who has studied the *Judensau* image extensively, sums up, "Jews are marked as belonging to the sow, as a different, and lesser form of being, as offspring of a beast. . . . Thus, the *Judensau* stresses the 'alien quality' of the Jews. . . . firmly establishing the distinct notion that Jews simply were 'another category of beings', a nonhuman life form."[42] Likewise, Claudine Fabre-Vassas, an expert on medieval porcine iconography, tells us that Jew-pig images were not just allegories. Their purpose was to point to the subhumanity of Jews: "The category of 'satirical allegory' under which these figurations are classified seems insufficient to account for their content: Jews and pigs placed together illustrate far more than a metaphor. . . . [The] metamorphoses of Jews reveal their 'true nature.' For the analogy does not stop at appearances. . . . This morphology reveals a hidden identity."[43]

The *Judensau* was still going strong eight centuries after it began, as Weidl describes:

Around 1900, the visitors of a fair in Saxony might have come across a traveling theater that was performing there, and if they stayed for the afterpiece, they might have been entertained with a puppet that is now kept at the Municipal Museum in Munich: a pig that, whenever the strings are pulled, is turned into a *Schacherjude*, the "classical" figure of a bearded Jew, bearing all the stereotyped facial features and extending a hand in a gesture that should evoke the idea of haggling, of reaching out for money. The swift transformations from sow to Jew to sow, enabled by a tilting mechanism, must have left a deep impression on the spectators who saw the two images blurring into one right in front of their eyes. . . . The Jew *per se* is equal to a sow, and therefore barely, if at all, human.[44]

Decades later, in the period following World War I, right-wing gangs marched through German streets protesting the fact that Foreign Minister Walther Rathenau was Jewish, chanting "Knallt ab de Walter Rathenau, die gottverdammte Judensau" ("Mow down Walter Rathenau, that God-damned Jew pig"). These were not empty words. In the summer of 1922 a terrorist unit ambushed Rathenau on a country road, and riddled him with bullets.

The *Judensau* lived on during the Third Reich, and was often featured in Nazi propaganda. In one cartoon published in the gutter-press Nazi newspaper *Der Stürmer* in 1934, prominent Jewish intellectuals Albert Einstein, Magnus Hirschfeld, Alfred Kerr, Thomas Mann, and Erich Maria Remarque are portrayed sucking milk from a sow, with the caption "Although the pig is dead, its piglets are yet to be eliminated."[45] And as Nazi terror increased, the word *Judensau* was scrawled on the windows of Jewish businesses. And the *Judensau* continues on in the neo-Nazi movements of today. In 2018, during a week of far-right demonstrations in the German town of Chemnitz, a gang of neo-Nazis smashed the front of a kosher restaurant, yelling at the Jewish proprietor "Get out of Germany, you *Judensau!*"[46]

The longevity of the *Judensau* illustrates the extraordinary staying power of ideological tropes. But the *Judensau* is not unique in this respect; many medieval anti-Semitic tropes persisted into the twentieth century and beyond.

Nazi racial ideology breathed new life into medieval representations of the Jew. The ground was already well prepared by an upsurge of German ethnonationalism in late nineteenth century. This strain of political anti-Semitism that took shape at that time included a secularized version of the image of the demonic Jew. Whereas in the Middle Ages Jews were regarded as opponents of Christianity, in the nineteenth-century iteration they were refigured as enemies of the German race. However, it was only after World War I that this brand of antisemitism got real political traction. "The main difference between the political anti-Semitism of the post- and pre-war periods lies not in its content," writes historian Peter Pulzer, "but in its success." Pulzer continues, "There were some changes in emphasis, a general increase of tone and unscrupulousness, and a growing acceptance of physical violence; but one would have to go a very long way through the anti-Semitic literature of the 1920's or 1930's to discover a point of argument which had not already been used before 1914. . . . What we need to know, therefore, is what changed in the political and social environment that turned the ravings of obscure sects into major prophecies."[47]

The resurgence and weaponization of age-old racist and dehumanizing tropes was fueled by a sequence of catastrophes—defeat in World War I and the humiliation of the Treaty of Versailles, the 1918 flu pandemic, and the political precarity of the Weimar era. These were coupled with anxiety caused by escalating liberalism and secularization. The postwar period brought "an increase in urban preponderance in politics, of the *avant-garde* in the arts, of mobility in the social structure . . . and, like any other emanation of modernity, they were anathema to the Right." These circumstances contributed to the radicalization of many on the right who had lost faith in conservatism's ability to stem encroachments on traditional German values and who resented the demise of the old social order. These "Right Radicals" were for the most part "recruited from persons whose social and economic position was either ruined or threatened with ruin . . . 'wanderers in the void.'"[48] What became the National Socialist Party began as one among many of these small extremist groups, and in the volatile social ecology of Weimar Germany, their propaganda ignited age-old anti-Semitic beliefs like a match to dry kindling.

Thematic Persistence

The electoral triumph of the National Socialists in 1930 and Hitler's subsequent rise to power ushered in a new era of dehumanization for the Jews. The medieval demon, the murderer of Christ, was reborn as the *Untermensch*—the subhuman adversary of German civilization. Although no longer described in religious or supernatural terms, the fourteenth-century conception of the Jew remained essentially unchanged in Nazi ideology: the legendary Red Jews were reincarnated as Communists, and Christian eschatology was replaced by a secular vision of an apocalyptic war between the races. Perhaps the most central of these themes was the idea of an international Jewish conspiracy. The historian Norman Cohn writes of twelfth-century Europe that "however helpless individual Jews might seem, Jewry possessed limitless powers for evil. And already then, there was talk of a secret Jewish government—a council of rabbis located in Moslem Spain, which was supposed to be directing an underground war against Christendom."[49] This conspiratorial fantasy reappeared at the dawn of the twentieth century in the notorious *Protocols of the Elders of Zion*, which found a home in the National Socialist canon. "The Jewish world-conspiracy," writes Cohn, "was seen as the product of an ineradicable destructiveness, a will to evil that was believed to be inborn in every Jew. A peculiar breed of sub-human beings, dark, earthbound, was working conspiratorially to destroy those sons of light, the 'Aryan' or German 'race'."[50]

The influential Nazi theorist Alfred Rosenberg warned that Jews posed an existential threat to the German *Volk*. His writings were peppered with demonological imagery, references to an apocalyptic battle between the forces of darkness and light, Jewish materialism versus German spirituality, and Jewish pollution versus Aryan purity.[51] Goebbels combined the themes of Jews as demonic and as enemies of the German people in a terrifying rhetorical cocktail at the 1937 Nuremburg rally. "Europe must see and recognize the danger. . . . We shall point fearlessly to the Jew as the inspirer and originator, the one who profits from these deadly catastrophes. . . . Look, there is the world's enemy, the destroyer of civilizations, the parasite among the peoples, the son of Chaos, the incarnation of evil, the ferment of decomposition, the demon who brings about the degeneration of mankind."[52]

Randall Bytwerk describes how the demonic character of Jews was portrayed in *Der Stürmer*, noting that its editor, Julius Streicher, "presented them as such evil creatures that it was difficult to allow them a place in the natural creation." Bytwerk continues,

> Just as God battled Satan in the heavenly realms, so on earth their respective allies joined battle. . . . To be the eternal enemy meant that Jews needed outside help, and that help had to be satanic. The precise nature of the relationship between the Devil and the Jews was not entirely clear. A 1935 article signed by Streicher was entitled "The Devil." It argued that the battle against the Jews had to be continued, since the Nazi takeover

had hurt but not destroyed the Jewish cause. The same year Ernst Heimer wrote "The Jew has the Devil in his blood."[53]

It is important to understand that references to the satanic nature of Jews were not exclusively meant as figures of speech, as Bytwerk goes on to point out: "The airship *Hindenberg* exploded in New Jersey in 1937. In the classic photograph of the disaster a *Stürmer* reader thought he saw the outline of a Jewish face in the smoke, and the *Stürmer* agreed: 'Nature has here shown clearly and with absolute correctness the Devil in human form.' Another lead article was headlined 'Light Against Darkness: The German Struggle for Freedom Against the World Devil.' The world Devil was of course the Jew."[54]

The Nazi appropriation of medieval beliefs also included the charge of ritual murder. This was not a novelty. The blood libel was very much alive during the late nineteenth and early twentieth centuries (there were more than one hundred such accusations in Central and Eastern Europe between 1880 and World War I—far more than between the twelfth and eighteenth centuries—some of which were taken to trial).[55] Streicher promoted the fantasy, from the 1920s onward, that Jews ritually murdered Christians. In 1934 he published a special issue of *Der Stürmer* devoted to it. One article from the special issue, after describing Jews as "criminals, murderers, and devils in human form," goes on to say that "they are charged with enticing Gentile children and Gentile adults, butchering them and draining their blood . . . and using it to practice superstitious magic. They are charged with torturing their victims, especially the children; and during the torture . . . they cast spells against the Gentiles."[56] Hitler suppressed the ritual murder issue of *Der Stürmer* after an international outcry. But this, too, was grist for the ideological mill. Streicher proclaimed that the international condemnation was proof that the sinister influence of international

Jewry was everywhere, and that the Jews would stop at nothing to keep the world from knowing the truth about their horrific blood practices—a truth that *Der Stürmer* was fearlessly determined to reveal.[57]

The vampiristic element of ritual murder also played an important metaphorical role in Nazi rhetoric. Hitler repeatedly describes Jews as blood-sucking creatures in *Mein Kampf* and often references Jews draining blood from the German people. Other Nazi writers followed suit. For example, a 1941 directive from the Office of Anti-Semitic Action of the Propaganda Ministry in Berlin stated, "The Jews in the USA hold power with the help of the Jewish government, *bleed the people white*, and oppress them. . . . The non-Jewish residents of the USA face extermination by the Jews" (emphasis added).[58] And it was linked to the claim that was promoted by some Nazi academics (for example, the historian Johann von Leers) that Jews conceive of gentiles as subhuman animals and therefore feel free to use them in rituals that call for the killing of animals. Political theorist Carl Schmitt drew on images of ritual murder and cannibalism when he wrote in a 1938 essay discussing Thomas Hobbes's *Leviathan*, "The Jews stand by and watch how the people of the world kill one another. This mutual 'ritual slaughter and massacre' is for them lawful and 'kosher,' and they therefore eat the flesh of the slaughtered peoples and are sustained by it."[59]

The thirteenth-century claim that Jews are the source of pestilence also occupied a prominent place in Nazi rhetoric. Goebbels's reference in the 1937 speech from which I have already quoted was just one of many descriptions of Jews as poisoners. These evoke the medieval belief that Jews spread the bubonic plague by poisoning water supplies. The closely related image of the Jew as the source of deadly infection was a major component of Nazi propaganda. As Felicity Rash observes in a study of the rhetorical architecture of *Mein Kampf*, "Jews, and to a lesser extent Marxists and other groups despised by Hitler, are portrayed as plague-like sicknesses (*Pest, Pestilenz, Verpestung, Seuche*) which might infect the German state and its people. Hitler was obsessed with the fear that the German *Volk* was sick and in need of a cure. In one passage, he accuses the cinema, the theater and the press, all supposedly under Jewish control, of infecting the German people. . . . 'This was pestilence, spiritual pestilence, worse than the Black Death of olden times, and the people was being infected with it.'"[60]

The age-old association between Jews and plague sealed an association with disease-carrying organisms. A comment in a 1938 article that appeared in *Der Stürmer* is typical. "Bacteria, vermin, and pests cannot be tolerated," it stated. "For reasons of cleanliness and hygiene we must make them harmless by *killing them off.*"[61] This point was made most graphically in a famous segment of the 1940 propaganda film *The Eternal Jew* showing rats swarming through cellars and sewers while the narrator intones, "Where rats turn up, they spread diseases and carry extermination into the land. They are cunning, cowardly and cruel, they travel in large packs, exactly the way the Jews infect the races of the world."[62]

Geographical Persistence

Lethal anti-Semitism also persisted geographically. In a fascinating study, economists Nico Voigtländer and Hans-Joachim Voth trace the continuity between the pogroms that took place in German lands during the Black Death and the Nazi persecutions of the twentieth century. Although very many German Jewish communities were massacred during the fourteenth century, some were entirely spared. The latter were often members of the Hanseatic League—a group of north German cities that banded together to protect and promote their collective commercial interests. Voigtländer and Voth found that the towns and cities where Jews were most persecuted during the fourteenth century were often *the very same places* where, almost seven hundred years later, there were strong anti-Semitic sentiments and acts of persecution during the Hitler regime (and also the places where earlier persecutions occurred, where *Judensau* images were displayed on buildings, and where, during the early nineteenth-century, Hep-Hep riots—riots provoked by the prospect of Jews being granted full citizenship rights—occurred). They conclude, "Localities that burned their Jews in 1348–50 showed markedly higher levels of anti-Semitism in the interwar period: attacks on Jews were 6 times more likely in the 1920s in towns and cities with Black Death pogroms; the Nazi Party's share of the vote in 1928—when it had a strong anti-Jewish focus—was 1.5 times higher; readers' letters to a virulently anti-Semitic Nazi newspaper (*Der Stürmer*) were more frequent; attacks on synagogues during the 'Night of Broken Glass' (*Reichskristallnacht*) in 1938 were more common; and a higher proportion of Jews was deported under the Nazis."[63]

Jews in these localities who had not been killed in the medieval plague pogroms fled, and by 1550 most of the remaining Jews had been expelled. They only began to trickle back in during the eighteenth century. However, despite the fact that Jews were long absent from these places, derogatory attitudes toward them persisted across the centuries.[64]

———

The kind of story that I have told about the persistence of dehumanizing anti-Semitic beliefs could have been told about many other dehumanizing ideologies. A similar story could have been told about African Americans, Roma, Native Americans, and many other oppressed populations. This points to a very disturbing fact about ideologies generally and dehumanizing ideologies in particular. Once established, they tend to persist. They become entrenched in ways of life, which makes them difficult to displace or disrupt. Even in cases where a dehumanizing ideology has seemingly gone into abeyance, changes in the social and political environment and the production of dehumanizing propaganda can reactivate it, sometimes with devastating results.

CHAPTER ELEVEN

Ambivalence

As I write these words, I am sitting on the deck overlooking acres of woodland behind my New England home. Two handsome red-tailed hawks have taken up residence in a tall tree, and, every once in a while, I see one swooping down to pick up some hapless mammal in its talons—a squirrel, a chipmunk, or a vole—carry it to its perch, tear the still-living creature to shreds, and gorge on its flesh. Closer to me, I see dragonflies flitting over the yard. It is a beautiful spectacle, but I know that these aerial acrobats are ferocious predators—tiny killing machines on the prowl for mosquitos and other insects to devour. And many of the mosquitos that the dragonflies eat are fat with blood drawn from the deer that roam the woods. Closer still, a team of tiny ants drags a writhing caterpillar across the decking boards by my feet. They will carry it to their nest, and consume it alive.

The natural world is anything but harmonious. It is wonderful and terrible, a place where life incessantly feeds upon life. Many animals depend on the flesh of others, and even the gentle herbivores dismember and devour plants. If plants could scream, their cries would be unrelenting. Some creatures have worked out cooperative relationships with their prey. Fruit-eaters are paid in calories for the job of spreading seeds. But for most of the rest, their existence demands destruction or exploitation. That is why Arthur Schopenhauer described nature as "a playground of tortured and anguish-ridden beings that endure only by eating one another, where consequently every vicious animal is the living grave of thousands of others, who only continue to exist by devouring each other . . . a chain of torturing deaths." Or, as Philip Kitcher succinctly put it, "Suffering is not incidental to life but written into the script."[1] Violence is a condition of life.

Homo sapiens are no exception to this pattern. From deep in prehistory onward, we have taken the lives of other organisms for food, for protection, for materials such as animal hides and plant fibers for clothing, for wood, horn and bone to fashion tools and ornaments, and eventually for recreation, and we have ritually slaughtered them to please the bloodlust of our deities. In addition to all the killing, human beings have exploited the physiology and muscle power of nonhuman animals for thousands of years, using livestock as walking larders, producers of eggs and milk, pullers of the plow, and means of transportation.

We could not have gotten by without doing violence to other organisms. But it is equally true that we could not have gotten by as social animals without powerful restraints on violence against our own kind. For most social animals, striking the right balance between aggression and restraint does not present a problem because evolution has endowed them with a set of instincts to manage it. Chimpanzees are built not to kill other members of their troop and to relish the flesh of the colobus monkeys that they hunt. They do not have to wonder—and indeed are incapable of wondering—whether it is permissible to take the lives of others. They simply follow nature's way. But we *Homo sapiens* are different. We are not as instinct-bound as even our closest primate relatives, and we are endowed with immensely greater behavioral flexibility than is available to other animals. We must make choices, and are driven to seek reasons to justify what we choose.

At some point in our species' journey through time our ancestors were confronted with the conundrum of why it is allowable to do kill some living things but not others. They needed a rationalizing story—an explanation, however mythical, for the rules surrounding the act of killing. One such story, found among some foraging cultures today and which was probably common in our prehistoric, hunter-gatherer past, is that human hunters and their prey exist in a cooperative relationship. Animals present themselves to hunters because they *want* to killed. Killing an animal therefore fulfills its wishes, because the animal gives it is life rather than the hunter taking it.[2] Religious studies scholar Graham Harvey writes,

> In some places, one role and employment of shamans is the persuading of animals to allow themselves to be found by hunters and to give up their lives for the good of humans. That is, shamans persuade animals and humans that hunting and being hunted is sacrificial. Death is unwelcome and often meaningless. But sacrifice is sacramental, transcendent, above life. Therefore, shamans might learn how to find that which is hidden to other humans: animals at a distance. Once they know where suitable animals are, shamans often attempt to persuade the potential prey to meet the hunters and to give themselves up. Culturally appropriate forms of respect are offered, and further respectful acts are promised at and after death.[3]

In some versions, the souls of animals that are killed continue their existence in an afterlife and must be propitiated. In others, they are reincarnated as other animals in an endless cycle of death and rebirth.

Of course, every hunter really knows that animals try to avoid being killed and are terrified of those that seek to kill them. And every hunter knows and that an animal with a spear piercing its side suffers agonies before it dies. The idea that animals offer themselves as prey is an ideological construction to legitimate killing them. It is a system of belief with the function of benefiting one group—in this case, human communities—and the expense of another—in this case, the nonhuman animals that they kill and exploit. Although it may sound odd, beliefs like these have the function of oppressing animals. The term "oppression" might strike you as an inappropriate way to characterize our relationship with nonhuman organisms. Surely, you might think, it is a term that should only be applied to our relations with other human beings. But this way of thinking betrays a commitment to the hierarchical framework that I described in Chapter 9. The intuition that only humans can be oppressed rests on the deep and perhaps inescapable bias that we humans occupy a higher rank in the cosmic order than other sorts of living things.

At some point, perhaps with the advent of domestication, agriculture, and socially stratified societies—a different ideology of killing emerged, one that proved to be very powerful—so powerful, in fact, that it is still with us today. The idea of a natural hierarchy provided an elegant solution to the problem of interspecies violence. The legitimacy of doing violence to other living things came to be considered as a function of their rank on the Great Chain of Being. Antelopes may be killed and eaten because they are less than human, but killing and eating fellow community members is impermissible. Like the idea that animals offer themselves as prey, the Great Chain of Being is an ideology. It is a system of belief that was and is reproduced because it underwrites practices that systematically advantages human being by legitimating violence to other organisms.

This, I suggest, is why the idea of the Great Chain of Being became so widespread and why it has such a tenacious grip on the human imagination. Life feeds upon life, and the idea of a hierarchy of nature is a tool for legitimating those acts of violence that we depend upon to flourish and survive.

Ultrasociality

We are ultrasocial animals. There is no other primate—indeed, no other mammal—that is anywhere near as social as *Homo sapiens* are.

And to thrive in the intensely social groups that we depend upon for our survival, we must have minds that are configured to be attuned to social interactions. Studies of the impact of solitary confinement on prisoners leave one in no doubt about its effects, which include "anxiety, withdrawal, hypersensitivity, ruminations, cognitive dysfunction, hallucinations, loss of control, irritability, aggression, rage, paranoia, hopelessness, a sense of impending emotional breakdown, self-mutilation, and suicidal ideation and behavior."[4] In fact, we are so strongly biased toward social interactions that we are inclined to see human beings that are not even there. "We find human faces in the moon, armies in the clouds," David Hume observed, "and by a natural propensity, if not corrected by experience and reflection, ascribe malice and good will to everything that hurts or pleases us."[5]

Social animals must avoid lethal or near-lethal aggression against members of their communities because otherwise a communal is impossible. So, human ultrasociality constrains human-on-human violence. People the world over have a natural preference for smoothly flowing, cooperative behavior. "The basic tendency is for persons to get caught up in the mutual focus of attention," writes sociologist Randall Collins, in his voluminous study of human violence, "and to become entrained in each other's bodily rhythms and emotional tones." Collins argues that

> these processes are unconscious and automatic. They are also highly attractive; the most pleasurable kinds of human activity are where persons become caught in a pronounced micro-interactional rhythm: a smoothly flowing conversation to the beat of a common intonational punctuation; shared laughter; crowd enthusiasm; mutual sexual arousal. Ordinarily these processes constitute an interaction ritual bringing feelings of inter-subjectivity and moral solidarity, at least for the present moment. Face-to-face conflict is difficult above all because it violates this

shared consciousness and bodily-emotional entrainment. . . . There is a palpable barrier to getting into a violent confrontation. It goes against one's physiological hard-wiring, the human propensity to become caught up in . . . rituals of solidarity.[6]

The extreme form of violent confrontation is physical violence, and its zenith is the act of killing. So, if Collins is right, the human preference for social solidarity must present a problem for motivating military combat. And it does. US Army historian S. L. A. Marshall made this very point in his immensely influential 1947 book *Men against Fire: The Problem of Battle Command*, which led to an overhaul of US military training. Marshall interviewed troops in the immediate aftermath of firefights and found that many infantrymen experienced difficulty firing their weapons. The problem was not mechanical. It was psychological. He claimed that these interviews convinced him soldiers all too often cannot bring themselves to use lethal force because "the average and normally healthy individual—the man who can endure the mental and physical stresses of combat—still has such an inner and usually unrealized resistance to killing a fellow man that he will not of his own volition take life if it is possible to turn away from that responsibility. . . . At the vital point he becomes a conscientious objector, unknowing."[7] In Marshall's view, a soldier's psychological resistance to killing is the result of socialization:

He is what his home, his religion, his schooling, and the moral code and ideals of his society have made him. The Army cannot unmake him. It must reckon with the fact that he comes from a civilization in which aggression, connected with the taking of life, is prohibited and unacceptable. The fear of aggression has been expressed to him so strongly and absorbed by him so deeply and pervadingly—practically with his mother's milk— that it is part of the normal man's emotional make-up. This is his great handicap when he enters combat. It stays his trigger finger even though he is hardly conscious that it is a restraint upon him. Because it is an emotional rather than an intellectual handicap, it is not removable by intellectual reasoning, such as "Kill or be killed."[8]

Marshall's explanation of soldiers' psychological resistance to killing accorded with the behaviorist orthodoxy of his day—the view that, apart from a few primitive reflexes, all human behavior is acquired by conditioning. But on the face of it, this explanation seems implausible. Children are rarely or ever taught not to kill others, and are certainly not rewarded for refraining from killing their playmates. And the evidence from developmental psychology points to infants being naturally cooperative and altruistic.[9] Psychology professor and combat veteran David Grossman, who more than anyone else has brought Marshall's ideas to a broader public, disagrees with Marshall's explanation of why soldiers so often find it difficult to take the lives of others. He argues that the resistance to killing other people is innate. It is a resistance that is so great, Grossman asserts, "that it is often sufficient to overcome the cumulative influences of the instinct for self-protection, the coercive forces of leadership, the expectancy of peers, and the obligation to preserve the lives of comrades."[10]

Although rich in insight, neither Marshall's nor Grossman's works are scholarly publications, and the evidence that they present is at best anecdotal. And Marshall's claim about soldiers having difficulty firing has been strongly criticized. However, the broad contours of their thinking cohere well with the work of others. For example, Harry Holbert Turney-High, an anthropologist and expert on pre-state warfare, wrote about primitive humans' "dread of taking enemy life, a feeling that if the life of a member of the we-group was precious, so was that of a member of the other-group. Fear of death-contamination has demanded expiation or purifica-

tion among many folk."[11] The work of influential Austrian etholo-
gist Irenäus Eibl-Eibesfelt provides another example. He argued
that we *Homo sapiens* are fitted out with *Tötungshemmungen*—
biologically based inhibitions against killing members of our species: "Human aggression is effectively held in check by a number
of phylogenetic adaptations. In all cultures there is a marked inhibition against killing a fellow human being, and if it is desired to
ignore it, as in war, for instance, special indoctrination is necessary
if the sympathetic appeal of common humanity is to be disregarded.
Sympathy as the subjective correlative of the inhibition on killing
is felt in all cultures, and is everywhere released by the same signals.
Thus inhibitions on aggression are innate in us."[12]

Inhibitions on aggression are nicely described in a paper by
psychologist Fiery Cushman and colleagues entitled "Simulating
Murder," which documents an experiment they conducted to determine whether the aversion to violence is entirely based on empathic concern for the victim or sometimes based on an aversion
to the violent action itself. Subjects were asked to perform, and also
to watch others perform, simulated violent acts. One was to take a
hammer and forcefully whack the experimenter's phony shin (the
"shin" was really a plastic pipe in the experimenter's empty pants
leg). Another was to pick up a hefty rock and bring it down hard on
a rubber hand protruding from an experimenter's shirtsleeve. The
third was to "shoot" the experimenter in the face with a realistic
toy gun; the fourth was to "cut" the experimenter's throat with a
rubber knife, and the fifth was to smash a lifelike baby doll's head
against a table.

The psychologists monitored their subjects' blood pressure and
cardiac activity while these things were going on. They found that
even though the participants knew full well that nobody was being
hurt, they showed strong physiological signs of distress—especially
when they performed the actions themselves rather than watching

somebody else do them. The experiment demonstrated that it was the actions rather than their moral consequences that elicited aversion. Of course, this does not imply that our behavior is not influenced by worries about the harmful effects of what we might do, but it does imply that focusing on empathic concern does not tell us the whole story. In their conclusion, Cushman and his colleagues spell out that "a forceful, automatic aversive response to the surface properties of harmful actions may explain otherwise puzzling human behaviors. In battlefield behavior and hypothetical moral judgment, people resist doing direct harm despite explicit knowledge that it could save many lives. Similarly, in our study, people experienced a strong aversive response to performing pretend harmful actions despite the explicit knowledge that no harm would be caused. These cases highlight a dissociation between our explicit knowledge of the consequences of our actions and our automatic affective responses to actions."[13]

These observations suggest that normal human beings are equipped with a psychological mechanism for regulating aggression that operates automatically, and is not subject to direct conscious control. It may be innate and genetically specified, it may be socially acquired, or it may be something that we are disposed to learn quickly and easily. The question of the origin of the mechanism is not important for this discussion. The point is that such a mechanism exists, and that it has the job of constraining interpersonal violence.

Perpetration-Induced Traumatic Stress

Several researchers have argued that overriding inhibitions against violence can be psychologically harmful. For instance, Grossman writes that "looking another human being in the eye, making an independent decision to kill him, and watching as he dies due to your action combine to form the most basic, important, primal, and potentially traumatic occurrence of war."[14] Psychologist Rachel McNair concurs. She argues that the act of killing often leads to severe traumatic stress, which she calls "perpetration-induced traumatic stress," that can lead to mental disorder. This sort of trauma is nowadays often called "moral injury." The idea is that killing in combat causes psychological harm because it violates deeply held moral beliefs and elicits immensely powerful feelings of guilt and shame.

The notion of moral injury is related to what genocide scholars sometimes call "perpetrator abhorrence," "perpetrator disgust," or "perpetrator trauma."[15] These are names for the abject horror that perpetrators sometimes feel about their own actions. Perpetrator abhorrence is linked to the moral injury thesis because the former is often interpreted as an effect of what sociologist Zygmunt Bauman calls "the impact of primeval moral drives."[16] According to this way of looking at the matter, genocidal killers have explicit ideological beliefs which coexist with and contradict their deeper, implicit belief that taking human life is wrong. Perpetrator abhorrence occurs when this deeper awareness bubbles to the surface, and causes them to recoil in horror from their own actions. Holocaust scholar Christopher Browning provides a vivid example of perpetrator abhorrence in the testimony of the pseudonymous Franz Kastenbaum, a German who took part in mass executions of Jews in Poland during World War II. Kastenbaum recalled,

> The shooting of the men was so repugnant to me that I missed the fourth man. It was simply no longer possible for me to aim accurately. I suddenly felt nauseous and ran away from the shooting site. I have expressed myself incorrectly just now. It was not that I could no longer aim accurately, rather the fourth time I intentionally missed. I then ran into the woods, vomited, and sat down against a tree. To make sure that no one was

nearby, I called loudly into the woods, because I wanted to be alone. Today I can say that my nerves were totally finished. I think that I remained alone in the woods for some two to three hours.[17]

Browning attributes these reactions to Kastenbaum's struggle with his moral sensibilities. But others, such as political scientist Daniel Goldhagen, deny that morality plays any role at all in such reactions. Goldhagen argues that the feelings of horror that experienced by people like Kastenbaum are often better understood as "aesthetic revulsion at the ghastliness of the scene." Being disturbed by "the exploded skulls, the flying blood and bone, the sight of so many freshly killed corpses of their own making" is quite different from being morally opposed to implementing atrocities.[18] There is something to be said for Goldhagen's objection. Perpetrators of atrocity who report being disturbed by the horrific acts that they performed or participated in very often do not describe suffering from feelings of guilt or remorse. Their reaction often consists of physical symptoms such as vomiting or trembling, dissociation, or feelings of horror—and horror is not a moral emotion. But saying that these responses are merely aesthetic does not explain very much. If people are intensely repelled by "the exploded skulls, the flying blood and bone, the sight of so many freshly killed corpses of their own making" there must be some reason *why* this is the case. There must be something *about* such scenes that triggers this response.

Goldhagen's comment about freshly killed corpses *of their own making* points to something more than aesthetics being involved, as the cause of something has no bearing on its aesthetic properties. Further, his explanation ignores similar reactions to the *act* of killing, which precedes any repugnant effects.

Neither of the two explanations of perpetrator abhorrence—moral reservations or aesthetic repugnance—seems to be entirely satisfactory, even though both probably do play a role. Hannah Arendt alluded to a third way to make sense of perpetrator abhorrence. She did not describe the horror as merely aesthetic, and she did not attribute it to the Nazi killers' moral conscience. Instead, she stated that in order to accomplish their genocidal goal, Nazis had to "overcome not so much their conscience but the animal pity by which all men are affected in the presence of physical suffering," which she characterized as an "instinctive reaction."[19] I take her to mean that this is an automatic, premoral response to physical suffering, albeit one that can be disabled or suppressed, and can be at odds with a person's moral convictions.

Pollution

So far, we have been looking only at individual psychology. But certain cultural beliefs, practices, and institutions also provide compelling evidence about attitudes to killing. Their details vary from place to place and from time to time, but all of them are variations on the idea that the act of killing contaminates the killer, who is in danger of becoming ill, going insane, or harming his community unless he is purified. Turney-High pointed this out as early as 1949, but there has been relatively little serious consideration of its implications since then. The fact that these ideas and practices have been very widespread, and have been taken so seriously—even in highly militaristic cultures that glorify the warrior—says something about the anxieties that suffuse the act of killing.

The idea that killing makes the killer unclean goes back thousands of years to the ancient world. Biblical scholar Jason A. Riley remarks, "Postbattle purification rituals for human warriors, including those intended to purify warriors from defilement, are commonly attested throughout the ancient near east and beyond."[20] In the Old Testament, Moses requires warriors who had slaughtered Midianite men, women, and children to cleanse themselves: "Camp outside the camp seven days; whoever of you has killed any person or touched a corpse, purify yourselves and your captives on the third and on the seventh day. You shall purify every garment, every article of skin, everything made of goats' hair, and every article of wood."[21] In a gloss of this passage, Susan Niditch writes, "The very act of killing in war renders the Israelite soldier unclean. He too must be purified before resuming his life as a whole member of the people of Israel. In this way, a late-Biblical ideology of war acknowledges the humanity of the enemy whose death tears the ordinary fabric of the Israelite universe even while insisting on the necessity of eliminating the impure 'Other.'"[22]

Other ancient cultures had similar views. The Greeks believed that the act of homicide could produce a highly contagious kind of pollution called, in English, miasma (from the Greek *miainein*—"to pollute"), which could infect anyone in the killer's proximity. This is why they held murder trials in the open air and required exiled murderers to plead their case from a boat to judges sitting on the shore. Anyone who was contaminated with miasma had undergo ritual purification "catharsis." If they were not cleansed, or if the lustration was unsuccessful, they were in danger of going mad.[23]

I am not aware of any evidence that the Greeks thought that killing in battle attracted the dreaded miasma, but there is ample evidence that the Romans did. Romans held that returning soldiers needed to be spiritually cleansed, and they instituted a public ceremony for this purpose. On October 19, at the conclusion of the fighting season, the entire Roman army underwent "purification (or disinfection) from the taint of bloodshed."[24]

The Roman idea that killing in combat stains the soul continued into the European middle ages. The philosopher Bernard Verkamp notes that medieval Christians "generally assumed that warriors returning from battle would or should be feeling guilty and ashamed for all the wartime killing they had done. Far from having such feelings dismissed as insignificant or irrelevant, returning warriors were encouraged to seek resolution of them through rituals of purification, expiation, and reconciliation. To accommodate these latter needs, religious authorities of the period not infrequently imposed various and sundry penances on returning warriors, depending on the kind of war they had been engaged in, the number of their killings, and the intention with which they had been carried out."[25] For example, the eleventh-century decree set out by Norman bishops specifying penances for knights who had fought with William the Conqueror at the Battle of Hastings required any knight who had killed an enemy combatant to do penance for a year, or for forty days if he did know whether the person survived the injuries that he inflicted on them. Those who lost track of how many people they killed had to do penance one day a week for the rest of their lives.[26]

Leaving Europe, there were similar beliefs among many indigenous American cultures. For example, Maricopa warriors returning home from military expeditions forced themselves to vomit because of having been exposed to "enemy sickness" which they needed to expel, and then spent twenty days undergoing purification.[27] After battle, Mohave warriors isolated themselves in their houses to undergo purification rituals that involved dietary restrictions and daily bathing. Their families and captives were also ritually cleansed to prevent the spread of fatal illness.[28] The Gila River Pima considered killing an enemy to be such a spiritually dangerous act that warriors withdrew from battle the moment they killed, to begin sixteen days of purification.[29] Similar beliefs and practices were common in Africa. For instance, the Zulu believed that a man who had killed was in fatal danger of contracting iZembe, a disease that could result in insanity. He was required to undergo purification, and be subject to certain restrictions for the rest of his life.[30] Thonga warriors believed that the vengeful spirits of those whom they had killed could make them ill or drive them mad, and that elaborate ritual procedures were required to protect them.[31] These are just a few examples of very many that can be culled from the anthropological literature.

There is an obvious relationship between the resistance to killing in combat, the destructive psychological consequences of overriding inhibitions against killing, and cultural beliefs that killing contaminates and endangers the killer and their entire community. And all three of these factors make sense in light of the ultrasocial character of our species. However, all of this leaves us with an explanatory puzzle. If human beings have such a powerful aversion to acts of violence, then how does this square with the fact that we indulge in them so frequently?

Disabling Inhibitions against Violence

Being the clever primates that we are, we are able to recognize that group-on-group violence often promises advantages—appropriating the resources of one's neighbors, enslaving and exploiting them, securing territory, and so on. Consequently, our ancestors developed and refined cultural practices that selectively disable inhibitions against performing acts of violence. One is the use of disinhibiting, mind-altering drugs prior to combat.[32] Another is the use of rituals, often involving rhythmic, dancing, drumming and chanting, to induce altered states of consciousness in the warrior.[33] Yet another involves religious ideologies, such as the promise of an eternity in paradise. But the most effective methods for liberating lethal violence are those that create distance between the aggressors and their victims.[34] Some distancing techniques create *perceptual* distance that shields the aggressor from the sights, sounds, and smells that would spark perpetrator abhorrence. One way to do this is by using long-range weapons. Progress in military technology, from the fourteenth-century longbow to today's Hellfire missiles, have made killing easier and less traumatic for combatants. Another method is to insulate the killer's sense organs from the stimuli that normally activate inhibitions. Chief among these is the sight of the human face—especially, the experience of looking into another person's eyes. The human face is by far the richest source of social information and the most intimate channel of connection between people, so it is not surprising that faces are especially significant for us. Even tiny infants preferentially gaze at faces. Our brains are equipped with cognitive systems that are specialized for visually processing facial information. Unlike other animals, that avoid eye contact with one another, we seek out the eyes of others when interacting with them.[35] When we gaze into a person's eyes, we cannot help responding to that person as a human being. We cannot help but see them as human—to automatically regard the face's bearer as *one of our own kind*.[36] Hence, the sight of the human face is a very powerful inhibitor of aggression, and avoiding or obscuring victims' faces can block this response. "The essence of the whole physical distance spectrum may simply revolve around the degree to which the killer can see the face of the victim," Grossman explains. "The eyes are the windows of the soul, and if one does not have to look into the eyes while killing, it is much easier to deny the humanity of the victim."[37] This is exemplified by the practice of hooding or blindfolding a person during their execution. It was also a feature of the Holocaust. The mass shootings of Jews by German Einsatzgruppen and police battalions were psychologically devastating for many of the killers, resulting in what they called *Seelenbelastung* ("burdening of the soul"), as well as physical reactions such as vomiting, trembling, and severe psychosomatic symptoms.[38] Some of these men refused to participate in the killing, and when an infuriated Heinrich Himmler, the head of the SS, decided to witness a mass execution at Minsk, he himself found it unbearable. According to SS general Erich von dem Bach-Zelewski, Himmler "was extremely nervous. He couldn't stand still. His face was white as cheese, his eyes went wild and with each burst of gunfire he always looked at the ground." On this occasion, two women were forced to lay down on the ground to be shot in the back of the head, but the shooters were so shaken that even at close range they missed and injured them. Himmler panicked and screamed, "Don't torture these women! Fire! Hurry up and kill them!" Bach-Zelewski then said to him, "Look at the men, how deeply shaken they are! Such men are finished for the rest of their lives!"[39]

It was the horror of this form of killing that led Himmler to explore alternative methods of mass murder. Inspired by the techniques that were developed for killing disabled people, the Nazis developed other means for mass extermination, beginning with carbon monoxide vans and ending in the gas chambers. These methods relied on avoiding any encounter that might lead perpetrators to respond to their victims as human beings. Tzvetan Todorov observes that "all possible measures were taken in the concentration camps to ensure that face-to-face encounters did not occur, to prevent the executioner from meeting his victim's gaze. Only an individual can look at us. . . . By avoiding his gaze, we can all the more easily ignore him as a person. In recognizing the other, even the most hardened individual risks moments of weakness." Todorov continues, "The gas chambers were invented to avoid this kind of 'human' reaction, to which even Himmler and Eichmann were not immune, and to keep the members of the *Einsatzkommandos*, who shot prisoners by the thousands, from losing their minds. Once the machine had replaced the man, the executioner could avoid all contact with the victim."[40]

In a similar vein, criminologist Nestar Russell discusses in detail how Nazi executioners managed to distance themselves from their victims. Bizarre as it might sound, senior Nazis, including Himmler and Rudolf Höss, the commandant of Auschwitz, spoke of the importance of exterminating Jews "humanely." As Russell notes, "The Nazi regime's pursuit of a method of killing capable of destroying large numbers of civilians gradually moved in a direction that allowed German perpetrators to emotionally distance themselves from their victims. By the time Crematorium II was completed at Auschwitz, the Germans most directly involved in the killing process need not touch, see, or hear their victims die."[41]

However, physical distancing can only take one so far. Mass violence inevitably involves some measure of person-to-person contact—some awareness that one is extinguishing the lives of human beings. Psychological distancing then becomes a second line of defense against perpetrator abhorrence. We can see it at work in Himmler's response to the horrific mass killing described above. After he regained his composure, Himmler gathered the men around him and made a speech, which Bach-Zelewski paraphrased:

They surely had noticed that even he was revolted by this bloody activity and had been aroused to the depth of his soul. But he too was obeying the highest law by doing his duty and he was acting from a deep understanding of the necessity of this operation. We should observe nature: everywhere there was war, not only among human beings, but also in the animal and plant worlds. Whatever did not want to fight was destroyed. . . . Primitive man said that the horse is good, but the bug is bad, or wheat is good but the thistle is bad. Humans characterize that which is useful to them as good, but that which is harmful as bad.

His final comment is especially significant. "Don't bugs, rats and other vermin have a purpose in life to fulfill?" Himmler continued, "But we humans are correct when we defend ourselves against vermin." This was not the only time that Himmler compared Jews to bugs. It was a popular Nazi trope. For instance, in a 1943 speech he said, "Antisemitism is exactly the same as delousing. Getting rid of lice is not a question of ideology. It is a matter of cleanliness. In just the same way, antisemitism, for us, has not been a question of ideology, but a matter of cleanliness, which now will soon have been dealt with. We shall soon be deloused. We have only 20,000 lice left and then the matter is finished within the whole of Germany."[42]

Dehumanization is a powerful way of creating psychological distance. It does this by creating conceptual, rather than perceptual, distance. And it can *motivate* violence rather than simply disinhibit it. Describing Jews as vermin does not just render violence against them permissible. It encourages their extermination. Appallingly, Zyklon B—the poison gas used in the killing chambers of the camps—was originally developed as an agent for exterminating lice.

CHAPTER TWELVE

Making Monsters

It has taken me eleven chapters to explain my view of what dehumanization is, how it works, what its function is, and why we should take it very seriously. But the journey is not yet over. There is another whole layer of dehumanization that needs explaining, and this requires adding some new and very important elements to the story that I have so far told.

My own thinking on these matters was stimulated by the need to address two important objections to the theory of dehumanization presented in my 2011 book *Less Than Human*. One of these, which I call the *problem of humanity*, has been discussed by several writers. It is well known and is often regarded as a knock-down refutation of the claim that dehumanization is real. The other, which I call the *problem of monstrosity*, has been largely unrecognized. After grappling with these issues for several years, I came to realize that they are both solved by a single theoretical stroke—one that dramatically deepens our understanding of what dehumanization is and how it works.

The Problem of Humanity

The *problem of humanity* is this: people who think of and talk about others as less than human also think and talk about them as human. This implies that, whatever is going on when people ostensibly dehumanize others, it is not accurate to say that they consider those they dehumanize to be nothing but subhuman animals. I addressed this problem in passing in Chapter 1, in the discussion of Winthrop Jordan's claim that White slaveholders did not literally regard enslaved Black people as subhumans. Jordan's incredulity about the animalization of Black people turned on the fact that slaveholders implicitly acknowledged the human status of those they held in bondage. I noted in that discussion that an even stronger argument can be made. The White people who described Black people as animals also often referred to them not merely implicitly, but *explicitly*, as human beings. This is typical of dehumanizing discourse. Nazis referred to Jews both as vermin and as criminals, but the category "criminal" is applicable only to human beings and not to vermin. And Islamophobes say that Muslims are both bloodthirsty beasts and religiously motivated terrorists, but only humans can be terrorists. The practice of referring to dehumanized people *as people* suggests either that there is something missing from theories of dehumanization or that the whole notion of dehumanization is seriously misguided and that people do not really conceive of other people as less than human.

The earliest statement of the problem of humanity dates back to Morgan Godwyn's writings, in particular his 1680 work *The Negro's and Indians Advocate*, which I cited in Chapters 4 and 8. The word "dehumanization" did not exist during Godwyn's lifetime. It was introduced early in the nineteenth century. But Godwyn certainly had a concept of dehumanization; he referred to it using terms such as "brutifying" and "soul murdering," and he wrote of Black people being "unsoul'd" and "unman'd." Godwyn was not interested in dehumanization as such. His mission was to show that it is factually, morally, and spiritually wrong to think of Black people as subhuman creatures. In the service of this goal, he sought to demonstrate that the White people who claimed that Black people were nothing more than "brutes" contradicted themselves by also implicitly affirming that Africans were human beings. Godwyn had a remarkably sophisticated understanding of the dehumanizing process. For instance, unlike many people today, he recognized that dehumanization is not a "failure" to see the humanness of others or merely a natural response to "difference." He was aware that dehumanizing beliefs about Black people are ideological constructions for legitimating oppression, and charged that slaveholders "infer their *Negro's Brutality*, justifie their reduction of them under Bondage; disable them from all *Rights and Claims;* even to *Religion* itself, pronounce them *Reprobates;* and upon a sudden (with greater speed and cunning than either the nimblest juggler or witch) *transmute* them into whatsoever substance the *exigence* of their wild reasonings shall drive them to."[1]

Godwyn notes that despite this seeming transmutation, slaveholders were unable to fully relinquish their awareness of the humanity of the people whose souls they tried to murder. If Black people were not human, then

> why should they be tormented and whipt almost (and sometimes quite) to death, upon any, whether *small or great* Miscarriages . . . were they (like Brutes) naturally destitute of *Capacities* equal to such undertakings? Or why, should their *Owners,* Men of Reason no doubt, conceive them fit to exercise the place of Governours and *Overseers* to their *fellow Slaves,* which is frequently done, if they were mere Brutes? . . . It would certainly be a pretty kind of *Comical* Frenzie, to imploy Cattel about business, and constitute them *Lieutenants, Overseers,* and *Governours,* like as *Domitian* is said to have made his horse a Consul.[2]

And what about the implications of their rape and sexual exploitation of enslaved people at the hands of their White overlords?

> If slavery hath such a faculty or power to turn men into beasts, or if all *Negro's* be naturally such, may we not be bold to demand what will become of those *Debauches,* that so frequently

228 ‡ MAKING MONSTERS

do make use of them for their *unnatural* Pleasures and Lusts? Or such of our People who have intermarried with them? Surely they would be loth to be endited of *Sodomy*, as for lying with a Beast. It would therefore be convenient for them to renounce that Beastly opinion; or else that the law may have its free Course *and be let loose upon them.*[3]

Finally, Godwyn points out that Whites' claim that slaves are livestock does not pass muster, because slavers are guilty of "treating their Slaves with far less Humanity than they do their *Cattel*. For they do not use to starve their *Horse*, which they expect shall both carry and credit them upon the Road; nor to *pinch the cow* of her fodder, by whose milk their *Families* are sustained: Which yet (to their eternal shame) is too frequently the lot and condition of these *poor People*, from whose labour their Wealth and *Livelihoods* do wholly arise."[4]

Godwyn anticipated most of the points raised in present-day discussions of the problem of humanity. For instance, we find the philosopher Stanley Cavell writing nearly three centuries later that "it is sometimes said that slaveowners did not see or treat their slaves as human beings, but rather, say, as livestock; some slaveowners themselves have been known to say so. . . . But does one really believe such assertions?"[5] His answer is "no," which he justifies thus:

When he wants to be served at a table by a black hand, he would not be satisfied to be served by a black paw. When he rapes a slave or takes her as a concubine, he does not feel that he has, by that fact itself, embraced sodomy. When he tips a black taxi driver . . . it does not occur to him that he might more appropriately have patted the creature fondly on the back of the neck. He does not go to great lengths either to convert his horses to Christianity or to prevent their getting wind of it. Everything in his relation to his slaves shows that he treats them as more or less human—his humiliations of them, his disappointments, his jealousies, his fears, his punishments, his attachments.[6]

Leaving aside the disturbing claim about Black taxi drivers, whom Cavell seems to regard as slaves, and leaving aside the fact that he does not draw on any historical evidence about the beliefs and attitudes of real White supremacists (in contrast to his story about a "more or less mythical slave owner"), it is clear that Cavell denies that racists regard Black people as subhuman animals. In his view, the slave owner really just believes that the slave is "indefinitely different" from himself, and that "what he really believes is not that slaves are not human beings, but that some human beings are slaves."[7]

Philosopher Kwame Anthony Appiah voiced related concerns in his book *Experiments in Ethics* nearly a decade after Cavell. He argues that the claim that genocidaires think of their victims as subhuman animals is "not quite right" because "it doesn't explain the immense cruelty . . . that are their characteristic feature. The persecutors may liken the objects of their enmity to cockroaches or germs, but they acknowledge their victims' humanity in the very act of humiliating, stigmatizing, reviling, and torturing them. Such treatments—and the voluble justifications the persecutors invariably offer for such treatment—is reserved for creatures we recognize to have intentions, and desires, and projects."[8]

Appiah points out that dehumanizers say that their victims *deserve* punishment, but that the notion of "deserving punishment" is applicable only to human beings—not to vermin. However, he does not move from this to the conclusion that genocidaires really think of their victims as human beings and not subhuman animals. If a conception of dehumanization is "not quite right," it is partially or largely right, and therefore incomplete rather than entirely mistaken. As you will see, I think that Appiah was on the right track.

The philosopher Kate Manne is the most prominent contemporary critic of theories of dehumanization. She argues that
dehumanization does not exist, and what seems like dehumanization is really something else. Manne's main target is a view that she
calls *humanism*, a central component of which is that "when we recognize another human being as such . . . then this is not only a
necessary condition for treating her humanely, in interpersonal contexts, but also strongly *motivates* and *disposes* us to do so."[9] She
points out that recognizing others as human is entirely compatible
with hostility toward them, and that seeing that they are human
often involves recognizing that they are threatening in distinctively
human ways. Human beings can be malicious, cruel, oppressive,
envious, rivalrous, and so on—therefore, recognizing others as
human does not translate into treating them kindly. What, then, is
the purpose served by referring to them as subhuman? Here is
Manne's answer: "One simple point is that dehumanizing speech
can function to *intimidate, insult, demean, belittle*, and so on . . . since
it helps itself to certain powerfully encoded *social meanings*. And
given that human beings are widely (if erroneously) held to be *superior* to nonhuman animals, denying someone's humanity can serve
as a particularly humiliating kind of put-down. When a white police officer in Ferguson called a group of black political protesters
'fucking animals' . . . he was using this trope to demean and degrade
the protesters and reassert his own dominance."

Manne points out that the police officer's use of an animalistic
slur to degrade and humiliate the protestors indicates that even
though he called them "animals," he regarded them as human. If
we assume otherwise, this scenario would simply not make sense,
Manne argues, because "such put-downs would hardly be apropos
when it comes to *actual* non-human animals, who could neither
comprehend the insult nor *be* successfully put down by having their
nonhuman status correctly identified. This requires human com-

prehension, not to mention an incipient human status to be degraded *from*. There is nothing to object to in being called a rat if, in fact, you are one."[10]

Let me put Manne's point in a slightly different way. Dehumanization is normally diagnosed on the basis of what people *say*—usually, their use of animalistic slurs. Such slurs are intended to derogate others—to humiliate them, to assert their inferiority, and so on. But people who slur others in this way could not possibly have such an intention if they *really believed* that the objects of their hostility were subhuman animals. The use of animalistic slurs presupposes that the speaker recognizes both that the person whom they are targeting is a human being and also that that person is aware of their status as a human being.

It should be evident that many of Manne's critical points are not applicable to the theory of dehumanization that I have set out in this book. I do not advocate humanism as she defines it, as I do not hold that recognizing others as human makes one favorably disposed toward them. I do not claim that the use of animalistic slurs always, or even mostly, indicates that the speaker has dehumanizing beliefs. And I reject the idea that dehumanization is a *failure* to notice the humanity of others. Nevertheless, Manne's characterization of the problem of humanity deserves serious attention, if only to address the problem of distinguishing slurs that express genuinely dehumanizing attitudes from those that do not.[11]

The Problem of Monstrosity

So far, I have explained dehumanization as the attribution of a subhuman essence to others. From the dehumanizer's perspective, the other person might appear to be human on the "outside," but they are actually subhuman animals on the "inside." However, there are many examples of dehumanization that do not fit this model.

Consider the victims of lynching described in Chapter 1, who were regularly described in racist literature of the day not simply as predatory animals, but also as monsters and fiends. And consider the putatively Satanic Jews described in Chapter 10, or the description of Jews in the SS booklet *Der Untermensch*, which stated, "Inside of this creature lies wild and unrestrained passions: an incessant need to destroy, filled with the most primitive desires, chaos and coldhearted villainy. . . . The subhuman thrives in chaos and darkness, he is frightened by the light. These subhuman creatures dwell in the cesspools, and swamps, preferring a hell on earth, to the light of the sun."[12] Taking this line of enquiry further, it is not necessary to use words like "monster" or "demon" to refer to and conceive of others as demonic or monstrous. Words like "superpredator" and "terrorist" can do exactly the same job. So, when considering the *problem of monstrosity*, we need to look below the surface of the manifest message.

Monstrousness does not fit into the theoretical framework that I have so far described, because monsters are not subhuman animals. They are *unnatural* entities: outsiders to the Great Chain of Being. The tenth-century *Liber Monstrorum de Diversis Generibus* (*The Book of Monsters of Various Kinds*) captures this point perfectly: "Made as they were, the order of creation must keep them on the outside."[13]

Thinking of others as monsters is quite different from thinking of them as animals. An animal might be frightening or disgusting, but monsters are horrifying, and they are felt to be much more dangerous than any animal because of their extraordinary powers. Monsters are malevolent and uncanny, whereas nonhuman animals are neither. And most importantly, monsters have no place in the order of nature. They embody its subversion.

Unlike the problem of humanity, the problem of monstrosity is hardly ever mentioned in the dehumanization literature *as a problem*.

Although many writers point out that members of dehumanized groups are often "demonized," they do not offer any explanation for this, and do not seem to notice that it does not comport with theories of dehumanization. This overlooking has large implications, because the challenge that it poses is not exclusive to theories like mine, which draw on the concept of the Great Chain of Being.

Researchers into dehumanization have not given demonization its proper due. None of the social psychological theories of dehumanization that I have discussed in this book have a place for it. On Nick Haslam's account, we dehumanize others by attributing machine-like or animal-like characteristics to them. But demons are neither machine-like or animal-like. And theorists who think of dehumanization as the denial of mental states to others also have no place for the demonic. Demons are evil, but they are not mindless. Others causally refer to demonization as a kind of dehumanization, without giving any account of what this amounts to or how it occurs. Things are no better in social political science. It is of course recognized that demonization plays an important role in international relations, but such analyses take the concept of the demonic as given, rather than subjecting it to analysis.[14]

Ambivalence

As I reconstruct it, the argument that moves from the premise that dehumanizers recognize the humanness of those whom they seem to dehumanize to the conclusion that they do not really think of these others as nonhuman proceeds like this. The first premise states that some people refer to some other people as subhuman creatures, but they also seem to regard them as human beings. The second premise states that it is logically impossible, and therefore inconceivable, for any being to be both human and subhuman,

234 ‡ MAKING MONSTERS

because these two categories exclude one another. The third premise states that, given the truth of the first and second premises, those who speak of others as human and as subhuman must be conceiving of them as either human or subhuman, but not as both. The fourth premise states that it is much more likely that these people conceive of those whom they seem to dehumanize as human than as subhuman. This premise might be justified in all sorts of ways, for example commonsensically (they don't look human) or through a sophisticated argument like Manne's. And all of this leads to the final conclusion that it is overwhelmingly likely that perpetrators do not really believe that those whom they describe as animals are really less than human.

This is a flawed argument. Its problem lies in the transition from the second premise to the third one. The second premise is a special case of the general truth that nothing can simultaneously possess a property and lack that very same property. This is true as a matter of logic. It cannot be true, for example, both that I am over six feet tall and that I am less than six feet tall, or that the tumbler on my desk both contains whiskey and does not contain whiskey. But the third premise, which is supposed to follow on from it, is a *psychological* claim rather than a logical one. It would only follow from the second premise there was another, intermediate premise stating something like "Human psychology always conforms to the rules of logic." That would be a ridiculous claim to make, because it is a truism that human psychology can and often does defy logic. We are adept at irrationality, and are often able to entertain contradictory beliefs side by side. So, unless there is good reason to think that beliefs about humanity and subhumanity are insulated from this sort of irrationality, the premises of this argument fall short of establishing its conclusion.

Versions of this argument that rely on animalistic slurs as their sole evidential base also suffer from another weakness. It is true that inferences about dehumanization rest largely on what people say. And, as I have pointed out, we cannot legitimately conclude that a person conceives of another as a subhuman just because they use this sort of speech against them. In Manne's example, the White cop who called Black protesters "fucking animals" may not have actually thought of them as animals, and may have said this just to put them down, just as she argues. But the evidential base for the reality of dehumanization is much broader than examples like this. There are many, many instances of people claiming that other people are subhuman, where this is meant to be taken literally as a statement of fact. I have supplied quite a few of them in this book. Here is yet another, from the anthropologist Hugh Raffles, who points out, drawing on historical documents, that "in early modern France . . . 'since coition with a Jewess is *precisely the same* as if a man should copulate with a dog,' Christians who had heterosexual sex with Jews could be prosecuted for the capital crime of sodomy and burned alive with their partners—'such persons in the eye of the law and our holy faith differ[ing] in no wise from beasts.'"[15]

Even if animalistic slurs never express dehumanizing beliefs (which is surely not the case), that does not undermine the evidential base for the reality of dehumanization. And once we accept that there are examples that, by any reasonable criterion, point to the existence of true dehumanization, it becomes an open question whether the dehumanizing mentality lurks behind any given episode of animalistic derogation.

However, the problem of humanity remains. Why is it that those who conceive of others as subhumans also conceive of them as humans? What does this tell us about the nature of dehumanization? Consider the passage that I just quoted. Even though the statements about the subhumanity of Jewish women were clearly meant to be taken at face value, the quoted text states that "such *persons*" differ in no wise from beasts. It seems strange to say that there are *persons* that are no different from beasts. If they are persons, they are not beasts, and if they are beasts, they are not persons.

Look again at the flawed argument that I gave a few paragraphs back. The argument can be repaired by eliminating the dubious premise "So it must be the case that those who speak of others in this way think of them as either human or subhuman, but not both" and adding in its place "So it must be the case that those who speak of others in this way believe them to be both human and subhuman." Once that is done, the rest of the argument falls away, leaving us with the conclusion that when people dehumanize others they *regard them as being human and subhuman simultaneously*. This should not be interpreted to mean that dehumanizers conceive of others as partly human and partly subhuman, like mermaids or centaurs. It should be understood to mean that they conceive of dehumanized people as *completely* human and *completely* subhuman, both at once. I am aware that this sounds bizarre, and perhaps even unintelligible. But I will do my best to dispel this aura of strangeness.

Understanding ambivalence is crucial for making sense of the contradiction that lies at the heart of the dehumanizing mind. Swiss psychiatrist Eugen Bleuler coined the term "ambivalence" in 1910. Bleuler identified three kinds of ambivalence: "affective ambivalence" (conflicting emotions toward the same person), "ambivalence of the will" (the desire to pursue some course of action coexisting with the desire not to pursue it) and "intellectual ambivalence" (belief in contradictory propositions). Freud picked up the term in 1912, and it soon became a mainstay of the theoretical vocabulary of psychoanalysis.[16]

Freud's major discussion of ambivalence appears in the second of four essays published in 1912–1913 that were pulled together as the book *Totem and Taboo*. *Totem and Taboo* is Freud's main foray into speculative anthropology. It is a work in which he attempted to theorize the phenomenon of taboo—forceful and often puzzling restrictions on certain kinds of behavior often found in traditional societies. As Freud put it, "Behind all these prohibitions there seems to be something in the nature of a theory that they are necessary because certain persons and things are charged with a dangerous power, which can be transferred through contact with them, almost like an infection. . . . The strangest fact seems to be that anyone who has transgressed one of these prohibitions himself acquires the characteristic of being prohibited—as though the whole of the dangerous charge has been transferred over to him."[17]

Freud argued that taboos arise from ambivalent attitudes that become sedimented into a culture, and he used the ambivalent attitudes of individuals to throw light on them. In particular, Freud was interested in the striking similarities between taboos and the strange private rituals and prohibitions found in cases of obsessional neurosis (nowadays known as obsessive-compulsive disorder). He treats these cultural taboos as obsessional neuroses writ large, extrapolating as best he can from one to the other. "Obsessional patients," he writes, "behave as though . . . persons and things were carriers of a dangerous infection liable to be spread by contact onto everything in their neighborhood." He continues, comparing the ritual purifications associated with cultural taboos with the private rituals of those suffering from obsessional neurosis: "Obsessional prohibitions involve just as extensive renunciations and restrictions in the lives of those who are subject to them as do taboo prohibitions; but some of them can be lifted if certain actions are performed. Thereafter these actions *must* be performed. They become compulsive or obsessive acts, and there can be no doubt that they are in the nature of expiation, penance, defensive measures and purification."[18]

Freud then goes on to argue that, in both cases, it is ambivalent attitudes that causally underwrite beliefs about a dangerous, contagious power that must be met by social isolation and rituals of purification. This attitude is not just a matter of mixed feelings, desires, or beliefs. If that were the case, the conflict between them could be resolved by deliberation bringing the incompatible ideas into relation to one another. But resolution is impossible because the incompatible attitudes are mentally segregated from one another. As Freud says, "The conflict between these two currents cannot be promptly settled because—there is no other way of putting it—they are localized in the subject's mind in such a manner that they cannot come up against each other."[19]

I think that something like what Freud describes goes on in episodes of dehumanization. There are two contradictory beliefs or mental representations of the dehumanized person present in the dehumanizer's mind. One of these is a conception of that person as a human being and the other is a conception of them as a subhuman animal. These are walled off from one another and cannot interact.[20]

Epistemic Deference

The next task is to explain how and why this occurs. Consider the ways that we normally come to categorize things. We usually do so on the basis of what our senses tell us. We think something is blue if it looks blue, we think something is a porcupine if it looks like a porcupine, we think someone is our best friend if they look like our best friend. But there is also another basis for categorization: expert opinion. Experts are people, or groups of people, whom we regard as having authoritative knowledge of some domain. *They are the ones who are supposed to know.*

We often accept as true what the experts tell us about the world even if what they tell us contradicts what our senses tell us. For example, solid objects like the chair on which you are sitting look and feel gapless. But physicists tell us that such objects consist mostly of empty space. Even though our eyes tell us that solid objects are gapless, we defer to the physicists because, in our culture, they are supposed to know.

There is no necessary connection between having the status of expert and having genuine knowledge. This is because being an expert is ultimately a political status, a position of power and authority. Sometimes, those who are supposed to know do not really know, or they conceal what they really know in the service of some political agenda. But because we defer to those who occupy the cultural role of expert, we are likely to trust even these claims and accept them as true.

I have been talking about scientists as experts, but there are many other figures who can and do occupy this role. Academics, members of the clergy, celebrities, athletes, politicians, motivational speakers, and even radio talk-show hosts may all be accorded the status of expert. Today, in the age of the internet, anyone with an attractive enough message can be presented as an expert, and accumulate followers who regard them as one. And purported expertise is often distributed through the whole of a society rather than being lodged in certain individuals. In such cases, pervasive, taken-for-granted ideological beliefs have the status of "common knowledge" that defines reality, even when these beliefs do not correspond to the deliverances of our senses.

However, the configuration of the human mind sometimes presents an obstacle to adopting expert opinion. "The Party told you to reject the evidence of your eyes and ears," wrote George Orwell in *1984*, but sometimes expert testimony does not cause us to relinquish what our senses tell us. Sometimes, we are unable to abandon these perceptual beliefs, even though we *also* accept what the experts claim. Consider again the example of the solid objects. Even though you and I both accept what physicists tell us about solid objects, it is impossible for us to stop regarding the chair and other such objects as gapless. We hold both beliefs—the belief in the chair's gaplessness and the belief in its gappiness—simultaneously, even though they are contradictory. Optical illusions are a great illustration. Consider the Müller-Lyer illusion. The illusion consists of two horizontal lines, one placed above the other. The two lines are exactly the same length, but the top line terminates with arrows at each end, and the bottom line terminates with inverted arrows at each end. Even though you *know* that the two horizontal lines in the illusion are precisely the same length, you cannot help seeing the one at the bottom as longer than the one at the top. Even though you know that what you are "seeing" is not really there, you just can't help seeing it that way.

This is how dehumanizing beliefs come about. At its heart, dehumanization involves a contradiction between the perceptual categorization of others as human and the more "theoretical" categorization, acquired from others, that they are subhuman.

As I explained in Chapter 11, when we encounter other human beings we tend to rapidly and reflexively perceive them as human beings.[21] So, when we are told by someone that certain people are less than human, and we accept this on their epistemic authority, this does not prevent us from also seeing them as human beings. Under these circumstances, we think of these others as fully human in one "part" of the mind and as fully subhuman in another "part" that is segregated from the first. As Freud wrote, "They are localized in the subject's mind in such a manner that they cannot come up against each other."

This way of looking at things resolves the problem of humanity. Dehumanizers implicitly or explicitly regard those whom they dehumanize as human beings because it is impossible for them to shake that belief, which sits side by side with their belief that these others are subhuman creatures. Even though the mind of the dehumanizer harbors both beliefs, only one of them can be salient at any given time. And when one is in the mental foreground, the other one retreats into the background. This is why dehumanizing discourse tends to alternate between characterizing the other as human and characterizing them as subhuman. The historian of American racism David Brion Davis observed this, although he did not theorize it. I quoted him in Chapter 2 as arguing that "since the victims of [lynching] are perceived as 'animalized humans,' this double consciousness would probably involve a contradictory shifting back and forth in the recognition of humanity."[22] An interview with a woman who participated in a lethal attack on Roma residents of the town of Hadereni, Romania, in which a man was burned to death and many homes were destroyed by arson, provides a very clear example of Davis's "contradictory shifting back and forth." The interviewee told a journalist, shortly after the pogrom, "On reflection . . . it would have been better if we had burnt more of the people, not just the houses. . . . We did not commit murder—how could you call killing Gypsies murder? Gypsies are not really people, you see. They are always killing each other. They are criminals, sub-human, vermin."[23] Notice that she starts off by saying that she regrets not having burned more of the *people* (that is, human beings) to death, but next says that killing Roma is not murder because Roma are *not people* (they are not human beings). Then she says that they are *criminals* (only human beings can be criminals) but asserts right afterward that they are subhuman *vermin* (once again, not human).

If I am right, the problem of humanity is not really a problem at all. Given the way that the human mind works, it is an expectable aspect of the dehumanization. But there are further ramifications of this idea—ramifications that both throw a great deal of unexpected light on the phenomenology of dehumanization and pave the way for a solution to the problem of monstrosity.

Uncanny Dehumanization

I begin with a point that is obvious but that is all too often overlooked. Consider the Nazis' claims that Jews are creatures rather
like rats. People have lots of different attitudes to rats. My grand-
mother, who spent her teenage years in a rat-infested tenement
building, was terrified of them. But my daughter adored rats as a
child, and kept two of them as pets. Psychologists who use rats
in maze-running experiments regard them dispassionately, as do
medical scientists who use them to test the effects of experimental
drugs. My point is that there is nothing intrinsically disgusting about
these rodents. But the Nazis did not say that Jews were simply rats.
That would have been delusional (Jews are not small furry creatures with naked tails). Instead, they described them as *human*
vermin. For all their ideological ardor, committed Nazis could not
help seeing Jews as human beings. But at the same time, they held
fast to the ideological belief that Jews were *Untermenschen*. So, Jews
were not just rats in the eyes of true believers of Nazi ideology.
They were rat/humans. Understanding this is vital for theorizing
dehumanization, because there is an important research literature
spanning several disciplines that suggests that contradictory beings like rat/humans elicit a distinctive and highly disturbing
psychological response. They are felt to be what in German is
called *Unheimlich*, a word that is conventionally (if imperfectly)
translated as "uncanny." Freud pointed out in an article that he
wrote on this topic that the uncanny "is undoubtedly related to what
is frightening. . . . Yet we may expect that a special core of feeling
is present which justifies the use of a special conceptual term. One
is curious to know what this common core is which allows us to
distinguish as 'uncanny' certain things which lie within the field
of what is frightening."[24]

Freud had his own ideas about how feelings of uncanniness come about, but it will be more productive for us to turn to the work of his contemporary, a German psychiatrist named Ernst Jentsch. In his 1906 paper "On the Psychology of the Uncanny," Jentsch set out to determine exactly what it is to experience something as uncanny, what sorts of things elicit this response, and why they do so. He argued that uncanny things produce a sense of disorientation and uncertainty. But he was aware that not all uncertainties generate the uncanny feeling, or produce it to the same degree. There must be a special sort of uncertainty involved: "Among all the psychical uncertainties that can become a cause for the uncanny feeling to arise, there is one in particular that is able to develop a fairly regular, powerful and very general effect: namely, doubt as to whether an apparently living being really is animate and, conversely, doubt as to whether a lifeless object may not in fact be animate—and more precisely, when this doubt only makes itself felt obscurely in one's consciousness. The mood lasts until these doubts are resolved and then usually makes way for another kind of feeling."[25]

Skillfully crafted human figures in a wax museum are one of his prime examples. Even though one knows that these are inanimate figures, they are so lifelike that one cannot help regarding them as real people. The outcome is seeing them as both animate and inanimate. But nothing can be wholly animate *and* wholly inanimate, and it is this that produces the uncanny feeling. To the extent that the uncanny feeling persists, he conjectures, "it is probably a matter of semi-conscious secondary doubts which are repeatedly and automatically aroused anew" or "the lively recollection of the first awkward impression lingering in one's mind."[26]

Having got to this point it is helpful to push back at the translation of *Unheimlich* as "uncanny." The English word does not quite capture the state of mind that Jentsch is gesturing toward.

Something "uncanny" can be simply odd or astonishing—even enjoyably fascinating, as is exemplified by open-mouthed wonder at the "uncanny" feats of a champion athlete. But Jentsch is clearly talking about a *disturbing* quality of experience, one that sends chills down your spine and makes your blood run cold. To find a good English equivalent, just ask yourself how uncanny things such as wax figures in a dimly lit room strike you. One word that is likely to come to mind is "creepy." Uncanny things are creepy things, and the state of mind that they produce is the state of being "creeped out." Now, imagine that the wax figures in the dimly lit room begin to move. They turn their heads toward you, open their mouths, and blink their waxy eyes. How would that make you feel? Here is how Jentsch discusses this kind of scenario, using the example of humanoid automata:

> This peculiar effect makes its appearance even more clearly when imitations of the human form not only reach one's perception, but when on top of everything they appear to be united with certain bodily or mental functions. This is where the impression easily produced by the automatic figures belongs that is so awkward for many people. Once again, those cases must here be discounted in which the objects are very small or very familiar in the course of daily usage. A doll which closes and opens its eyes by itself, or a small automatic toy, will cause no notable sensation of this kind, while on the other hand, for example, the life-size machines that perform complicated tasks, blow trumpets, dance and so forth, very easily give one a feeling of unease.

Sixty-four years after Jentsch's paper, Japanese roboticist Masahiro Mori published a paper that drew the same conclusion. Although very short and highly speculative, Mori's paper has been immensely influential, especially in the cognitive sciences. It is titled "Bukimi No Tani," which was translated into English by the art critic Jasia Reichardt as "The Uncanny Valley."[27] Like the German *Unheimlich*, the Japanese *bukimi* can be rendered as "creepy"—so the title of Mori's paper can equally well be translated as "The Valley of Creepiness." The thrust of the article is straightforward. Mori speculated that as robots become more and more human-like, we will feel more and more comfortable with them until technology reaches the point where robots are almost, but not quite, indistinguishable from human beings. At that point, he suggested, there will be a precipitous drop in the feeling of affinity, and the humanoid robot will be experienced as *bukimi*. He called this "the uncanny valley." Mori made the same prediction about prosthetic limbs. An artificial hand that is not quite indistinguishable from a flesh-and-blood hand will, he supposed, produce feelings of re-pugnance. And just like Jentsch, Mori argued that adding move-ment will only augment the disturbing effect. "Since the negative effects of movement are apparent even with a prosthetic hand," he wrote, "to build a whole robot would magnify the creepiness. This is just one robot. Imagine a craftsman being awakened suddenly in the dead of the night. He searches downstairs for something among a crowd of mannequins in his workshop. If the mannequins started to move, it would be like a horror story."[28]

Mori's use of the expression "horror story" is significant, because there is a quantitative dimension to the uncanny. Uncanny things are on a spectrum extending from the merely creepy (for example, a prosthetic hand) to those that elicit feelings of sheer horror (for example, the moving mannequins). The feeling of horror is not the same as the feeling of fear. As we proceed, I will articulate more clearly what it is that separates horror from fear. For now, though, I want to focus on just one element—one that applies in equal mea-sure to all uncanny things. Things that are uncanny, whether creepy or horrifying, have a peculiar allure that distinguishes them from things that are merely repulsive or terrifying. This is nicely illustrated by Plato's story about Leontius in the *Republic:*

> Leontius, the son of Aglaeon, was on his way up to the town from the Piraeus. As he was walking below the North Wall, on the outside, he saw the public executioner with some dead bodies lying beside him. He wanted to look at the bodies, but at the same time felt disgust and held himself back, but at the same time he was disgusted and turned away. For a time he struggled and covered his eyes. Then, desire got the better of him. He rushed over to where the bodies were, and forced his eyes wide open saying "There you are, curse you. Have a really good look. Isn't it a lovely sight?"[29]

I do not think that "disgust" is the right word for what drove Leontius's rubbernecking impulse. Truly disgusting things do not draw the eye toward them, as these corpses did. Instead of being repelled, Leontius behaved like a person watching a horror film who covers their eyes with their hands when things get intense, but then just can't resist peeking out through the gaps between their fingers.[30]

For all their insightfulness, neither Jentsch nor Mori got to the bottom of the uncanny. To get closer to the core of the kind of uncertainty or ambiguity that makes things seem uncanny, consider this chillingly evocative passage from Arthur Machen's novel *The House of Souls:* "What would your feelings be, seriously, if your cat or your dog began to talk to you, and to dispute with you in human accents? You would be overwhelmed with horror. I am sure of it. And if the roses in your garden sang a weird song, you would go mad. And suppose the stones in the road began to swell and grow before your eyes, and if the pebble that you noticed at night had shot out stony blossoms in the morning?"[31]

Machen's examples are at the horror end of the uncanniness spectrum. He was, after all, a writer of horror fiction. Consider the first example—that of a talking pet. Being confronted with a talking dog would certainly be disorienting, but this would not be because you are uncertain whether this entity is a dog or a human being. Rather, it would be because the talking dog has properties that are unique to dogs (its canine appearance) as well as properties that are unique to humans (the ability to speak). You are not wondering whether this creature is a dog or a human. Your reaction is driven by the fact that it seems to be both, but being a dog is incompatible with being a human. It is not uncertainty that elicits the uncanny feeling, it is *contradiction*. Similar considerations apply to singing roses, and the examples of stones that grow and shoot out blossoms similarly involve an impossible combination of the mineral and the botanical.

Machen's passage points to several fundamental features of uncanny things. The first is that they all involve *categorical contradiction*. Uncanny things seem to transgress the categories that we use to make sense of the world. Whereas Mori's paper was about the categorical boundary between humans and robots (and human limbs and prosthetic limbs), Jentsch had a more expansive view of the sources of uncanniness, and allowed that other kinds of categorical contradiction can elicit this disturbing feeling. This more general conception of categorical contradiction has received experimental support from a study conducted by Eva and Patrick Weiss showing that cognitive conflict occurring at category boundaries need not always involve the category "human," but also that ambiguity about whether or not an entity is human produces the most pronounced effect.

The second feature of Machen's examples is that they all involve things that we think of as natural kinds (although artifacts can figure in them, as is shown by the wax museum and robot examples). And third, they all involve living things (although nonliving things can figure in them, as is shown by the example of the sprouting stones). Now, putting these three elements together, we get the following specification: a thing is uncanny if and only if it is a contradictory living (or once living) thing that violates the boundaries that we take to demarcate biological natural kinds from one another.

A moment's reflection reveals why this might be. As I explained in Chapter 4, we tend to essentialize natural biological kinds, and because essences do not come in degrees—a thing cannot have more or less of them—we take essences to demarcate those kinds *absolutely*. So, if a single entity is categorized as belonging to two different natural kinds, these representations are irreconcilable. A being classified as an insect and as a human being is not felt to be "sort of" an insect and "sort of" a human being—an insect-like human or a humanoid insect—but is represented as completely an insect and completely a human being. Dehumanized people are experienced as uncanny by their dehumanizers, because they violate the human/subhuman boundary. They are conceived as wholly human and as wholly subhuman, but these two representations of the dehumanized person cannot be reconciled with one another. The dehumanizer's mind is pulled in two directions at once, and it cannot settle on either of the two mutually exclusive alternatives. The dehumanizer's consciousness oscillates between them, thereby giving rise to the problem of humanity.

Why are these contradictory, metaphysically transgressive representations so disturbing? To answer that question, we need to draw on the work of a different thinker, who approaches the same conceptual territory from a different direction.

Mary Douglas was a British anthropologist who wrote an extraordinarily influential book, published in 1966, entitled *Purity and Danger*. The book is an anthropological study of ritual uncleanliness. Its basic insight is that whatever does not fit into the framework of categories that one's culture uses to order the world is felt to be dirty, abominable, and polluting. "Dirt is never a unique, isolated event," Douglas writes. "Where there is dirt there is a system. Dirt is the by-product of a systematic ordering and classification of matter, in so far as ordering involves rejecting inappropriate elements. Dirt is the by-product of the systematic ordering and classification of matter. . . . In short, our pollution behavior is the reaction which condemns any object or idea likely to confuse or contradict cherished classifications."[32]

Every culture has some conception of the natural order: a framework of categories that are used to make the world intelligible. And these concepts of the natural order are used to underwrite the social order. Normally, we think of claims as either descriptive or normative. They state either how things are or how they should be. But the form of thinking that Douglas describes does not conform to this pattern. The natural order is how the world is arranged, and it is how the world should be arranged. But there is also a realm of the unnatural. These are unnatural things—things that exist but are outside the natural order. They are harbingers of pollution and chaos. The idea of the unnatural inevitably accompanies systems that purport to describe the natural order, because there are always things that have no proper place in the framework. These anomalous things are experienced as powerful and dangerous, and must therefore be segregated, marginalized, controlled, or destroyed.

Douglas's formulation goes significantly further than those set out by Jentsch and Mori. Unlike theirs, it attends to the social and political underpinnings of classificatory schemes and does not limit the disturbing effect to clashing perceptual (primarily *visual*) signals. For Douglas, abomination is primarily a matter of how we classify things rather than how they appear to us. This comports very well with my theory of dehumanization. Dehumanized people are regarded as anomalous beings, but this is not because of how they appear. We classify them as human on the basis of their appearance, and as subhuman on the basis of what we have been told. And it is this double consciousness of the dehumanized other that derives the most toxic consequences of the dehumanizing process, because it turns people into monsters.

Solving the Problem of Monstrosity

Addressing the problem of humanity in this way goes well beyond the problem itself, and opens the door to a much deeper understanding of facets of the dehumanizing process. Because dehumanizers conceive of those whom they dehumanize as simultaneously human and subhuman, they also think of them as creepy, horrifying, defiling, and this helps to explain why they are driven to dominate, or exterminate, them and why these people are so strongly associated with filth and disease. But it also tells us a lot more, because the solution to the problem of humanity also turns out to be a solution to the problem of monstrosity.

As I mentioned in the preface to this book, there are at least two kinds of dehumanization. Sometimes, dehumanized people are experienced as docile creatures, as beasts of burden or objects of ridicule. We can see it, to give but one example, in the Nazis dehumanization of disabled people. Johann Chapoutot begins his book *The Law of Blood: Thinking and Acting as a Nazi* with the example of eighteen Nazi physicians who were put on trial for murdering fifty-six disabled children as part of the Nazi euthanasia program. The charges against them were dismissed by the Hamburg regional court in 1949. Chapoutot writes, "The hospital's director, Dr. Wilhelm Bayer, objected strenuously to the charge of 'crimes against humanity.' Such a crime, he asserted, 'can only be committed against people, whereas the living creatures that we were required to treat could not be qualified as "human beings."'" Another Nazi physician, Werner Catel, who also participated in the Aktion T4 euthanasia program was interviewed in 1964 in the German magazine *Der Spiegel*. When the journalist pointed out that the death penalty had been abolished in West Germany, Catel responded, "But don't you see that when a jury makes a decision it is always judging human beings, even if they are criminals? We are not talking about humans here, but rather beings that were merely procreated by humans and that will never themselves become humans endowed with reason and a soul."[33]

I call this kind of dehumanization "enfeebling dehumanization." When people are dehumanized in this way, they are not considered to be horrifying, dangerous monsters (the sense of "monster" that I have been using in this book). This qualification is important, because there is a long history of referring to disabled people as "monstrous." I have not had much to say in this book about enfeebling dehumanization. This is not because it is unimportant. It is because it has a different phenomenology and different dynamics from the kind of dehumanization that I have concentrated on here, which I call "demonizing dehumanization." When people are dehumanized in this way, they are regarded as sinister and malevolent. It is in these cases that the problem of monstrosity arises.

Daniel Jonah Goldhagen is one of the few writers who tries to explain the relation between dehumanization and demonization. Goldhagen objects to the use of "dehumanization" in very general sense because it elides two "separate conceptual dimensions." So, instead of subsuming demonization under an umbrella concept of dehumanization, he contrasts the former with the latter:

> A belief (really an assemblage of beliefs) exists that can be properly said to be the *dehumanizing* of others. It is that other people inherently lack qualities fundamental to being fully human in the sense of deserving moral respect, rights, and protection. Such beings are said to lack human capacities and powers and, as

a definitional matter, do not need to be treated as humans. . . . A second belief (also complex and various) is the *demonization* of others. The belief is about other people's moral quality, including their moral intentions. It holds the people to be, literally or figuratively, demonic, morally evil. . . . The dimension of dehumanization is mainly about biological (cognitive, physical, etc.) capacity, held to be impaired. The dimension of dehumanization is mainly about moral character, held to be depraved, or so debased the people might as well be depraved.[34]

I do not think that this way of characterizing the relation between dehumanization and demonization is very helpful. One reason is that it is purely descriptive, without any underlying theoretical structure—rather like classifying chemical elements on the basis of their color rather than on the basis of their microstructure. Second, it does not work very well descriptively. People who are demonized are not simply seen as having poor moral character. In fact, they may be regarded as amoral. What is crucial is that they are regarded as *predatory*—as physically threatening. My third worry about Goldhagen's schema is that the term "demonic" does not have any real theoretical heft. He might just as well have used an ordinary, vernacular term such as "immoral" or "depraved."

Goldhagen's framework leads him to miss or misrepresent certain aspects of dehumanization (in my sense of the word): "Dehumanization and demonization do not necessarily go hand in hand. The dehumanized are not always demonized. Whites enslaving blacks in the American South, and later repressing them with Jim Crow, dehumanized them, deeming them subhumans with diminished intellectual (and moral) capabilities, akin to domesticated, semi-wild animals that, when kept in check, were useful but if let loose could be dangerous. Whites did not construe their slaves, or freed blacks, as malevolent demons bent upon harming them."[35] This passage is accurate up until the final sentence. Think back to my account in Chapter 1 of how Black male victims of lynching (and Black Americans generally) were represented in the mass media of the day. Black men were, unequivocally, represented as dangerous beasts, bent on rape and murder—a dehumanizing stereotype that persists to this day. To claim that Black males, conceived as super-predators, were not demonized is bizarre. In the United States, the image of the Black male is the *paradigmatic* case of demonizing dehumanization.

Goldhagen's misstep here may be due to his thin, atheoretical notion of the demonic. Unlike Jews, who for centuries have been described as literally demonic, Black Americans have rarely been referred to explicitly as demons. This shows how important it is for a theory of dehumanization to have a theoretically rich notion of the demonic. As I use it, "demonic" is a theoretical term of art that is closely connected to but not exactly coextensive with its vernacular meaning. As I use the terms, the demonic is synonymous with the monstrous, and I therefore use them more or less interchangeably.

To give an analysis of what a demon/monster is that can address the problem of monstrosity, it is helpful to turn to the writings of the philosopher Noël Carroll. Carroll is well known for his work on horror fiction. One of the questions that he investigates, and at-tempts to answer, is that of what distinguishes monsters—or in his terminology, "horrific monsters"—from other kinds of beings. Car-roll draws on Douglas's theory of uncleanliness to explain what it is for a thing to be a monster. To count as a monster, he argues, an entity must be physically threatening. If an entity does not pose a physical threat to human beings, then it is not a monster. But phys-ical menace is not sufficient, because there are many physically threatening beings that are not monsters. The female anopheles mosquito—a tiny insect that carries malaria—is physically threat-ening, but it is not a monster. Neither are venomous snakes, or people who commit homicide. All of these beings can be frightening, because fear is the natural response to perceived threat. But they are not *horrifying*, as monsters are.

Carroll argues that monsters have got to be *cognitively* as well as physically threatening. What makes a monster cognitively threatening is its subversion of the natural order. A monster is a being that belongs to two or more incompatible natural kinds simultaneously, "a composite that unites attributes held to be categorically distinct and/or at odds with the cultural scheme of things in unambiguously one, spatio-temporally discrete entity."[36] For Carroll, "Demonically possessed characters typically involve the superimposition of two categorically distinct individuals, the possessee and the possessor, the latter usually a demon, who, in turn, is often a categorically transgressive figure (e.g., a goat-god). Stevenson's most famous monster is two men, Jekyll and Hyde, where Hyde is described as having a simian aspect which makes him appear not quite human. Werewolves mix man and wolf, while shape changers of other sorts compound humans with other species."[37]

I prefer the term "metaphysical threat" to Carroll's "cognitive threat." "Cognitive threat" suggests a threat to a person's mental representations of the world, but the kind of threat that monsters pose *is a threat to the natural order itself.*

Carroll's analysis of fictional monsters is immensely important for the analysis of dehumanization. The most dangerous and destructive kind of dehumanization transforms others into monsters. Members of the dehumanized group are thought to be dangerous. They are said to be vicious, predatory, cruel, destructive. And they are also felt to be metaphysically threatening because they are seen as both human and subhuman. This makes them seem immensely dangerous in the eyes of their dehumanizers, and explains why it is that although dehumanized people are typically among the most vulnerable members of a population, they are typically regarded as overwhelmingly dangerous. Also, because it is almost always male members of the dehumanized group that are regarded as *physically* threatening, these human monsters are almost always male.[38]

It is important to bear in mind that, in my view, making people into monsters is a *consequence* of dehumanization rather than its *aim*. The aim of dehumanization is the demotion of others to a lower-than-human metaphysical rank, to disactivate inhibitions against harming them. The aim of dehumanization is to turn people into animals, but because it is next to impossible to completely shut off awareness of their humanity, it turns them into monsters instead.

CHAPTER THIRTEEN

Last Words and Loose Ends

We are nearly at the end now. In this, the final chapter, I want to recap some of the main points that I have made, and then draw out some of their further implications, which I could not seamlessly incorporate elsewhere in the text.

First, the recapitulation. *Homo sapiens* are ultrasocial animals, with powerful inhibitions against performing acts of violence against members of our own kind. However, we also have the capacity for means-ends deliberation, and the imaginative horsepower to envisage future possibilities. Because of our cognitive gifts, we are aware that harming, killing, or oppressing others can be advantageous to ourselves and members of our own community. We can take their resources for ourselves, create Lebensraum, exploit their bodies and their labor, and so on. The function of dehumanization is to selectively disable inhibitions against performing acts like these. Dehumanizing beliefs are often entrenched ideological beliefs that proliferated because at some point in time they advantaged one group of people at the expense of another. Such beliefs can lose their causal efficacy, and become latent, but they can be reignited by changes in a social ecology that is hospitable to them, including effective dehumanizing propaganda.

Thanks to our ultrasocial nature, we cannot help responding to other members of our species as human beings. When we look into the eyes of another, we cannot help but see another human being. And this experience of "seeing human" triggers inhibitions against doing violence to them. These inhibitions are strong, but they are not insurmountable. Our deference to epistemic authority, combined with a propensity for psychological essentialism and hierarchical thinking, leaves us open to accepting that some of these others who appear human are not really human, and this helps us to disable or override the inhibitions against doing violence against them. However, even when we adopt the view that these others are subhuman under the influence of ideology or propaganda, we cannot help also seeing them as human. In consequence of this, when we dehumanize others we conceive of them both as completely human and completely subhuman. And, as I explained in Chapter 12, we experience them as transgressing natural boundaries, and therefore as uncanny (per Ernst Jentsch and Masahiro Mori) or abominable (per Mary Douglas). When we also believe them to be physically dangerous, we experience them as monsters (per Noël Carroll).

This account of dehumanization provides a response to the challenge posed by Stanley Cavell, Kwame Anthony Appiah, and Kate Manne, among others. Once we recognize that dehumanized people are conceived not just as less than human animals, but as disturbing amalgams of humanity and subhumanity, their dehumanizers' recognition of their humanity is no longer puzzling, and need not lead to doubts about the reality of dehumanizing states of mind. And it is no longer difficult to understand why dehumanizers so often think of their victims as monstrous or demonic beings. It is the dehumanizer's nagging awareness of the other's humanity that gives dehumanization its distinctive psychological flavor. Ironically, it is our inability to regard other people as nothing but animals that leads to unimaginable cruelty and destructiveness.

Partial Humanity

Often, people who write about dehumanization claim that we think of dehumanized people as not being *fully* human or as *less* human than ourselves. They write about humanness as a property that is attributed to others in degrees: just as a person can be more or less tall, or more or less sunburned, they can be more or less human. I pointed out in Chapter 8 that this way of looking at things flies in the face of the basic premise of psychological essentialism, which demands that essences are an all-or-nothing affair—you either have one or you don't—with no gray area in between. So, if people think that belonging to a natural kind is the same as possessing the essence of that kind, and being human is belonging to the natural kind "human," then the idea of a semihuman being does not make sense.

However, if we listen to what people actually say, they sometimes speak as if they see humanness as an incremental property. This way of speaking even shows up in dehumanizing propaganda. For example, the SS booklet *Der Untermensch* discussed in Chapter 12 states, "The subhuman is a biological creature, crafted by nature, which has hands, legs, eyes and mouth, even the semblance of a brain. Nevertheless, this terrible creature *is only a partial human being*" (emphasis added). The idea that humanness comes in degrees is a challenge to my account of dehumanization, which is predicated on the idea that attributions of essences—including the human essence—are absolute and categorical. To meet this challenge, I need to give a plausible account of how the notion of a partial human being can be squared with the claim that attributing humanness to a person is attributing a human essence to them. We can start with the example from *Der Untermensch*. The authors say that the *Untermensch* outwardly resembles a human being (has hands, legs, eyes, and so on), but they also say, quite explicitly, that the *Untermensch* is not a human being at all. ("Not all of those, who appear human are in fact so. Woe to him who forgets it!") I cannot see any way to explain this contradiction except by the thesis that the monstrous *Untermensch* is simultaneously human and subhuman, and therefore "partially" human only in an extended and misleading sense.

My account of dehumanization also clarifies another puzzling statement in *Der Untermensch*: "Although it has features similar to a human, the subhuman is lower on the spiritual and psychological scale than any animal." If dehumanizing others means conceiving of them simply as animals, asserting that they are "lower" than any animal does not make any sense. How can an animal be lower than any animal? However, this sentence does make sense when considered against the background of the transformation of dehumanized people into monsters, because no matter how repugnant nonhuman animals might seem, they are nowhere near as vile as monsters are.

There is a different way of looking at talk about partial humanity, which does not really apply to cases of dehumanization (in my strict sense) but does apply to cases that are easily mistaken for them. Sometimes, "not fully human" is used in a way similar to "not fully grown" or "not fully cooked." In such contexts, full humanity is understood as an outcome of a process of development. This view holds that people become human by degrees over time. But it allows that some people are developmentally arrested and therefore only incompletely human. This is how Aristotle conceived of those whom he called barbarians.[1] This notion of incompleteness has often been used to characterize marginalized or oppressed groups, including people with disabilities and women. The idea that humanness is a state that one attains, if at all, to a greater or lesser extent is bound up with the idea that being human is having a human essence. I pointed out in Chapter 4 that the notion of development plays an important role in the essentialist framework. Insofar as people are psychological essentialists, they picture development as the unfolding of an essence over time. The oak is concealed in the acorn. Over time, the oak unpacks itself, emerging from its tiny shell, drawing resources from its environment. But this process can go wrong, resulting in a deformed oak. There are two ways that this can happen. One is that there are insufficient or unsuitable resources to facilitate normal development—there is not enough sunlight, or water, or nutrients in the soil, or whatever. The other is that there is something defective inside the acorn itself, which no amount of environmental provision can fix. And the same is supposed to hold true of human development according to folk theory. The whole human being is supposed to be contained in the genes (or some other stand-in for the human essence), and the process of development resulting in a fully-fledged human being is understood as the unfolding of that essence over time.

Once upon a time, scientists and philosophers endorsed this picture. From the days of Aristotle right up to the nineteenth century, many serious thinkers were "preformationists" who believed that the form of a whole organism was contained in miniature in its father's semen (the mother's only role was to fill that form out with matter). Much later, preformationism gave way to the no less essentialistic thesis of "hereditarianism," which is the view that the form of the whole organism is located in the genome. For many (probably most) of us, this is a very intuitive way of looking at development, even though it is egregiously wrong. In reality, development is a complex, multifactorial, causal process. The human being is not latent "in" their genes, and the genes do not "unfold." Each of us is an ongoing *construction* from multiple resources, including but not limited to our genes and the intracellular machinery that builds protein from them.

Sometimes, when people talk about some people being more human or less human than others, this makes most sense in the context of this essentialist version of development. Looked at through an essentialist lens, a person is said to be human—that is, to manifest humanness—to the degree that they realize their human essence. A person who has realized that essence more fully than another person will consequently be considered to be "more human" than that other person. This idea plays into certain versions of sexism and ableism: women and disabled people are considered categorically human—by which I mean human by virtue of possessing a human essence—but chronically defective, incomplete, or deformed because they are unable to fully realize that essence.

Abortion

People who are morally opposed to abortion sometimes recruit the notion of dehumanization to bolster their case. From time to time my own work has been appropriated to that end. The pattern of reasoning involved is that people who support the right to choose are in fact supporting murdering unborn infants. Murdering infants is unequivocally wrong, so to dodge moral blame, these people dehumanize unborn children, a tactic that is reflected in the language that they use. Journalist Kathleen Parker, for one, writes: "When we use language to disguise reality—whether the developing human baby is a 'clump of cells, a 'fetus,' or, even, a 'product of termination'—we move ever-closer to the dehumanization of us all."[2]

In an article titled "Is Dehumanization Always and Intrinsically Unjust?," Michael Spielman describes having written an email to me with the following question: "Socially speaking, have you ever encountered a scenario in which you found 'subhuman' to be a legitimate classification? Your book is saturated with examples of human beings who have been erroneously categorized as 'less than human,' for all sorts of despotic ends. But did you ever come across a case of dehumanization that you found to be morally defensible? If not, would it be fair to say that any effort to dehumanize a group of human beings is always and intrinsically unjust?"[3] I remember Spielman's email. It was polite and respectful, unlike some messages that I have received from people who are opposed to abortion on moral grounds. As he mentions in his article, I did not respond to it, but this was neither because I would have been forced to grapple with a challenge to my own views nor because I was too busy. It was because I did not want to become entangled in what I took then (and take now) to be an important issue for a dehumanization theorist to address without having thought it through properly.

In spite of its title, Spielman's article does not address the question of whether dehumanization is *always* unjust. It answers that question in the affirmative, asserts that abortion is predicated on the dehumanization of the unborn, and concludes that abortion is intrinsically unjust: "It is no exaggeration to say that abortion is ground zero in the contemporary intersect between public policy and dehumanization. Can you think of any other institution that is propped up on the explicit dehumanization of its victims? Though racism remains a massive global problem, nobody argues in public that immigrants, refugees, or ethnic minorities are less than fully human—and yet this is exactly the argument that's being made in the context of abortion."[4]

Spielman's argument is quite similar to that of others who have used my work to underwrite a "pro-life" position. But whatever the merits or demerits of the pro-life position, my theory of dehumanization does not justify it. The central problem with the argument that people who are pro-choice dehumanize unborn children (to use the language preferred by pro-life advocates) is the claim that unborn children are dehumanized *as such*. I say "as such" because it is true that the unborn are sometimes dehumanized. During the Third Reich, Nazis dehumanized embryos gestating in the wombs of Jewish women. But (and this is crucial) these Jews-to-be were not dehumanized because of their embryonic status. They were dehumanized because of the racial status of their parent. I was clear in *Less Than Human* that in my view dehumanization should be understood as the attribution of the essence of a subhuman animal to a member of our species. But this is not what is going on when someone describes the contents of a woman's womb as a blob of tissue rather than a baby. A blob of tissue is not a subhuman animal, and referring to it as such is not tantamount to referring to it as a cockroach. Terms like "blob of tissue" might come under the heading of "dehumanization" according to some theories of dehumanization, but not according to mine. In saying this I am not denying that abortion is inherently immoral (and I am not affirming it either). I am saying that it is a mistake to infer the wrongness of abortion from the wrongness of dehumanization.

There is a further question to ask about this. Why might this person, and others who use my work in this way, have thought that the unborn are dehumanized? I suspect that it springs from an essentialist conception of the human. If that is the case, then a pregnant woman has a human being growing inside of her from the moment of conception, and from that point onward, that human's growth and differentiation is the unfolding of its human essence over time. From this perspective, referring to the embryo as anything other than a human being sounds like a denial of its humanity. And, arguably, it is this denial that makes taking its life seem to be permissible.

Of course, I reject both essentialism and the idea that the term "human" functions as a natural kind term. There is no such thing as a human essence of the sort that psychological essentialism postulates, and it is therefore false to claim that from conception onward, there is a being with a human essence growing inside a woman's womb. What *is* true is that at some point or other, this thing inside of the woman comes to be regarded as a human being. However, if my analysis of the concept of the human is correct, it is wrong-headed to ask at what point the developing embryo becomes a human being. As I argued in Chapter 8, "human" is a status that we accord to those whom we regard as one of us. Strange as it sounds, there are no purely biological facts that distinguish what beings are human from what beings are not, and that means that there are no facts to adjudicate the question of when an embryo becomes a human being. The dispute between those who believe that *human* life begins at conception and those who believe that it starts at some later point, and the related dispute about at what point, if any, it is illegitimate to terminate a pregnancy, is ultimately—like all ethical conflicts—a dispute about the kind of world the disputing parties want to live in.

Superhumans

Although dehumanized people are typically some of the most vulnerable and marginalized members of a society, they are often thought of as formidably threatening, because they are both malevolent and endowed with powers that exceed those of ordinary human beings. In persecuting the dehumanized group, those in power usually see themselves as acting in their own self-defense rather than as bearing down on a marginalized minority. My account of dehumanization explains why this is the case.

We can begin with the Jews. During the Middle Ages, Christians commonly believed that Jews possessed supernatural powers, which they received from their master, the devil, who gave them a talent for sorcery. Joshua Trachtenberg writes,

> Magic was the technique whereby Satan promoted the designs of those evil humans who fought with him to destroy and overthrow Christendom. The widely heralded collusion between Satan and the Jews in bringing about the death of Jesus lent itself perfectly to the elaboration of this theme. Several medieval dramatic versions of the Passion exhibit the Jews, instigated by Satan, working their most potent charms against Jesus, mixing a typical witches' potion with all the lurid ceremonial of the well-known witch-cults, while the devil solicitously su-

pervises the operation. What more natural, in these circumstances, than that the Jews should be feared and hated as
Europe's peerless sorcerers.[5]

The idea that Jews possessed occult powers persisted for centuries. From around the late eighteenth century onward, it morphed
into the secular fantasy of a mysterious, international Jewish conspiracy that holds the world in its sinister grip.[6] The particulars of
the image of the evil, supremely powerful Jew—its properties and
the web of associations surrounding it—was the outcome of the
unique cultural and historical circumstances of European Jewry.

Other dehumanized groups with different histories and dwelling
in different cultural and historical circumstances are demonized
differently. But the common thread running through all of these
demonizations is the attribution of unnatural powers to members
of the dehumanized group. The idea that some people have such
powers can take two forms. It can involve supernatural powers, such
as we find in medieval beliefs about Jews and Roma. However, the
notion that whole groups of people have supernatural powers has
not survived the transformation of the medieval world into the
modern one. The image of the Jew as literally demonic and adept
at the black arts is virtually extinct in today's secular societies. But
people persist in attributing what I call *preternatural* abilities to
members of dehumanized populations. Preternatural abilities are
ordinary abilities taken to an extraordinary degree. So, to continue
with the example, at some point between the late middle ages and
the twentieth century, Jews lost their supernatural aura, but came
to be seen as diabolically intelligent.

The preternatural powers attributed by Whites to Black Americans were of a different kind. In the decades following the civil war,
and in particular after the collapse of reconstruction, there emerged
an image of the Black male as preternaturally strong, sexually

voracious, violent, and insensitive to pain. It is still part of the White American imaginary today. In 2014, three psychologists, Adam Waytz, Kelly Marie Hoffman, and Sophie Trawalter, published research purporting to show that White Americans tend to attribute extraordinary powers to Black people, a phenomenon that they called "superhumanization."[7] And in an article that they subsequently contributed to the *Washington Post*, they argued that Darren Wilson, the police officer who fatally shot Black teenager Michael Brown in Ferguson, Missouri, on August 9, 2014, may have superhumanized Brown. The authors quote Wilson's testimony to the grand jury:

> The only way I can describe it, it looks like a demon, how angry he looked. . . . He turns, and when he looked at me, he made like a grunting, like aggravated sound and he starts, he turns and he's coming back towards me. . . . At this point it looked like he was almost bulking up to run through the shots, like it was making him mad that I'm shooting at him. And the face that he had was looking straight through me, like I wasn't even there, I wasn't even anything in his way.

They conclude that although it is "unclear whether Wilson's 'it' refers to Brown's facial expression, or Brown himself, the use of the term, 'demon,' both sub-humanizes and super-humanizes Brown, clearly casting him outside of humanity."[8] Of course, this is highly speculative. But there are other, unambiguous cases of White police officers seeing Black males as larger and more formidable than they really are.

Psychologists John Paul Wilson, Kurt Hugenberg, and Nicolas O. Rule conducted an experimental study that demonstrated that White people tend to have exaggerated perceptions of the size and strength of young Black men. They begin their paper describing the study with this example: "On April 30th, 2014, an unarmed

Black man named Dontre Hamilton was shot 14 times and killed by a White police officer in Milwaukee, Wisconsin. The officer later testified that Hamilton had a 'muscular build' and 'most definitely would have overpowered . . . me or pretty much any officer I can think of, to tell you the truth. He was just that big, that muscular' . . . . This account is contradicted by the autopsy, in which the medical examiner reported that Hamilton was 5'7" and 169 pounds."[9] This sort of bias also infects White people's perceptions of Black children, as is illustrated by the examples of Tamir Rice and Trayvon Martin:

> Tamir Rice was a 12-year-old Black boy shot and killed by a Cleveland police officer in November, 2014, while he played with a toy gun in a park. A representative of the Cleveland Police later explained the shooting by saying "Tamir Rice is in the wrong. He's menacing. He's 5-feet-7, 191 pounds. He wasn't that little kid you're seeing in pictures. He's a 12-year-old in an adult body." . . . In the wake of the 2012 shooting of Trayvon Martin (an unarmed Black teen in Florida), images circulated depicting Martin as older and larger than he was. In one notorious example, people widely shared a photograph of a man with facial tattoos in what was purported to be an up-to-date representation of Martin. In fact, it was a rap musician known as Game who was in his 30s in the photograph. . . . In each of these cases, people attempting to explain the events post hoc included appeals to the size and threat posed by the targets.[10]

In a related vein, psychologist Philip Atiba Goff and his colleagues examined the question of whether Black boys are granted the same childhood protections as their White peers in encounters with law enforcement. They found that police officers who implicitly associate Black people with apes, which the psychologists reasonably interpreted as a sign of dehumanization, also regarded Black boys as less childlike and innocent than White boys. Unsurprisingly, those police officers who associated Black people with apes also tended to treat Black children in custody more harshly than those who didn't. In a related study, Goff and his colleagues found that mainly White female undergraduate students who unconsciously associated Black people with apes overestimated the age of Black boys, sometimes by more than four years.[11]

Why do dehumanizers overattribute powers to those whom they regard as less than human? On the face of it, it seems deeply puzzling, but Carroll's theory of monstrosity points us toward a solution. Carroll addresses the seeming paradox in the context of horror fiction:

> It is a remarkable fact about creatures of horror that they do not seem to be of sufficient strength to make a grown man cower. A teetering zombie or a severed hand would appear incapable of mustering enough force to overpower a coordinated six-year-old. Nevertheless, they are presented as unstoppable, and this seems psychologically acceptable to audiences. This might be explained by noting Douglas' claim that culturally impure objects are generally taken to be invested with magical powers. . . . Monsters in works of horror, by extension, then, may be similarly imbued with awesome powers in virtue of their impurity.[12]

Transplanting Carroll's thoughts from the imaginary realm of horror fiction to the real-world horror of dehumanization, it seems that the metaphysically threatening character of dehumanized people amplifies whatever physical threat they are imagined to present. An ordinary Black male is transformed into a horrifically violent superpredator, bent on rape and destruction, and a normal Jew is morphed into a fiendishly intelligent and scheming one. The process leading to dehumanization almost always begins with the image of the members of a marginalized group as physically threatening. But once they are dehumanized they are transformed into entities that are even more terrifying to their persecutors, who then implement more and more extreme methods against them in an ascending spiral of violence.

Although it might seem very strange, I think that it is helpful to think about the transformation of dehumanized people into monsters with the help of a principle from formal logic called the "principle of explosion." The principle of explosion states that anything follows from a contradiction. In other words, you can infer anything from a contradiction. So, if I were to assert that I am over six feet tall and that I am under six feet tall, I could infer any other statement (for example, "Elephants live on Jupiter") from it. The principle of explosion sounds bizarre, and is certainly not intuitive. But I think it has an intuitive counterpart that explains more fully why the metaphysically threatening character of dehumanized people amplifies their perceived dangerousness. Suppose that you were to encounter a contradictory being—an impossible fusion of natural kinds. For instance, imagine glancing across the room where you are sitting, and seeing a severed hand scuttling toward you like a large, fleshy spider. This would be terrifying, but it is not obvious why. How much damage could a severed hand do? But then the thought occurs, "If a hand can be a spider, then who knows what damage it could do?" In other words, once the natural order has been violated, then there is no safety. Some of the most effective horror films effectively trade on this response. For instance, in Wes Craven's *A Nightmare on Elm Street* the sense of the collapse of any reliable order makes the antagonist Freddie Kruger even more terrifying than he would otherwise be.[13] The metaphysical counterpart of "Anything (logically) follows from a contradiction" is "If a contradictory being exists, then anything can happen."

Managing Monsters

This last point leads me to my final topic. Throughout the book, I have stressed that dehumanization is something that happens in people's heads. It is a way of thinking about others, rather than a way of treating them. But, as many of the examples in this book illustrate, the strange folk metaphysics of dehumanization is intimately bound up with horrifically cruel and destructive forms of human behavior. It is this causal connection between dehumanizing thought and the behavior it motivates that makes the investigation into dehumanization so urgent and so necessary.

There are various social practices that are underpinned by dehumanizing states of mind. Some of them, such as the institution of slavery, are enshrined in ancient tradition, while others, like the gas chambers of Auschwitz, are recent innovations. In the remainder of this chapter, I want to take a bird's-eye view of the ways that dehumanized people are "managed," with the help of Mary Douglas's account of how traditional societies manage ritually impure, boundary-transgressing things. Douglas lists five ways that such societies handle "aberrant forms," and each of them maps onto ways that "aberrant" dehumanized people have been, and sometimes continue to be, treated by their persecutors.

One method is to try to *eliminate* the anomalousness of the thing, so that it fits neatly into an accepted metaphysical category and loses its threatening character. For example, Douglas tells us that the Nuer of Sudan regard deformed babies—so-called monstrous births—as violating the distinction between human beings and subhuman animals. They resolve the contradiction by relegating these babies completely to the animal category, in a manner that makes it permissible to kill them. She says, "the Nuer treat monstrous births as baby hippopotamuses, accidentally born to humans and, with this labelling, the appropriate action is clear. They gently lay them in the river where they belong."[14]

As we have seen, dehumanized people are felt to be metaphysically threatening because they are believed to transgress the human/subhuman boundary, and therefore violate the natural order. Although the dehumanizing impulse seeks to demote them to a lower rank on the natural hierarchy, this has the consequence of removing them from the natural order entirely. As Johann Chapoutot astutely points out, Nazi writings "sketched out a hierarchy of living things that was unique to Nazism. Contrary to what is often claimed, this hierarchy was not a scale with Aryans at the top and Jews at the bottom. Rather, it was a far more complex topology, with Aryans . . . at the top, followed by mixed peoples, and then, at the bottom, Slavic, Black, and Asian individuals. Jews had no place in it at all."[15]

Likewise, in the United States free Black people had no place in either the natural order or the social order that was imagined to reflect it. In the aftermath of the Civil War, Whites demonized Black Americans explicitly in relation to Satan, the ultimate transgressor of natural law. For example, Hinton Rowan Helper—whom Lincoln appointed as US consul in Buenos Aires—wrote in his virulently racist 1867 book *Nojoque:*

> If, in a spirit of rebellion against the laws of nature, we love the negroes and other black things, we shall thereby only gain the low distinction of gratifying the devil; but if, on the other hand, assuming antagonism toward the imps of Africa, toward the prince of darkness, and toward all the other monstrous representatives of blackness and abomination, "we hate them with perfect hatred," as they deserve to be hated, and as we are required and expected to hate them, we shall thereby render highly acceptable and pleasing service to the Deity; and, continuing to

please him, will secure for ourselves unlimited and everlasting felicity in heaven.[16]

In his masterful essay on spectacle lynchings as rituals of human sacrifice, Orlando Patterson emphasizes that this practice grew out of southern Whites' contradictory mental representations of recently emancipated Blacks. "The association of 'blackness' first with humans, then with beasts, leads to the dissociation of 'blackness' from both, thereby becoming an object of intense contemplation." To the White southerner, a black person was "a black beast, the archetypal *bête noire*." Patterson continues: "Then, with the horror of the slave's legal emancipation and employment as a soldier during the Civil War, several incongruous associations took place: black = beast = free; black = beast = man; black = beast = white status (soldier). It was enough to drive all good Southerners into a frenzy not only of outrage but of fear. . . . The ritual of sacrifice violently emphasized and dissociated the incongruity, in the process first isolating and then reconstructing the only acceptable association of qualities: freedom = manhood = white status."[17]

Like the Nuer's solution to the problem of so-called monstrous births, one way that dehumanizers try to remove the element of metaphysical threat is by stripping others of their humanity entirely. This has the function of transforming frightening monsters into tractable animals, and often involves extremely degrading and humiliating practices. For example, historian Mia Bay points out that formerly enslaved African Americans reported "being fed like pigs, bred like hogs, sold like horses, driven like cattle, worked like dogs, and beaten like mules."[18] Frederick Douglass recounted in his autobiography, "Our food was coarse corn meal boiled. This was called mush. It was put into a large wooden tray or trough, and set down upon the ground. The children were then called, like so many pigs, and like so many pigs they would come and devour the mush; some with oyster-shells, others with pieces of shingle, some with naked hands, and none with spoons." Others told interviewers, "Dey was a trough out in de yard [where] dey poured de mush and milk in an us chillum an de dogs would all crowd 'roun it and eat together . . . we sho' had to be in a hurry 'bout it cause de dogs would get it all if we didn't," and "The white folks et the white flour and the niggers et the shorts . . . the hogs was also fed the shorts."[19]

The hypothesis that these acts were attempts to put these people in their metaphysical place by stripping away their humanity and reducing them completely to a condition of animality may add another layer of complexity to the response to Kate Manne's skeptical argument that I described in Chapter 12. Recall that Manne argued that when a White cop called Black protesters "fucking animals" he was trying to put them down rather than make a claim about the type of beings they are. But he might have been doing both. He might have been engaging in the verbal equivalent of forcing Black people to eat out of pig troughs, denuding them of their threatening humanness (threatening, because it makes them monsters), and trying to turn them into animals. Of course, I am not claiming knowledge of what was really going on in this man's mind. None of us can know that. I am only opening up an alternative possibility for making sense of his behavior, as well as other behaviors like it.

Another approach is to exert *control* over the anomalous item. Douglas tells us, by way of illustration, that in some cultures cocks that crow at night rather than in the morning are regarded as anomalous. "If their necks are promptly wrung," she writes, "they do not live to contradict the definition of a cock as a bird that crows at dawn."[20] Dehumanizers exercise control over dehumanized people in so many ways that it would take whole volumes to fully enumerate them. To give just one example, the practice of slave branding, which has been practiced for thousands of years, was a means for asserting control over enslaved people. As Frederick Douglass described it, "A person was tied to a post, and his back, or such other part as was to be branded, laid bare; the iron was then delivered red hot, and applied to the quivering flesh, imprinting upon it the name of the monster who claimed the slave."[21] Murder, torture, incarceration, threats, discriminatory laws, and economic exploitation are just a few of the ways that dehumanizers have brought dehumanized people to heel.

The third strategy is *avoidance*. We see this in practices such as apartheid and in laws against miscegenation. The fourth is *labeling*. Sometimes these labels are tangible, physical things, especially in cases where it is hard to distinguish members of the dehumanized group from those who dehumanize them. During the thirteenth century, and then again during the Third Reich, Jews were forced to wear distinctive clothing and cloth badges to set them apart from Aryans. And during the Jim Crow era, "To dress ostentatiously (that is, like middle-class whites) . . . was to risk attack and derision." Whites would wait at railway stations to meet uniformed Black veterans returning from World War I and "cut the buttons and armaments off their clothes, make em get out of them clothes, make em pull them uniforms off and if they didn't have another suit of clothes . . . make em walk in their underwear."[22] But labeling does not require physical tokens like branding, yellow stars, or shabby clothes to be effective. Dehumanized people are labeled through the vocabulary that the dominant group imposes on them.

The final technique that Douglas mentions is the mastery achieved by *ritual practices* that restore order. Anyone familiar with the relevant historical literature will know that lynchings are often described as "rituals" with the purpose of affirming and restoring the White supremacist social order in the wake of emancipation. Lynchings and other kinds of anti-Black terrorism were motivated by what historian Joel Williamson aptly called "a rage for order."[23] They were rites designed to restore harmony to the world by putting Black men—human animals—back in their social-cum-metaphysical place, and thereby confirming White people, those putatively superior human beings, in theirs. As historian of lynching Amy Louise Wood observes, "Lynching spectacles . . . did more than dramatize or reflect an undisputed white supremacy or attest to an uncontested white solidarity. . . . The rituals of lynching themselves, in their torturous dehumanization of black men, enacted and embodied the core beliefs of white supremacist ideology, creating public displays of bestial black men in visible contrast to strong and commanding white men. Lynching allowed white southerners to perform and attach themselves to these beliefs—to literally inhabit them."[24]

Some lynchings were elaborately ritualized events. These were spectacles such as the lynchings of Henry Smith and Sam Hose that I described in Chapter 1. In the essay quoted above, Patterson communicates the religious character of lynchings.[25] Spectacle lynchings were part of the southern religion of the "lost cause." They were rites with the purpose of affirming, and trying to bring about, the return of a way of life that southern Whites had lost with their defeat in the Civil War. "Although rarely made explicit," Patterson writes, "there is no denying the profound religious significance that these sacrificial murders had for Southerners. . . . Fundamentalist preachers not only condoned the sacrifices but actively incited many of them. They were at the vanguard of such organizations as the Ku Klux Klan."[26] Patterson perfectly captures the ritualistic core of lynching and the socially and metaphysically anomalous position of the free Black man in White Southern society when he writes, "Spiritually, the degenerate masterless slave who dared to assert his manhood or freedom became the ideal sacrificial victim. As ex-slave, he symbolized the human wickedness and sin that haunted the fundamentalist souls of his executioners. And as 'black beast,' he could be horribly sacrificed, without any sense of guilt, to a wrathful, vengeful God as a prime offering of blood and human flesh and as the soul of his enemy, Satan."[27]

———

When writing a book, it is difficult to know when to stop. This is especially true of a book like this one. The ideas that I have set out here, and the examples that I have gathered together, have occupied my mind for more than a decade. Dehumanization is a subject that is very important to understand, but which few people have tried seriously to understand. In this book, I have told the best story about it that I have been able to muster, but I am sure that, despite my most strenuous intellectual efforts, some of my thinking is mistaken. Hopefully, others will join in the conversation, correct my errors, make new discoveries, and move the story further toward the truth.

NOTES

INDEX

NOTES

Epigraph: Karl Jaspers, *The Origin and Goal of History* (London: Rout-ledge and K. Paul, 1953), 149.

Preface

1. Elie Ngarambe interviewed in Mike DeWitt, dir., *Worse Than War* (Sherman Oaks, CA: JTN Productions, 2009), aired October 18, 2009, on PBS. *Worse Than War* can be viewed online at Loriann Clod, "Geno-cide Worse Than War Full Length Documentary Pbs," YouTube video, 1:54:16, May 24, 2015, https://www.youtube.com/watch?v=vsMe7QvqpaU. The film is based on Daniel Jonah Goldhagen, *Worse Than War: Geno-cide, Eliminationism, and the Ongoing Assault on Humanity* (New York: Public Affairs, 2009).

2. One might query this interpretation of "same flesh" as indicating "same kind of being." See, for example, the discussion in Peter Swirski, *From Literature to Biterature: Lem, Turing, Darwin, and Explorations in Com-puter Literature, Philosophy of Mind, and Cultural Evolution* (Toronto: McGill-Queen's University Press, 2013), 92–93. I have assumed—I be-lieve plausibly—that Ngarambe used the term in much the same way as it was used in premodern Europe to indicate affinity. See David Warren Sabean, "Descent and Alliance: Cultural Meanings of Blood in the Baroque," in *Blood and Kinship: Matter for Metaphor from Ancient Rome to the Present,* ed. Christopher H. Johnson, Bernhard Jussen, David Warren Sabean, and Simon Teuscher (London: Berghahn, 2013), 144–174.

1. What Is Dehumanization?

1. I capitalize "Black" and "White" to indicate that I am using them as racial categories and use the lower case when I am talking about color categories.

2. Several accounts give a figure of 10,000 onlookers. According to the description published in the *Dallas News,* there were 15,000. See Henry

Vance, *Facts in the Case of the Horrible Murder of Little Myrtle Vance and Its Fearful Expiation at Paris, Texas, February 1st, 1893* (Paris, TX: P. L. James, 1893). Ida B. Wells's informant, the Reverend King, who was present at the lynching, reported that there were 20,000 people present. See Ida B. Wells, *The Red Record: Lynchings in the United States, 1892–1893–1894* (Chicago: Donohue and Henneberry, 1894). Smith's dying agonies were recorded on a primitive gramophone roll for further entertainment, and as late as 1909 White New Yorkers were entertained in movie theaters with photographic displays of Smith's lynching and the recording of his dying screams. See Amy Louise Wood, *Lynching and Spectacle: Witnessing Racial Violence in America, 1890–1940* (Durham, NC: University of North Carolina Press, 2011). However, this recording may have been a reenactment. See Gustavus Stadler, "Never Heard Such a Thing: Lynching and Phonographic Modernity," *Social Text* 28, no. 102 (2010): 87–105.

3. "Burned at the Stake," *Saint Paul Daily Globe.* February 2, 1893.

4. "Burned at the Stake," 1.

5. Grace Elizabeth Hale, *Making Whiteness: The Culture of Segregation in the South, 1890–1940* (New York: Vintage, 1999); Orlando Patterson, *Rituals of Blood: Consequences of Slavery in Two American Centuries* (New York: Civitas, 1998).

6. "Tortured Him at the Stake," *New York Sun*, 1, https://www.loc.gov/resource/sn83030272/1893-02-02/ed-1/?sp=1&r=0.504,0.091,0.221,0.08,0.

7. Wells hired a Pinkerton detective to investigate the case. He informed her that the claim that the murdered child had been mutilated was false, and she believed that the falsification was for the sake of whipping up enthusiasm for mob violence. See Wells, *The Red Record*, 19.

8. Cited in Wood, *Making Whiteness*, 65.

9. Cited in Vance, *Facts in the Case*, 93.

10. Cited in Vance, *Facts in the Case*, 97–98.

11. Cited in Vance, *Facts in the Case*, 100.

12. Cited in Phillip Dray, *At the Hands of Persons Unknown: The Lynching of Black America* (New York: Modern Library, 2003), 78.

13. Junius M. Early, *An Eye for an Eye; or, The Fiend and the Fagot: An Unvarnished Account of the Burning of Henry Smith at Paris, Texas, February 1, 1893, and the Reason He Was Tortured* (Paris, TX: Marshall's Printing House, 1893), 36.

14. Atticus G. Haygood, "The Black Shadow in the South," *Forum* (October 1893): 167–175.

15. Vance, *Facts in the Case*, 3.

16. For a powerful, historically rich, and conceptually nuanced study of the social construction of black masculinity and the derogation of Black males, see Tommy J. Curry, *The Man-Not: Race, Class, Gender and the Dilemmas of Black Manhood* (Philadelphia: Temple University Press, 2017).

17. Dray, *At the Hands of Persons Unknown*, 4–5 and 14.

18. This was relatively brief. The torture of lynching victims could last as long as twelve hours.

19. Dray, *At the Hands of Persons Unknown*, 13.

20. "Negro Tortured and Burned to Death at Stake," *San Francisco Call* 85, no. 145 (April 24, 1899).

21. W. E. B. DuBois, "My Evolving Program for Negro Freedom," in *What the Negro Wants*, ed. Rayford W. Logan (Notre Dame, IN: University of Notre Dame Press, 1944), 53.

22. It is relevant that the English term "maroon," which was by slaveholders to denote escaped slaves, was derived from the Spanish *cimarrón* meaning "wild"—a term that was used for cattle that had escaped and gone feral.

23. Cited in Leon F. Litwack, *Trouble in Mind: Black Southerners in the Age of Jim Crow* (New York: Vintage Books, 1999), 284.

24. William Cowart, letter to the editor, *The Crisis* 2, no. 1 (May 1911): 32.

25. Cited in Vance, *Facts in the Case*, 98–99. Notice the use of the word "infested," which would normally be used to refer to destructive vermin or insects, and also notice that the word "communities"—which is used only with reference to human beings—seems here to be restricted to Whites.

26. *Congressional Record*, 57th Congress, 2nd Session (February 19, 1903), 2564.

27. Charles H. Smith, "Have Negroes Too Much Liberty?," *Forum* 16 (1893): 181; George T. Winston, "The Relations of the Whites to the Negroes," *Annals of the American Academy of Political and Social Science* 17 (1901): 108–109.

28. Phillip Alexander Bruce, *The Plantation Negro as a Freeman: His Character, Condition, and Prospects in Virginia* (New York: G. P. Putnam's Sons, 1889), 86.

29. Thomas Dixon Jr., *The Clansman: An Historical Romance of the Ku Klux Klan* (New York: A. Wessels, 1907), 249.

30. Dixon, *Clansman*, 234.

31. *Paris News*, February 14, 1893, cited in Vance, *Facts in the Case*, 108–109.

32. Arthur O. Lovejoy, *The Great Chain of Being: A Study of the History of an Idea* (Cambridge, MA: Harvard University Press, 1936).

33. See, for example, Khalil Gibran Muhammad, *The Condemnation of Blackness: Race, Crime, and the Making of Modern Urban America* (Cambridge, MA: Harvard University Press, 2019).

34. Robin B. Jeshion, "Slurs, Dehumanization, and the Expression of Contempt," in *Bad Words: Philosophical Perspectives on Slurs*, ed. David Sosa (New York: Oxford University Press, 2018), 79.

35. Jeshion, "Slurs, Dehumanization, and the Expression of Contempt," 80.

36. Daniel Bar-Tal, *Shared Beliefs in a Society* (London: SAGE, 2000), 122.

37. Jeshion, "Slurs, Dehumanization, and the Expression of Contempt," 77–108.

38. Richard Boyle, *The Flower of the Dragon: The Breakdown of the U.S. Army in Vietnam* (San Francisco: Ramparts Press, 1972).

39. Transcript of Record at 1246–1247, *State of Texas v. Kerry Max Cook* (1978) (No. 1-177-179); Kerry Max Cook, *Chasing Justice: My Story of Freeing Myself after Two Decades on Death Row for a Crime I Did Not Commit* (New York: William Morrow, 2008).

40. Gilbert Ryle, *The Concept of Mind* (Chicago: University of Chicago Press, 1949), 16.

41. The term "objectification" is found the writings by Hegel, Marx, and Sir William Hamilton, among others, during the nineteenth century, but these writers did not seem to use it to denote the act of treating or conceiving of human beings as things.

42. For detailed discussions, see Barbara Herman, "Could It Be Worth Thinking about Kant on Sex and Marriage?," in *A Mind of One's Own: Feminist Essays on Reason and Objectivity*, ed. Louise M. Antony and Charlotte Witt (Oxford: Westview Press, 1993), 53–72; Lina Papadaki, "Sexual Objectification: From Kant to Contemporary Feminism," *Contemporary Political Theory* 6, no. 3 (2007): 330–348.

43. Immanuel Kant, *Lectures on Anthropology*, ed. Alan Wood and Robert Louden (Cambridge: Cambridge University Press, 2013), 127. This, of course, raises disturbing questions not only about the moral status of nonhuman animals, but also about the moral status of infants and the mentally impaired.

44. Catherine A. MacKinnon, "Sexuality, Pornography, and Method: Pleasure under Patriarchy," *Ethics* 99, no. 2 (1989): 327; Rae Langton, *Sexual Solipsism: Philosophical Essays on Pornography and Objectification* (New York: Oxford University Press, 2009), 316.

45. Catherine A. MacKinnon, *"Are Women Human?" and Other International Essays* (Cambridge, MA: Harvard University Press, 2006), 4.

46. Not all medical objectification is so benign; see Jacques-Philippe Leyens, "Humanity Forever in Medical Dehumanization," in *Humanness and Dehumanization*, ed. Paul G. Bain, Jeroen Vaes, and Jacques-Philippe Leyens (New York: Psychology Press, 2013), 167–185.

47. Martha Nussbaum, "Objectification," *Philosophy and Public Affairs* 24, no. 4 (1995): 2251. See also Lina Papadaki, "Feminist Perspectives on Objectification," in *The Stanford Encyclopedia of Philosophy* (Winter 2015 Edition), ed. Edward N. Zalta, https://plato.stanford.edu/archives /win2015/entries/feminism-objectification/.

48. Although her conception of dehumanization is quite different from mine, this argument is also used by Mari Mikkola to distinguish objectification from dehumanization. See Mari Mikkola, *The Wrong of Injustice: Dehumanization and Its Role in Feminist Philosophy* (Oxford: Oxford University Press, 2016), 145.

49. Jeremy Waldron, "Cruel, Inhuman, and Degrading Treatment: The Words Themselves," *New York University Public Law and Legal Theory Working Papers* 98 (2008): 37–38.

50. See, for instance, Jean Améry (1980), *At the Mind's Limits: Contemplations by a Survivor of Auschwitz and Its Realities*, trans. Sidney Rosenfeld and Stella P. Rosenfeld (Bloomington: Indiana University Press, 2008).

51. Nicholas Haslam, "Dehumanization: An Integrative Review," *Personality and Social Psychology Review* 10, no. 3 (2006): 252–264.

52. Andrea Dworkin, "Against the Male Flood: Censorship, Pornography, and Equality," in *Oxford Readings in Feminism: Feminism and Pornography*, ed. Drucilla Cornell (New York: Oxford University Press, 2000), 19–44.

53. Linda LeMoncheck, *Dehumanizing Women: Treating Persons as Sex Objects* (New York: Rowman and Littlefield, 1985), 32.

54. LeMoncheck claims that there are actually two forms of dehumanization. She also thinks of dehumanization as the treatment of others as nonpersons.

55. Mikkola, *Wrong of Injustice*, 145.

56. Nicholas Epley and Adam Waytz, "Mind Perception," in *The Handbook of Social Psychology*, 5th ed., ed. Susan T. Fiske, Daniel T. Gilbert, and Gardner Lindzey (New York: Wiley, 2009), 498–541. See also Lasana T. Harris and Susan T. Fiske, "Dehumanizing the Lowest of the Low: Neuroimaging Responses to Extreme Out-Groups," *Psychological Science* 17, no. 10 (2006): 847–853; Lasana T. Harris and Susan T. Fiske, "Social Neuroscience Evidence for Dehumanized Perception," *European Review of Social Psychology* 20, no. 1 (2009): 192–231; Lasana T. Harris and Susan T. Fiske, "Dehumanized Perception," *Zeitschrift Für Psychologie* 219, no. 3 (2011): 175–181.

57. Adam Waytz and Nicholas Epley, "Social Connection Enables Dehumanization," *Journal of Experimental Social Psychology* 48, no. 1 (2012): 70. The quoted passage is somewhat confusing as the authors begin with a claim about the failure to attribute mental properties (a cognitive state) but then move on to talk about "treatment," which usually refers to behavior. I assume that Epley and Waytz are using "treating" broadly to include attitudes.

58. Waytz and Epley, "Social Connection Enables Dehumanization," 70.

59. Quoted in Bettina Stangneth, *Eichmann before Jerusalem: The Unexamined Life of a Mass Murderer* (New York: Vintage, 2015), 304.

60. Susan T. Fiske, "Varieties of (De)Humanization: Divided by Competition and Status," in *Objectification and (De)Humanization: 60th Nebraska Symposium on Motivation*, ed. Sarah J. Gervais (New York: Springer, 2013), 53.

61. Kelly M. Hoffman, Sophie Trawalter, Jordan R. Axt, and M. Norman Oliver, "Racial Bias in Pain Assessment and Treatment Recommendations, and False Beliefs about Biological Differences between Blacks and Whites," *Journal of the National Academy of the Sciences* 113, no. 16 (2016): 4296–4301; Phillip Atiba Goff, Christian Jackson, Carmen Marie Culotta, Brooke Allison, Lewis Di Leone, and Natalie Ann DiTomasso, "The Essence of Innocence: Consequences of Dehumanizing Black Children," *Journal of Personality and Social Psychology* 106, no. 4 (2014): 526–545; Colin Holbrook, Daniel M. T. Fessler, and Carlos David Navarete, "Looming Large in Others' Eyes: Racial Stereotypes Illuminate Dual Adaptations for Representing Threat versus Prestige as Physical Size," *Evolution and Human Behavior* 37, no. 1 (2016): 67–78.

62. David Hume, *A Treatise of Human Nature* (New York: Oxford University Press, 2003), 223.

63. Adam Waytz, Kelly Marie Hoffman, and Sophie Trawalter, "A Super-humanization Bias in Whites' Perceptions of Blacks," *Social Psychological and Personality Science* 6, no. 3 (2014): 352.
64. Daniel Jonah Goldhagen, *Worse Than War: Genocide, Eliminationism, and the Ongoing Assault on Humanity* (New York: Public Affairs, 2009), 229.
65. Cited in "Opinion," *The Crisis* 3, no. 3 (January 1912): 108.
66. Herbert C. Kelman, "Violence without Moral Restraint: Reflections on the Dehumanization of Victims and Victimizers," *Journal of Social Issues* 29 (1973): 25–61; Albert Bandura, "Social Cognitive Theory of Moral Thought and Action," in *Handbook of Moral Behavior and Development: Theory, Research and Applications*, vol. 1, ed. William M. Kurtines and Jacob L. Gewirtz (Washington, DC: Psychology Press, 1991), 71–129.

2. Dehumanization Is Real

1. The Phrygian hat was an emblem of Jewishness in medieval art.
2. Debra Higgs Strickland, *Saracens, Demons, and Jews: Making Monsters in Medieval Art* (Princeton, NJ: Princeton University Press, 2003), 136.
3. Strickland, *Saracens, Demons, and Jews*, 133.
4. David Gordon White, *Myths of the Dog-Man* (Chicago: University of Chicago Press, 1991), 69.
5. Strickland, *Saracens, Demons, and Jews*, 122.
6. Cited in Strickland, *Saracens, Demons, and Jews*, 52. From Peter the Venerable, *Against the Inveterate Obduracy of the Jews*, trans. Irven M. Resnick (Washington, DC: Catholic University of America Press, 2013).
7. See, for example, reproductions of propaganda posters in Sam Keen, *Faces of the Enemy: Reflections of the Hostile Imagination* (New York: Harper and Row, 1991).
8. Strickland, *Saracens, Demons, and Jews*, 251.
9. Strickland, *Saracens, Demons, and Jews*, 251.
10. Moshe Zimmerman, "Two Generations of in the History of German Antisemitism: The Letters of Theodor Fritsch to Wilhelm Marr," *Yearbook of the Leo Baeck Institute* 23 (1978), 95–97.
11. Ludwig Klages, *Rhythmen und Runen* (Leipzig: Johann Ambrosius Barth, 1944), 330.

12. Eleonora Sterling, *Judenhass: Die Anfänge des politischen Antisemitismus in Deutschland (1815–1850)* (Europäische Verlagsanstalt: Frankfurt-am-Main, 1969).

13. Joachim C. Fest, *Hitler*, trans. Richard Winston and Clara Winston (New York: Harcourt, 1973).

14. The proverb is cited in Jay Geller, *Bestiarium Judaicum: Unnatural Histories of the Jews* (New York: Fordham University Press, 2018), 49. Schmitt's version was a response to the expression from Fichte used to open the Weimar National Assembly: "Gleichheit alles dessen, was Menschenanlitz trägt" ("Everyone with a human face is equal"); Carl Schmitt, "Das gute Recht der deutschen Revolution," *Westdeutscher Beobachter*, May 12, 1933, cited in Claudia Koonz, *The Nazi Conscience* (Cambridge, MA: Harvard University Press, 2003), 277.

15. Winthrop D. Jordan, *White over Black: American Attitudes toward the Negro, 1550–1812* (Baltimore: Pelican, 1969), 232.

16. Jordan, *White over Black*, 234.

17. C. L. R. James, *The Black Jacobins: Toussaint L'Ouverture and the San Domingo Revolutions* (New York: Vintage, 1989), 11–12.

18. James, *Black Jacobins*, 17.

19. Jordan, *White over Black*, 233.

20. Georg W. F. Hegel, *Lectures on the Philosophy of World History* (Cambridge: Cambridge University Press, 1975), 177, 178.

21. See David N. Livingstone, *Adam's Ancestors: Race, Religion, and the Politics of Human Origins* (Baltimore: Johns Hopkins University Press, 2011).

22. Although the definitive history of the dehumanization of Black people has yet to be written, there are some useful sources. I particularly recommend Wulf D. Hund, Charles W. Mills, and Silvia Sebastiani, *Simianization: Apes, Gender, Class, and Race* (Zürich: Lit Verlag, 2016).

23. Cited in Gustav Jahoda, *Images of Savages: Ancient Roots of Modern Prejudice in Western Culture* (London: Routledge, 1998), 47.

24. Lydia Maria Child, *An Appeal in Favor of That Class of Americans Called Africans* (Boston: Allen and Ticknor, 1833), 156.

25. For Sojourner Truth, see *New York Tribune*, September 5, 1853, 5; Frederick Douglass, *The Claims of the Negro, Ethnologically Considered: An Address before the Literary Societies of Western Reserve College* (Rochester, NY: Printed by Lee, Mann & Co., Daily American Office, 1854), 6–7. For Black slaves' perceptions of the dehumanizing attitudes of Whites, see also Mia Bay, *The White Image in the Black Mind: African-American*

Ideas about White People, 1830–1925 (New York: Oxford University Press, 2000).

26. Samuel A. Cartwright, "Unity of the Human Race Disproved by the Hebrew Bible," *De Bow's Review* 29, no. 2 (August 1860): 129–130; Ariel [Buckner H. Payne], *The Negro: What Is His Ethnological Status? Is He a Progeny of Ham? Is He a Descendent of Adam and Eve? Has He a Soul? Or Is He a Beast in God's Nomenclature? What Is His Status as Fixed by God in Creation? What Is His Relation to the White Race?* (Cincinnati: Publisher for the Proprietor, 1867), 21; Gottlieb C. Hasskarl, *"The Missing Link"; or, the Negro's Ethnological Status. Is He a Descendant of Adam and Eve? Is He the Progeny of Ham? Has He a Soul? What Is His Relation to the White Race? Is He a Subject of the Church, of the State, Which?* (Chambersburg, PA: Democratic News, 1898), 9. For a detailed discussion for these and other racist works of the period, see Livingstone, *Adam's Ancestors*.

27. Curiously, Joel Williamson claimed in *The Crucible of Race: Black-White Relations in the American South since Emancipation* (New York: Oxford University Press, 1984) that Carroll was a Black man. I have been unable to find any documentation to support this claim.

28. H. Paul Douglass, *Christian Reconstruction in the South* (Boston: Pilgrim Press, 1909); Edward Atkinson, review of *The Negro: A Beast*, by Charles Carroll, *North American Review* (1905): 181. The book also prompted the publication of a whole book in response by W. S. Armistead entitled *The Negro Is A Man: A Reply to Professor Charles Carroll's Book "The Negro is a Beast or In the Image of God"* (Tifton, GA: Armistead and Vickers, 1908). For "enormously influential," see Jane Dailey, "Sex, Segregation, and the Sacred after Brown," *Journal of American History* 91 (2004): 119.

29. Josia C. Nott and George R. Gliddon, *Types of Mankind: or, Ethnological Researches Based upon the Ancient Monuments, Paintings, Sculptures, and Crania of Races, and upon Their Natural, Geographical, Philological and Biblical History: Illustrated by Selections from the Inedited Papers of Samuel George Morton and by Additional Contributions from L. Agassiz, W. Usher, and H.S. Patterson* (Philadelphia: Lippincott, Grambo, 1854), 81.

30. Nott and Gliddon, *Types of Mankind*, lxxv.

31. Josiah Nott, "The Mulatto a Hybrid—Probable Extermination of the Two Races If Whites and Blacks Are Allowed to Intermarry," *American Journal of Medical Sciences* 6 (1843): 254.

32. For comprehensive discussions of the history of the debate about hybridity and race, see Robert J. C. Young, *Colonial Desire: Hybridity in Theory, Culture, and Race* (London: Routledge, 1995); Werner Sollors, *Neither Black nor White Yet Both: Thematic Explorations of Interracial Literature* (New York: Oxford University Press, 1997).

33. Cited in Randall L. Bytwerk, *Julius Streicher: Nazi Editor of the Notorious Nazi Newspaper* Der Stürmer (New York: Cooper Square Press, 2001), 206.

34. Nott and Gliddon, *Types of Mankind*, 182. At the time, "orang-outan" referred to all of the species of great ape, rather than just one as it does today.

35. Josiah C. Nott, *Two Lectures on the Natural History of the Caucasian and Negro Races* (Mobile, AL: Dade and Thompson, 1844), 41.

36. Jahoda, *Images of Savages*, 46.

37. David Brion Davis, *The Problem of Slavery in the Age of Emancipation* (New York: Alfred A. Knopf, 2014), 15.

38. Davis, *Problem of Slavery*, 18.

3. In the Blood

1. Guenter Lewy, *Perpetrators: The World of the Holocaust Killers* (New York: Oxford University Press, 2017), 103. The statement that Jews are not to be regarded as human might be interpreted in two ways. It might be an order that the men take a certain *stance* toward Jews—to regard them *as if* they are not human, or it might me an order confirming that Jews are *not* human and therefore ought not to be regarded as human. Given the pervasiveness of the Nazi doctrine of Jewish subhumanity, the latter seems most plausible.

2. Frederick Douglass, "'Men and Brothers': An Address Delivered in New York, New York, on 7 May 1850," in *The Frederick Douglass Papers*, ser. 1, vol. 2, ed. John Blassingame and Peter P. Hinks (New Haven, CT: Yale University Press, 2002), 238.

3. Henry McNeal Turner, "I Claim the Rights of a Man," in *Lift Every Voice: African American Oratory, 1787–1900*, ed. Philip S. Foner and Robert J. Branham (Tuscaloosa, AL: University of Alabama Press, 1998), 477–478.

4. This example is inspired by of one Frank Keil's transformation experiments involving a coffeemaker that is transformed into a birdfeeder. See

Frank C. Keil, *Concepts, Kinds, and Cognitive Development* (Cambridge, MA: MIT Press, 1989).

5. I am assuming that the two coffeemakers make coffee in much the same way. In fact, it is possible for two artifacts to discharge the same function in quite different ways, and this may require differently constructed innards.

6. For one such incident of Germans being misidentified as Jews, see Jewish Telegraphic Agency, JTA Daily News Bulletin, August 18, 1943, http://pdfs.jta.org/1943/1943-08-18_192.pdf.

7. The quote is from *Poodle-Pug-Dachshund-Pinscher*, cited in Jay Geller, *Bestiarium Judaicum: Unnatural Histories of the Jews* (New York: Fordham University Press, 2018), 7. It is important in this connection that Nazi theorists often characterized Jews as a *Gegenrasse*—an "antirace"—because they were regarded as an impure and uncanny mixture of races. See, for example, Johannes Chapoutot, *The Law of Blood: Thinking and Acting as a Nazi* (Cambridge, MA: The Belknap Press of Harvard University Press, 2018). The full significance of this will be made clear in Chapter 12.

8. James Q. Whitman, *Hitler's American Model: The United States and the Making of Nazi Race Law* (Princeton, NJ: Princeton University Press, 2017).

9. For a very detailed discussion, see Eric Ehrenreich, *The Nazi Ancestral Proof: Genealogy, Racial Science, and the Final Solution* (Bloomington: Indiana University Press, 2007).

10. Steven E. Aschheim, "Reflections on Theatricality, Identity, and Modern Jewish Experience," in *Jews and the Making of Modern German Theatre*, ed. Jeanette R. Malkin and Freddie Rokem (Iowa City: University of Iowa Press, 2010), 26–27.

11. Christopher H. Johnson, Bernhard B. Jussen, David W. Sabean, and Simon Teuscher, *Blood and Kinship: Matter for Metaphor from Ancient Rome to the Present* (New York: Berghahn, 2013).

12. Rachel E. Boaz, *In Search of "Aryan Blood": Serology in Interwar and National Socialist Germany* (Budapest: Central European University Press, 2012), 14. We find a similar theme in the Sherlock Holmes story "The Adventure of the Creeping Man," which features a professor who develops monkey-like characteristics on account of injecting himself with a serum extracted from monkeys. See Arthur Conan Doyle, *The Case-Book of Sherlock Holmes* (Looe, UK: House of Stratus, 2001), 75–108. Recent psychological research shows there is a tendency to think that

cross-species organ transplants might have similar effects. See Meredith Meyer, Sarah-Jane Leslie, Susan Gelman, and Sarah M. Stilwell, "Essentialist Beliefs about Body Transplants in the United States and India," *Cognitive Science* 37 (2013): 668–617. In this connection, see also Lesley Alexandra Sharp, *Strange Harvest: Organ Transplants, Denatured Bodies, and the Transformed Self* (Berkeley: University of California Press, 2006).

13. Letter from Townes to Lister, August 1674, cited in Raymond P. Stearnes, *Science in the British Colonies of America* (Urbana: University of Illinois Press, 1970), 216.

14. Doug Kiel, "Bleeding Out: Histories and Legacies of Indian Blood," in *The Great Vanishing Act: Blood Quantum and the Future of Native Nations*, ed. Norbert Hill Jr. and Kathleen Ratteree (Golden, CO: Fulcrum Press, 2017), 80–97.

15. Russell Thornton, "Tribal Membership Requirements and the Demography of 'Old' and 'New' Native Americans," in *Changing Numbers, Changing Needs: American Indian Demography and Public Health*, ed. Gary D. Sandefur, Ronald R. Rindfuss, and Barney Cohen, (Washington, DC: National Academies Press, 1996), 103–112.

16. For an impressively detailed account of the rise and fall of Nazi sero-anthropology, see Boaz, *In Search of "Aryan Blood."*

17. The scientific quest for a reliable biological marker of race began with Francis Galton's invention of fingerprinting. Although subsequently appropriated by criminology, Galton's project was driven by the hope that a person's race is inscribed in their fingerprints. Galton was disappointed that he could discover no race-specific fingerprint patterns, but speculations about the possibility persisted well into the twentieth century. See Francis Galton, *Finger Prints* (London: Macmillan, 1892).

18. Cited in Boaz, *In Search of "Aryan Blood,"* 185.

19. Johann W. von Goethe, *Faust*, trans. Anna Swanwick (New York: Dover Press, 2011).

20. According to an unpublished dissertation by Konstantin Seifert, Serelman's blood was used to help a woman who subsequently died of placenta praevia. Seifert says that Serelman was arrested ten days later because he was a member of the Communist Party, and sent to Sachsenburg. So it may be that his internment was overdetermined (thanks to Wulf Hund for informing me of this). Konstantin Seifert, "Mediziner, 'Rassenschänder', Interbrigadist . . . ? Leben und Werk des Hans Serelman (1898–1944)" (PhD diss., Friedrich-Schiller-Universität Jena, 2017).

21. Robert N. Proctor, *Racial Hygiene: Medicine under the Nazis* (Cambridge, MA: Harvard University Press, 1988); Jewish Telegraphic Agency, "Nazi Order Prohibiting Jewish Blood for Transfusions Causing Death of Many Soldiers," March 2, 1942, http://www.jta.org/1942/03/02/archive /nazi-order-prohibiting-jewish-blood-for-transfusions-causing-death -of-many-soldiers.

22. This should come as no surprise, given that the Nazis modelled their racial policies on American Jim Crow laws. See Whitman, *Hitler's American Model.*

23. Allyson D. Polsky, "Blood, Race, and National Identity: Scientific and Popular Discourses," *Journal of Medical Humanities* 23, nos. 3–4 (2002): 180.

24. Judy Scales-Trent, "Racial Purity Laws in the United States and Nazi Germany: The Targeting Process," *Human Rights Quarterly* 23, no. 2 (2001): 266.

25. Cited in Randall L. Bytwerk, *Julius Streicher: Nazi Editor of the Notorious Nazi Newspaper* Der Stürmer (New York: Cooper Square Press, 2001), 145.

26. This folk conception of species membership is ultimately inconsistent with Darwinian thought. See Daniel C. Dennett, "Darwin and the Overdue Demise of Essentialism," in *How Biology Shapes Philosophy: New Foundations for Naturalism,* ed. David Livingstone Smith (Cambridge: Cambridge University Press, 2017), 9–22.

27. Ehrenreich, *Nazi Ancestral Proof.*

4. Essential Differences

1. There is a dauntingly large literature on psychological essentialism, but for an especially rich and sophisticated discussion, see Sarah-Jane Leslie, "Essence and Natural Kinds: When Science Meets Preschooler Intuition," in *Oxford Studies in Epistemology*, vol. 4, ed. Tamar S. Gendler and John Hawthorne (Oxford: Oxford University Press, 2013), 108–165.

2. Douglas Medin and Andrew Ortony, "Psychological Essentialism," in *Similarity and Analogical Reasoning*, ed. Stella Vosniadou and Andrew Ortony (Cambridge: Cambridge University Press, 1989), 179–195.

3. Whether psychological essentialism essentially applies to biological kinds remains an open question. However, it is clear that essentialistic

thinking is rampant in thinking about biological taxa. See Susan Gelman, *The Essential Child: Origins of Essentialism in Everyday Thought* (New York: Oxford University Press, 2003).

4. Leslie, "Essence and Natural Kinds."

5. For a good discussion of essentialism in chemistry, see Leslie, "Essence and Natural Kinds." For an account of why it does not work in biology, see Daniel C. Dennett, "Darwin and the Overdue Demise of Essentialism," in *How Biology Shapes Philosophy: New Foundations for Naturalism*, ed. David Livingstone Smith (Cambridge: Cambridge University Press, 2017), 9–22.

6. Paul E. Griffiths, "What Is Innateness?," in *Arguing about Human Nature: Contemporary Debates*, ed. Stephen M. Downes and Edouard Machery (New York: Routledge, 2013).

7. See Eliot Sober, "Evolution, Population Thinking and Essentialism," *Philosophy of Science* 47, no. 3 (1980): 350–383.

8. Griffiths, "What Is Innateness?"

9. Dan Sperber, "Why Are Perfect Animals, Hybrids, and Monsters Food for Symbolic Thought?," *Method & Theory in the Study of Religion* 8, no. 2 (1996): 157.

10. Griffiths, "What Is Innateness?," 123.

11. Gil Diesendruck and Susan A. Gelman, "Domain Differences in Absolute Judgments of Category Membership: Evidence for an Essentialist Account of Categorization," *Psychonomic Bulletin & Review* 6, no. 2 (1999): 338–339.

12. Aristotle, *Politics*, 1.5, 1254b20–23. Cited in Malcolm Heath, "Aristotle on Natural Slavery," *Phronesis: A Journal for Ancient Philosophy* 53, no. 3 (2008): 262.

13. *Quasi*-brutes because although Aristotle draws analogies between natural slaves and nonhuman animals, he considers natural slaves to be human beings. See Heath, "Aristotle on Natural Slavery," 258–259.

14. Heath, "Aristotle on Natural Slavery," 262.

15. Martha Nussbaum, "Aristotle on Human Nature and the Foundation of Ethics," in *World, Mind, and Ethics: Essays on the Ethical Philosophy of Bernard Williams*, ed. J. E. J. Altham and Ross Harrison (Cambridge: Cambridge University Press, 1995).

16. Peter Garnsey, *Ideas of Slavery from Aristotle to Augustine* (Cambridge: Cambridge University Press, 1996).

17. Cited in Siep Stuurman, *The Invention of Humanity: Equality and Cultural Difference in World History* (Cambridge, MA: Harvard University Press, 2017), 225.

18. William Harper, *Memoir on Slavery, Read before the Society for the Advancement of Learning, of South Carolina, at Its Annual Meeting at Columbia, 1837* (Charleston, SC: James Burger, 1838), 37.

19. Morgan Godwyn, *The Negro's & Indians Advocate, Suing for Their Admission into the Church, or, A Persuasive to the Instructing and Baptizing of the Negro's and Indians in Our Plantations* (London: J.D., 1680), 3; Morgan Godwyn, "A Brief Account of Religion, in the Plantations, with the Causes of the Neglect and Decay Thereof in Those Parts," in *Some Proposals towards Propagating of the Gospel in Our American Plantations*, ed. Francis Brokesby (London: G. Sawbridge, 1708), 3.

20. Mia Bay, *The White Image in the Black Mind: African-American Ideas about White People, 1830–1925* (New York: Oxford University Press, 2000), 124.

21. Ilan Dar Nimrod and Steven J. Heine, "Genetic Essentialism: On the Deceptive Determinism of DNA," *Psychological Bulletin* 137, no. 5 (2011): 800–818.

22. Dorothy Nelkin and M. Susan Lindee, *The DNA Mystique: The Gene as a Cultural Icon* (New York: W. H. Freeman, 1995), 40–43. For a readable, brief account of the ideological role of the gene, see Stuart Newman, "The Divisive Gene," *Monthly Review* 72, no. 8 (January 2020).

23. See, for example, Deborah A. Bolnick, "Individual Ancestry Inference and the Reification of Race as a Biological Phenomenon," in *Revisiting Race in the Genomic Age*, ed. Sarah S. Richardson, Sandra Soo-Jin Lee, and Barbara A. Koenig (New Brunswick, NJ: Rutgers University Press, 2008), 70–85; Jonathan M. Kaplan and Rasmus G. Winther, "Ontologies and Politics of Bio-Genomic 'Race,'" *Theoria* 60, no. 3 (2013): 54–80; Jonathan M. Kaplan and Rasmus G. Winther, "Prisoners of Abstraction? The Theory and Measure of Genetic Variation, and the Very Concept of 'Race,'" *Biological Theory* 7, no. 4 (2013): 401–412; Koffi N. Maglo, Tesfaye B. Mersha and Lisa J. Martin, "Population Genomics and the Statistical Values of Race: An Interdisciplinary Perspective on the Biological Classification of Human Populations and Implications for Clinical Genetic Epidemiological Research," *Frontiers in Genetics* 7, no. 22 (2016), https://www.frontiersin.org/articles/10.3389/fgene.2016.00022/full; Melissa Wills, "Are Clusters Races? A Discussion of the

Rhetorical Appropriation of Rosenberg et al.'s 'Genetic Structure of Human Populations,'" *Philosophy, Theory, and Practice in Biology*, 9, no. 12 (2017), http://dx.doi.org/10.3998/ptb.6959004.0009.012; Adam Hochman, "Against the New Racial Naturalism," *Journal of Philosophy* 110, no. 6 (2013): 331–351.

24. For one of many examples, see Sopan Deb, "Obama Portraits 'Push Us to Think More,' Readers Say," *New York Times*, February 18, 2018.

5. The Logic of Race

1. See Werner Sollors, *Neither Black nor White Yet Both: Thematic Explorations of Interracial Literature* (New York: Oxford University Press, 1997).

2. Oskar Panizza, "The Operated Jew," in *The Operated Jew: Two Tales of Anti-Semitism*, ed. Jack Zipes (New York: Routledge, 1991), 85–86.

3. Panizza, "Operated Jew," 52.

4. Panizza, "Operated Jew."

5. Panizza, "Operated Jew," 51.

6. Panizza, "Operated Jew," 72–73.

7. Joela Jacobs, "Assimilated Aliens: Imagining National Identity in Oskar Panizza's *Operated Jew* and Salomo Friedlaender's *Operated Goy*," in *Alien Imaginations: Science Fiction and Tales of Transnationalism*, ed. Ulrike Küchler, Silja Maehl, and Graeme Stout (New York: Bloomsbury, 2015), 59–61.

8. Panizza, "Operated Jew," 74.

9. Jack Zipes, "The Negative German-Jewish Symbiosis," in *Insiders and Outsiders: Jewish and Gentile Culture in Germany and Austria*, ed. Dagmar Lorenz, Gabriele Weinberger, and Alan Levenson (Detroit: Wayne State University Press, 1994), 154–164; *Kreutzwendedich*, which means "cross turn-around," may refer to the *Hackenkreutz* (swastika). "Rehsok" is the inversion of "kosher." See Jacobs, "Assimilated Aliens."

10. Salomo Friedlaender, "The Operated Goy," in *The Operated Jew: Two Tales of Anti-Semitism*, trans. Jack Zipes (New York: Routledge, 1991), 75.

11. Friedlaender, "Operated Goy," 76.

12. Friedlaender, "Operated Goy," 77. Friedlaender does not say that the dog was trained to attack Jews on command. He says that the dog was trained to "bite any Jews who came too close." When Rebecka Gold-Isaac subsequently approaches the count, the dog, but not its master, is aware that she is a Jew. The idea that the count's Great Dane could dis-

tinguish between Jews and gentiles indicates a subtle intrusion of race realism into Friedlaender's otherwise skeptical narrative. The "Borkum Hymn" was a song about the beautiful North Sea island resort of Borkum, which emphasized that its beaches were *Judenfrei* (free of Jews). The final verse states, "Those who come with flat feet, crooked noses, and curly hair must not enjoy the beach, but must be out! Be out! Out!" Singing the "Borkum Hymn" was a regular part of vacationing there. See Tom Blass, *The Naked Shore of the North Sea* (London: Bloomsbury, 2015), 114.

13. Friedlaender, "Operated Goy," 85–86.

14. Jacobs, "Assimilated Aliens," 69.

15. Friedlaender, "Operated Goy," 122.

16. George Schuyler, *Black No More: Being an Account of the Strange and Wonderful Workings of Science in the Land of the Free, AD 1933–1940* (Boston: Northeastern University Press, 1989), 31. Notice that Crookman appears to implicitly assert racial essentialism while explicitly denying it. In saying that Negros come packaged in a broad range of phenotypes, he implies that what it is that makes a person a Negro is something other than their phenotype.

17. Schuyler, *Black No More*, 130, 131.

18. This phrase may be a reference to the "new Christians" in fifteenth- and sixteenth-century Spain: Jews who converted to Christianity under duress but were nonetheless believed to have tainted Jewish blood.

19. Schuyler, *Black No More*, 219–221.

20. Sander L. Gilman, *The Jew's Body* (New York: Routledge), 191.

21. Robert Wilson Shufeldt, *The Negro: A Menace to American Civilization* (Boston: Richard G. Badger, 1907), 135. Republished as *America's Greatest Problem: The Negro* (Philadelphia: F. A. Davis, 2015).

22. This methodological taxonomy is from Julie L. Shulman and Joshua Glasgow, "Is Race-Thinking Biological or Social, and Does It Matter for Racism? An Exploratory Study," *Journal of Social Philosophy* 41, no. 3 (2010): 244–259.

23. For a good discussion of these, see Ann Morning, *The Nature of Race: How Scientists Teach and Think about Human Difference* (Berkeley: University of California Press, 2011). See also Joshua Glasgow, Julie L. Shulman, and Enrique Covarrubias, "The Ordinary Conception of Race in the United States and Its Relation to Racial Attitudes: A New Approach," *Journal of Cognition and Culture* 9, nos. 1–2 (2009): 15–38.

24. See Michael Brownstein and Jennifer Saul, *Implicit Bias and Philosophy, Volumes 1 and 2: Metaphysics and Epistemology; Moral Responsibility, Structural Injustice, and Ethics* (Oxford: Oxford University Press, 2016). The claim that implicit attitudes are prevalent and often fail to cohere with one's explicit attitudes is independent of debates surrounding the Implicit Association Test, which is an influential tool for tapping implicit biases. For an interesting discussion of criticisms of this approach, see John Schwenkler, "What Can We Learn from the Implicit Association Test? A Brains Blog Roundtable," *Brains Blog*, January 17, 2017, http://philosophyofbrains.com/2017/01/17/how-can-we-measure-implicit-bias-a-brains-blog-roundtable.aspx.

25. Glasgow, Shulman, and Covarrubias, "Ordinary Conception of Race." See also Shulman and Glasgow, "Is Race-Thinking Biological or Social."

26. Glasgow, Shulman, and Covarrubias, "Ordinary Conception of Race," 36.

27. Glasgow, Shulman, and Covarrubias, "Ordinary Conception of Race," 25.

28. Morning, *Nature of Race*.

6. Hierarchy

1. Evelin Lindner, *Making Enemies: Humiliation and International Conflict* (Westport, CT: Greenwood / Praeger Security International, 2006), 5–7. For the language of uprightness, see also Sander L. Gilman, *Stand Up Straight! A History of Posture* (London: Reaktion Books, 2018).

2. Arthur O. Lovejoy, *The Great Chain of Being: A Study of the History of an Idea* (Cambridge, MA: Harvard University Press, 1936); Oludamini Ogunnaike, "From Heathen to Sub-Human: A Genealogy of the Influence of the Decline of Religion on the Rise of Modern Racism," *Open Theology* 2 (2016): 785–803.

3. See Raymond Corbey, *The Metaphysics of Apes: Negotiating the Animal-Human Boundary* (Cambridge: Cambridge University Press, 2005).

4. For an excellent discussion of how the Great Chain of Being came to underpin racial hierarchies, see Ogunnaike, "From Heathen to Sub-Human."

5. Julien-Joseph Virey, "Art nègre," in *Dictionnaire des Sciences Mèdicales*, vol. 35 (Paris: Crapart, 1819), 385.

6. Charles Darwin, *On the Origin of Species by Means of Natural Selection, or the Preservation of Favoured Races in the Struggle for Life* (London: John Murray, 1859).

7. Karol Wojtyla, "On the Dignity of the Human Person," in *Person and Community: Selected Essays*, vol. 4, *Catholic Thought from Lublin*, ed. Andrew N. Woznicki (New York: Peter Lang, 1993), 178; George Kateb, *Human Dignity* (Cambridge, MA: Harvard University Press), 3–4. For a very informative discussion of the role of human supremacism in human rights discourse, see Will Kymlicka "Human Rights without Human Supremacism," *Canadian Journal of Philosophy* 48, no. 6 (2018): 763–792.

8. Harriet Ritvo, *The Platypus and the Mermaid: And Other Figments of the Classifying Imagination* (Cambridge, MA: Harvard University Press, 1998), 30–31. The embedded quote is from Robert Knox, *The Races of Men: A Philosophical Enquiry into the Influence of Race over the Destinies of Nations* (London: Henry Renshaw, 1862).

9. Emanuele Rigato and Alessandro Minelli, "The Great Chain of Being Is Still Here," *Evolution: Education and Outreach* 6, article no. 18 (2013), http://www.evolution-outreach.com/content/6/1/18.

10. Sean Nee, "The Great Chain of Being," *Nature* 435 (May 26, 2005): 429. See also Rigato and Minelli, "Great Chain of Being"; J. David Archibald, *Aristotle's Ladder, Darwin's Tree: The Evolution of Visual Metaphors for Biological Order* (New York: Columbia University Press, 2014).

11. A. J. Lowe and R. J. Abbott, "Reproductive Isolation of a New Hybrid Species, Senecio Eboracensis Abbott & Lowe (Asteraceae)," *Heredity (Edinb)* 92, no. 5 (2004): 386–395.

12. Lovejoy, *Great Chain of Being*, 55–59. Lovejoy interprets Aristotle's notion of continuity in terms of metaphysical vagueness: natural kinds are fuzzy rather than discrete, with each kind shading into it is neighbors, such that there might be borderland entities that belong to two natural kinds. However, Herbert Granger has shown that this is probably incorrect, arguing that Aristotle's essentialism precluded this sort of vagueness. In his view, Aristotle held that natural kinds are sharply bounded, but the boundaries between them may be impossible to discriminate. Herbert Granger, "The Scala Naturae and the Continuity of Kinds," *Phronesis* 30, no. 2 (1985): 181–200.

13. T. J. Kasperbauer, *Subhuman: The Moral Psychology of Human Attitudes to Animals* (New York: Oxford University Press, 2018), 74; H. Rae

Westbury and David L. Neumann, "Empathy-Related Responses to Moving Film Stimuli Depicting Human and Non-Human Animal Targets in Negative Circumstances," *Biological* Psychology 78 (2008): 66–74; S. Plous, "Psychological Mechanisms in the Human Use of Animals," *Journal of Social Issues* 49, no. 1 (1993), 11–52; Michael W. Allen, Matthew Hunstone, Jon Waerstad, Emma Foy, Thea Hobbins, Britt Wikner, and Joanne Wirrel, "Human-to-Animal Similarity and Participant Mood Influence Punishment Recommendations for Animal Abusers," *Society and Animals* 10, no. 3 (2002): 267–284.

14. Catherine Dupré, *The Age of Dignity: Human Rights and Constitutionalism in Europe* (Sydney: Hart, 2015). See also Lisa Guenther, "Beyond Dehumanization: A Post-Humanist Critique of Solitary Confinement," *Journal for Critical Animal Studies* 10, no. 2 (2012): 47–68.

15. Gen. 1:26–28 (New International Version).

16. Wilhelm Halbfass, *Tradition and Reflection: Explorations in Indian Thought* (Albany: SUNY Press, 1990), 349.

17. Francis E. Ekanem, "On the Ontology of African Philosophy," *International Journal of Humanities and Social Science Invention* 1, no. 1 (2012): 56. See also Francis Etim, "African Metaphysics," *Journal of Asian Scientific Research* 3, no. 1 (2013): 11–17; Placide Tempels, *Bantu Philosophy* (Paris: Presence Africaine, 1969); John S. Mbiti, *African Religions and Philosophy* (Nairobi: Heineman, 1969).

18. G. E. R. Lloyd, *Being, Humanity, and Understanding* (Oxford: Oxford University Press, 2012).

19. Peggy Reeves Sanday, *Divine Hunger: Cannibalism as a Cultural System* (Cambridge: Cambridge University Press, 1986), 294.

20. Eva Hunt, *The Transformation of the Hummingbird: Cultural Roots of a Zinacantican Mythical Poem* (Ithaca, NY: Cornell University Press, 1977), 89. For Mesoamerican phagiohierachy, see also John D. Monaghan, "Theology and History in the Study of Mesoamerican Religions," in *Handbook of Middle American Indians*, suppl. 6, *Ethnology*, ed. John D. Monaghan (Austin: University of Texas Press, 2000), 24–49.

7. The Order of Things

1. John Stuart Mill, "On Nature," in *Nature, the Utility of Religion, and Theism* (London: Longmans, Green, Reader, and Dyer, 1975), 12.

2. Mill had it that nonnaturalness, in this sense, requires modification by *voluntary* human intervention. If he meant to say by this that these modifications must be deliberate effects, then his criterion seems too restrictive, as anthropogenic climate change seems to be a good candidate for something that is nonnatural. So, I interpret Mill's criterion as referring to the *effects* of voluntary intervention, which may be intended or not.

3. See, for example, Sherry B. Ortner, "Is Female to Male as Nature Is to Culture?," *Feminist Studies* 1, no. 2 (1972): 5–31; William Cronon, "The Trouble with Wilderness, or, Getting Back to the Wrong Nature," *Environmental History* 1, no. 1 (January 1996): 7–28; Hermann Glaser, *The Cultural Roots of National Socialism* (Austin: University of Texas Press, 1978).

4. Stefaan Blancke, Frank Van Breusegem, Geert De Jaeger, Johan Braeckman, and Marc Van Montagu, "Fatal Attraction: The Intuitive Appeal of GMO Opposition," *Trends in Plant Science* 20, no. 7 (2015): 414–418.

5. Aristotle, *The Nicomachean Ethics*, in *The Complete Works of Aristotle*, vol. 2, ed. Jonathan Barnes (Princeton, NJ: Princeton University Press, 1984), 6–7. See also Plato's conception of ideal social stratification, and the "grand lie" to justify it, in *The Republic*, ed. G. R. F. Ferrari, trans. Tom Griffith (Cambridge: Cambridge University Press, 2000), 107.

6. See, for example, Jacques Maritain, *Christianity and Democracy* (San Francisco: Ignatius Press, 2012).

7. Mary Douglas, *How Institutions Think* (Syracuse, NY: Syracuse University Press, 1986), 48.

8. Williams did not use "prejudice" here in a pejorative sense. He believed that the mere fact of humanness provides grounds for us—that is, other human beings—to treat others as having special moral status. See Cora Diamond, "Bernard Williams on the Human Prejudice," *Philosophical Investigations* 41, no. 4 (2018): 379–398.

9. Aristotle, *Aristotle's Politics: Writings from the Complete Works*, ed. Jonathan Barnes (Princeton, NJ: Princeton University Press, 2016), 4.

10. Cicero, *On Obligations: De Officiis*, trans. P. G. Walsh (New York: Oxford University Press, 2000), 36–37.

11. Thomas Aquinas, *Summa Theologicae*, vol. 1, pt. 1, trans. Fathers of the English Dominican Province (New York: Cosimo Classics, 2007), 471.

12. For an insightful discussion, see Ann Phillips, *The Politics of the Human* (Cambridge: Cambridge University Press, 2015).

13. William Graham Summer, *Folkways: A Study of the Sociological Importance of Usages, Manners, Customs, Mores, and Morals* (Boston: Ginn, 1906), 13.

14. There is a very large literature on in-group / out-group biases. Some helpful contributions are Brad Pinter and Anthony G. Greenwald, "A Comparison of Minimal Group Induction Procedures," *Group Processes and Intergroup Relations* 14, no. 1 (2011): 81–98; Mark Bennett, Martyn Barrett, Rauf Karakozov, Giorgi Giorgi Kipiani, Evanthia Lyons, Valentyna Pavlenko, and Tatiana Riazanova, "Young Children's Evaluations of the Ingroup and of Outgroups: A Multi-National Study," *Social Development*, 13, no. 1 (2004): 124–141; Henri Tajfel, M. G. Billig, R. P. Bundy, and Claude Flament, "Social Categorization and Intergroup Behavior," *European Journal of Social Psychology* 1, no. 2 (1971): 149–178. For the Humean roots, see David Hume, *A Treatise of Human Nature: A Critical Edition*, ed. David Fate Norton and Mary J. Norton (Oxford: Clarendon Press, 2007). For chimpanzee aggression, see Dale Peterson and Richard Wrangham, *Demonic Males: Apes and the Origins of Human Violence* (Boston: Mariner Books, 1997).

15. Brian Hare and Vanessa Woods, *Survival of the Friendliest: Understanding Our Origins and Rediscovering Our Common Humanity* (New York: Random House, 2020), xxiv.

16. Thomas Hobbes, *Leviathan* (Harmondsworth, UK: Penguin, 1982), 186.

17. Hobbes, *Leviathan*, 127.

18. For an interesting discussion that is quite relevant to this point, see Carl Schmitt, *The Concept of the Political* (Chicago: University of Chicago Press, 1996). Schmitt understands the political as the sphere of collective friends and enemies. On this account, the political is uniquely human, and reflects the special significance that human beings accord to one another (although it does not exhaust that significance).

19. Roy A. Rappaport, *Ritual and Religion in the Making of Humanity* (Cambridge: Cambridge University Press, 1999); Oliver S. Curry, "Morality as Cooperation: A Problem-Centered Approach," in *The Evolution of Morality*, ed. Todd K. Shackelford and Ranald D. Hansen (New York: Springer, 2016), 27–52.

20. For justification of this claim, see the research summarized in T. J. Kasperbauer, *Subhuman: The Moral Psychology of Human Attitudes to Animals* (New York: Oxford University Press, 2018).

21. Ayal Halfon and Ran Barkai, "The Material and Mental Effects of Animal Disappearance on Indigenous Hunter-Gatherers, Past and Present," *Time and Mind* 13, no. 1 (2020): 1–29; Frédéric Laugrand and Jarich Oosten, *Hunters, Predators, and Prey: Inuit Perceptions of Animals* (New York: Berghahn, 2015); Ann Fienup-Riordan, *Eskimo Essays: Yup'ik Lives and How We See Them* (New Brunswick, NJ: Rutgers University Press, 1990); Edouardo Vivieros de Castro, "Cosmological Deixis and Amerindian Perspectivism," *Journal of the Royal Anthropological Institute* 4, no. 3 (1998): 469–488.

22. Harvey A. Feit, "Hunting, Nature, and Metaphor: Political and Discursive Strategies in James Bay Cree Resistance and Autonomy," *Indigenous Traditions and Ecology*, ed. John A. Grim (Cambridge, MA: Cambridge University Press, 2001), 421. Feit notes that the hierarchical conception of nature is not altogether absent in Cree metaphysics, but the division between kinds is neither rigid nor absolute. See also Robert A. Brightman, *Grateful Prey: Rock Cree Human-Animal Relationships* (Los Angeles: University of California Press, 1993); Adrian Tanner, *Bringing Home Animals: Religious Ideology and Mode of Production of the Mistassini Cree Hunters* (New York: St. Martin's Press, 1979).

23. Helga Vierich, "Why They Matter: Hunter-Gatherers Today," *Medium*, August 27, 2017, https://medium.com/@helgavierich/why-they-matter-hunter-gatherers-today-9af2a0d642df. Vierich also notes that the attitude of gratitude extends to plants: "During gathering trips, I observed women deliberately taking a handful of berries or nuts from their bags, and tossing them on the ground as they walked along, and then heeling them into the dirt. I asked why, and was told this was a way of thanking the plants for their bounty, by putting some of their 'babies' where they might grow."

24. Christopher Boehm, *Hierarchy in the Forest: The Evolution of Egalitarian Behavior* (Cambridge, MA: Harvard University Press, 1999).

8. Being Human

1. For a range of views, see, for example, Richard E. Leakey and Robert Lewin, *Origins Reconsidered: In Search of What Makes Us Human* (New York: Anchor, 1993); Christophe Falguères, Jean-Jacques Bahain, Yuji Yokoyama, Juan Luis Arsuaga, Jose Maria Bermudez de Castro, Eudald Carbonell, James L. Bischoff, and Jean-Michel Dolo, "The Earliest

Humans in Europe: The Age of TD6 Gran Dolina, Atapuerca, Spain," *Journal of Human Evolution*, 37, nos. 3–4 (September 1999): 343–352; Daniel Schmitt, "Insights into the Evolution of Human Bipedalism from Experimental Studies of Humans and Other Primates," *Journal of Experimental Biology* 206 (2003): 1437–1448; Richard Potts, "Early Human Predation," in *Predator-Prey Interactions in the Fossil Record*, ed. Patricia H. Kelley, Michael Kowalewski, and Thor A. Hansen (New York: Springer, 2003), 359–376; Tarjei S. Mikkelsen, "What Makes Us Human?," *Genome Biology* 5, no. 238 (2004), https://genomebiology.biomedcentral.com/articles/10.1186/gb-2004-5-8-238; Robert Andrew Foley and Roger Lewin, *Principles of Human Evolution* (London: Wiley-Blackwell, 2003); Katherine S. Pollard, "What Makes Us Human?" *Scientific American* 300, no. 5 (2009): 44–49.

2. Ian Tattersall, "The Genus *Homo*," *Inference: International Review of Science* 2, no. 1 (February 2016), http://inference-review.com/article/the-genus-homo.

3. Douglas Medin, "Concepts and Conceptual Structure," *American Psychologist* 44, no. 12 (1989): 1469–1481; Ernst Mayr, "A Tenderfoot Explorer in New Guinea: Reminiscences of an Expedition for Birds in the Primeval Forests of the Arfak Mountains," *Natural History* 32 (1932): 83–97; Ralph Bulmer, "Why Is the Cassowary Not a Bird? A Problem of Zoological Taxonomy among the Karam of the New Guinea Highlands," *Man* 2, no. 1 (1967): 5–25. For the question of whether whales are fish, see John Dupré, "Are Whales Fish?," in *Folkbiology*, ed. Douglas Medin and Scott Atran (Cambridge, MA: MIT Press), 461–476.

4. For an introduction to contemporary philosophical work on human nature, see Elisabeth Hannon and Tim Lewins, *Why We Disagree about Human Nature* (Oxford: Oxford University Press, 2018). For relevant transhumanist work, see David John Roden, "The Disconnection Thesis," in *Singularity Hypotheses: A Scientific and Philosophical Assessment*, ed. Amnon H. Eden, James H. Moor, Johnny H. Seraker, and Eric Steinhart (Berlin: Springer, 2013), 281–298. My historical sketch of the concept of personhood is obviously parochial, as it focuses exclusively on the Christian West. For as somewhat broader view, at least of the concept of personhood, see Michael Carrithers, Steven Collins, and Steven Lukes, *The Category of the Person: Anthropology, Philosophy, History* (Cambridge: Cambridge University Press, 1985).

5. Jack Turner, "John Locke, Christian Mission, and Colonial America," *Modern Intellectual History* 8, no. 2 (2011): 267–297; Alden T. Vaughan, *Roots of American Racism: Essays on the Colonial Experience* (Oxford: Oxford University Press, 1995).

6. Vaughan, *Roots of American Racism*, 66.

7. John Locke, *An Essay concerning Human Understanding*, ed. Peter A. Nidditch (Oxford: Clarendon Press, 1975), 335; Charles C. Taylor, "The Person," in Carrithers, Collins, and Lukes, *Category of the Person*, 257–281; Peter Singer and Paola Cavalieri, "Apes, Persons, and Bioethics," in *All Apes Great and Small*, vol. 1., *African Apes*, ed. Biruté M. F. Galdikas, Nancy Erickson Briggs, Lori K. Sheeran, Gary L. Shapiro, and Jane Goodall (New York: Springer, 2001), 283–291; Paola Cavalieri and Peter Singer, "The Great Ape Project," in *Peter Singer: Unsanctifying Human Life*, ed. Helge Kuhse (Oxford: Blackwell), 135.

8. Charles C. Taylor, *Sources of the Self: The Making of Modern Identity* (Cambridge: Cambridge University Press), 6–7.

9. In fact, philosophers who ostensibly support the human / person distinction often slip into using the two terms interchangeably. Judith Jarvis Thomson states, in a celebrated paper on the ethics of abortion, "Most opposition to abortion relies on the premise that the fetus is a human being, a person, from the moment of conception." Judith Jarvis Thomson, "A Defense of Abortion," *Philosophy and Public Affairs* 1, no. 1 (1971): 69. Sometimes, instead of "humanness" and "personhood," the contrast is between descriptive and evaluative notions of the human, but this boils down to the very same dichotomy. See, for example, Eric Juengst and Daniel Moseley, "Human Enhancement," in *The Stanford Encyclopedia of Philosophy* (Spring 2016 Edition), ed. Edward N. Zalta, https://plato.stanford.edu/archives/spr2016/entries/enhancement/.

10. Peter Singer, *Animal Liberation* (London: Pimlico, 1995), 238–239.

11. Nick Haslam, Stephen Loughnan, Kashima Yoshihisa, and Paul Bain, "Attributing and Denying Humanness to Others," *European Review of Social Psychology* 19, no. 1: 55–85.

12. Nick Haslam, Paul Bain, Lauren Douge, Max Lee, and Brock Bastian, "More Human Than You: Attributing Humanness to Self and Others," *Journal of Personality and Social Psychology*, 89, no. 6 (2005): 940.

13. Haslam et al., "More Human Than You." For a very sharp methodological critique of Haslam's approach, see Florence E. Enock, Jonathan

C. Flavell, Steven P. Tipper, and Harriet Over, "No Convincing Evidence Outgroups Are Denied Uniquely Human Characteristics: Distinguishing Intergroup Preference from Trait-Based Dehumanization," *Cognition* 212 (July 2021): https://doi.org/10.1016/j.cognition.2021.104682.

14. Lawrence A. Hirschfeld, "How Biological Is Essentialism?"; Medin and Atran, *Folkbiology*.

15. Haslam et al., "More Human Than You," 941.

16. Nick Haslam, "Genetic Essentialism, Neuroessentialism, and Stigma: Commentary on Dar-Nimrod and Heine," *Psychological Bulletin* 137, no. 5 (2011): 819–824.

17. Ann Phillips, *The Politics of the Human* (Cambridge: Cambridge University Press), 2015.

18. Phillips, *The Politics of the Human*, 9.

19. Michael Hauskeller, "Making Sense of What We Are: A Mythological Approach to Human Nature," *Philosophy* 84, no. 372 (2009): 97–98.

20. Claude Levi-Strauss, *Race and History* (New York: UNESCO, 1952), 12.

21. George Rippey Stewart, *Names on the Globe* (New York: Oxford University Press, 1975), 68.

22. For similar views, see Maria E. Kronfeldner, *What Is Left of Human Nature: A Post-Essentialist, Pluralist, and Interactive Account of a Contested Concept* (Cambridge, MA: MIT Press, 2018); Sylvia Wynter, "No Humans Involved: An Open Letter to My Colleagues," *Voices of the African Diaspora* 8, no. 2 (1992): 13; Tommy J. Curry, *The Man-Not: Race, Class, Gender and the Dilemmas of Black Manhood* (Philadelphia: Temple University Press, 2017); Kay Anderson, *Race and the Crisis of Humanism* (New York: Routledge, 2007); Reinhart Koselleck, *Begriffsgeschichten: Studien zur Semantik und Pragmatik der politischen und socialen Sprache* (Frankfurt-am-Main: Suhrkamp, 2006); Marshall Sahlins, *The Western Illusion of Human Nature* (Chicago: Prickly Paradigm Press, 2008).

23. This is even true of paleoanthropological disputes about what primate taxa count as human. See Raymond Corbey, *The Metaphysics of Apes: Negotiating the Animal-Human Boundary* (Cambridge: Cambridge University Press, 2005).

9. Ideology

1. Charles W. Mills and Danny Goldstick, "A New Old Meaning of 'Ideology,'" *Dialogue: Canadian Philosophical Revue* 28, no. 3 (1989): 417.

2. John Gerring, "Ideology: A Definitional Analysis," *Political Research Quarterly* 50, no. 4 (1997): 957–959.

3. Karl Marx and Friedrich Engels, *The German Ideology*, in *Marx and Engels Collected Works*, vol. 5, *Marx and Engels 1845–47*, ed. Jack Cohen et al., trans. Clemens Dutt, W. Lough, and C. P. Magill (London: Lawrence Wishart, 2010).

4. Karl Marx, "Preface to *A Contribution to the Critique of Political Economy*," trans. Rodney Livingstone, in *Karl Marx: Early Writings* (Harmondsworth: Penguin, 1975), 425.

5. As Joe McCarney points out, this phrase may have been intended to refer specifically to Hegelianism, as the book primarily targets the young Hegelians, rather than to ideology as such. He interprets "in die ganzen Ideologie" as "in the whole ideology" instead of "in all ideology." Joe McCarney, *The Real World of Ideology* (London: Harvester, 1980).

6. Marx and Engels, *German Ideology*, 59.

7. Tommie Shelby, "Race, Moralism, and Social Criticism," *Du Bois Revue: Social Science Research on Race* 11, no. 1 (2014): 66; Sally Haslanger, "Culture and Critique," *Proceedings of the Aristotelian Society Supplementary Volume* 91, no. 1 (2017): 150. Other functionalists are Alan W. Wood, "Ideology, False Consciousness, and Social Illusion," in *Perspectives on Self-Deception*, ed. Brian P. McLaughlin and Amelie Oksenberg Rorty (Berkeley: University of California Press, 1988), 345–363; Raymond Geuss, *The Idea of a Critical Theory: Habermas and the Frankfurt School* (Cambridge, MA: Cambridge University Press, 1981).

8. Marilyn Frye, *The Politics of Reality: Essays in Feminist Theory* (Freedom, CA: Crossing Press, 1983), 33.

9. Marion I. Young, *Justice and the Politics of Difference* (Princeton, NJ: Princeton University Press, 1990), 41.

10. The locus classicus for this conception of function is Robert Cummins, "Functional Analysis," *Journal of Philosophy* 72, no. 20 (1975): 741–765.

11. Barbara J. Fields, "Slavery, Race, and Ideology in the United States of America," in *Racecraft: The Soul of Inequality in American Life*, ed. Karen E. Fields and Barbara J. Fields (New York: Verso, 2012), 111–148.

12. Terry Eagleton, *Ideology: An Introduction* (London: Verso, 2007), 5.

13. There is a parallel with the notorious paradoxes of self-deception. In fact, the theory of ideology that I offer in this chapter is largely inspired by my analysis of self-deception. See David Livingstone Smith, "Form

and Function in Self-Deception: A Biological Model," *Sistemi Intelligenti* 3 (2013): 565–580; David Livingstone Smith, "Self-Deception: A Teleofunctional Approach," *Philosophia* 42, no. 1 (2013): 181–199.

14. See Ruth Garratt Millikan, *Language, Thought, and Other Biological Categories: New Foundations for Realism* (Cambridge, MA: MIT Press, 1984); Ruth Garratt Millikan, *White Queen Psychology and Other Essays for Alice* (Cambridge, MA: MIT Press, 1993); Ruth Garratt Millikan, *Varieties of Meaning: The 2002 Jean Nicod Lectures* (Cambridge, MA: MIT Press, 2004).

15. Millikan, *Language, Thought, and Other Biological Categories*.

16. John A. Byers, *American Pronghorn: Social Adaptations and the Ghosts of Predators Past* (Chicago: University of Chicago Press, 1997), xv–xvi.

17. Tommie Shelby, "Ideology, Racism, and Critical Social Theory," *Philosophical Forum* 34, no. 2 (2003): 159.

18. Geuss, *Idea of a Critical Theory*, 12.

19. Wood, "Ideology, False Consciousness, and Social Illusion."

20. Haslanger, "Culture and Critique," 150.

21. Shelby, "Race, Moralism, and Social Criticism," 60.

22. Shelby, "Ideology, Racism, and Critical Social Theory," 174.

23. This discussion owes a great deal to David J. Buller, "DeFreuding Evolutionary Psychology," in *Where Biology Meets Psychology: Philosophical Essays*, ed. Valerie G. Hardcastle (Cambridge, MA: MIT Press, 1999), 99–114.

24. I use "driving forces" rather than "motives" for *Triebkräfte*. Otherwise this is the Torr translation. Friedrich Engels, "Engels Letter to Franz Mehring, July 14, 1893," in *Karl Marx and Friedrich Engels: Correspondence, 1846–1895*, ed. and trans. Donna Torr (New York: International Publishers, 1968), 434–435.

25. John Torrance, *Karl Marx's Theory of Ideas* (Cambridge: Cambridge University Press, 1995).

26. Ernst Mayr, "Proximate and Ultimate Causation," *Biology and Philosophy* 8 (1993): 95–98.

10. Dehumanization as Ideology

1. The phrase "teaching of contempt" is from Jules Isaac, *The Teaching of Contempt: The Christian Roots of Anti-Semitism* (New York: Reinhart, Holt, and Winston, 1964). For early Christian anti-Semitism, see Rose-

mary Radford Reuther, *Faith and Fratricide: The Theological Roots of Anti-Semitism* (New York: Seabury Press, 1974).

2. John 8:44–45 (New Revised Standard Version).
3. Moshe Lazar, "The Lamb and the Scapegoat: The Dehumanization of the Jews in Medieval Propaganda Imagery," in *Anti-Semitism in Times of Crisis*, ed. Sander L. Gilman and Steven T. Katz (New York: New York University Press, 1991), 45.
4. John Chrysostom, *Discourses against Judaizing Christians*, trans. Paul W. Harkins, (Washington, DC: Catholic University of America Press, 1999), 8.
5. Robert Michael, *A History of Catholic Antisemitism: The Dark Side of the Church* (London: Palgrave Macmillan, 2008).
6. Jeremy Cohen, *The Friars and the Jews: The Evolution of Medieval Anti-Judaism* (Ithaca, NY: Cornell University Press, 1982). David Nirenberg, *Anti-Judaism: The History of a Way of Thinking* (London: Head of Zeus, 2013).
7. Peter the Venerable, *Letters of Peter the Venerable*, vol. 1, ed. Giles Constable (Cambridge, MA: Harvard University Press, 1967), 328.
8. See Joshua Trachtenberg, *The Devil and the Jews: The Medieval Conception of the Jew and Its Relation to Modern Anti-Semitism* (Philadelphia: Jewish Publication Society, 1983).
9. Dana Carleton Munro, "Urban and the Crusaders," *Translations and Reprints from the Original Sources of European History*, vol. 1 (Philadelphia: University of Pennsylvania, 1895), 5.
10. Robert Chasan, *In the Year 1096: The First Crusade and the Jews* (Jewish Publication Society: Philadelphia, 1996); Shlomo Eidelberg, *The Jews and the Crusaders* (Brooklyn, NY: KTAV Publishing House, 1996).
11. Robert Michael, *A History of Catholic Antisemitism: The Dark Side of the Church* (New York: Palgrave, 2008), 48.
12. David Nirenberg, *Anti-Judaism: The History of a Way of Thinking* (New York: W. W. Norton, 2013), 194.
13. Geraldine Heng, *The Invention of Race in the European Middle Ages* (Cambridge: Cambridge University Press, 2019), 61–62. Although Heng is explicitly referring to England in this passage, this was the pattern of the treatment of Jews throughout Western and Central Europe.
14. Heng, *Invention of Race*, 29–30.
15. Hannah Arendt, *The Origins of Totalitarianism* (New York: Harcourt Brace Jovanovich, 1973), xi–xii.

16. Max-Sebastián Hering Torres, María Elena Martínez, and David Nirenberg, *Race and Blood in the Iberian World* (Zürich: Lit Verlag, 2012).

17. See the discussion in Richard Cole, "Kyn / fólk / Þjóð / Ætt: Proto-Racial Thinking and Its Application to Jews in Old Norse Literature," in *Fear and Loathing in the North: Jews and Muslims in Medieval Scandinavia and the Baltic Region*, ed. Cordelia Heß and Jonathan Adams (De Gruyter: Berlin, 2015), 239–268.

18. For example, the philosopher Judah Ha-Levi (c1045–1141) argued that Jews possess a special divine faculty, passed down biologically from one generation to the next, that distinguishes them from gentiles. Raphael Jospe, "Teaching Judah Ha-Levi: Defining and Shattering Myths in Jewish Philosophy," in *Paradigms in Jewish Philosophy*, ed. Raphael Jospe (Cranbury, NJ: Associated University Presses, 1997): 112–128.

19. The placeholder conception was introduced in Douglas Medin and Andrew Ortony, "Psychological Essentialism," in *Similarity and Analogical Reasoning*, ed. Stella Vosniadou and Andrew Ortony (Cambridge: Cambridge University Press, 1989), 179–195.

20. See the discussion in David Livingstone Smith, *Less Than Human: Why We Demean, Enslave, and Exterminate Others* (New York: St. Martin's Press, 2011).

21. Heng, *Invention of Race*, 30. In addition to the characteristics mentioned in this passage by Heng, Jews were also thought to have tails and "goat beards" (goats were associated in the Medieval mind with the devil). See Trachtenberg, *Devil and the Jews*.

22. Lazar, "Lamb and the Scapegoat," 52.

23. Steven F. Kruger, "Conversion and Medieval Sexual, Religious, and Racial Categories," in *Constructing Medieval Sexuality*, ed. Karma Lochrie, Peggie McKracken, and James A. Schultz (Minneapolis: University of Minnesota Press, 1997), 159.

24. Isaiah Shachar, *The Judensau: A Medieval Anti-Jewish Motif and Its History* (London: Warburg Institute, 1974), 33.

25. Kruger, "Conversion," 164–165.

26. Sara Lipton, *Dark Mirror: The Medieval Origins of Anti-Jewish Iconography* (New York: Henry Holt, 2014), 176.

27. Albert Winkler, "The Medieval Holocaust: The Approach of the Plague and the Destruction of Jews in Germany, 1348–1349," *Federation of East European Family History Societies* 13 (2005): 6–24.

28. Jews were associated with plague at the 681 Council of Toledo. In 1320 anti-Semitic violence erupted in France and Aragon in the so-called Shepherd's Crusade, which set the stage for accusations that Jews (in league with Muslims) had plotted with lepers to poison water supplies. See Malcolm Barber, "Lepers, Jews and Moslems: The Plot to Overthrow Christendom in 1321," *History* 66, no. 216 (1981): 1–17.

29. Andrew Colin Gow, *The Red Jews: Antisemitism in the Apocalyptic Age, 1200–1600* (New York: E. J. Brill, 1994).

30. Samuel K. Cohn Jr., "The Black Death and the Burning of Jews," *Past and Present* 186 (2007): 16–17.

31. Nico Voigtländer and Hans-Joachim Voth, "Persecution Perpetuated: The Medieval Origins of Anti-Semitic Violence in Nazi Germany," *Quarterly Journal of Economics* 127, no. 3 (2012): 1339–1392.

32. Trachtenberg, *Devil and the Jews*, 12.

33. Magda Teter, *Blood Libel: On the Trail of an Antisemitic Myth* (Cambridge, MA: Harvard University Press, 2020).

34. See "The Canons of the Fourth Lateral Council," in *Internet Medieval Sourcebook*, ed. Paul Halsall, last modified January 20, 2021, https:// sourcebooks.fordham.edu/basis/lateran4.asp.

35. Peter the Venerable, *Against the Inveterate Obduracy of the Jews*, trans. Irven M. Resnick (Washington, DC: Catholic University of America Press, 2013). For images of Jews as demons, see Debra Higgs Strickland, *Saracens, Demons, and Jews: Making Monsters in Medieval Art* (Princeton, NJ: Princeton University Press, 2003).

36. Lazar, "Lamb and the Scapegoat," 55–56.

37. In addition to the many representations of Jews consuming the blood of murdered Christian children, there are also images of outright cannibalism—for instance, the statue that still stands in the city of Berne depicting a Jewish man greedily devouring a child, which was later exploited in Italian fascist and Nazi propaganda. See David I. Kertzerand and Gunnar Mokosh, "The Medieval in the Modern: Nazi And Italian Fascist Use of the Ritual Murder Charge," *Holocaust and Genocide Studies* 33, no. 2 (2019): 177–196. See the related discussion in the "Passing Strange" section of Chapter 2.

38. Ruth G. Millikan, *Language, Thought, and Other Biological Categories* (Cambridge, MA: MIT Press, 1984).

39. Birgit Weidl, "Laughing at the Beast: The *Judensau:* Anti-Jewish Propaganda and Humor from the Middle Ages to the Early Modern

Period," in *Laughter in the Middle Ages and Early Modern Times*, ed. Albrecht Classen and Marilyn Sandidge (Berlin: Walter de Gruyter, 2010), 325–364.

40. Shachar, *Judensau.*

41. Wiedl, "Laughing at the Beast," 345.

42. Wiedl, "Laughing at the Beast," 346.

43. Claudine Fabre-Vassas, *The Singular Beast: Jews, Christians, and the Pig*, trans. Carol Volk (New York: Columbia University Press, 1997), 101.

44. Wiedl, "Laughing at the Beast," 325.

45. Martina Pluda, *Animal Law in the Third Reich* (Barcelona: Servei de Publicacions de la Universitat Autònoma de Barcelona, 2019), 82.

46. Lucy S. Dawidowicz, *The War against the Jews, 1933–1945* (New York: Bantam, 1986); Michael Burleigh, *The Third Reich: A New History* (New York: Hill and Wang, 2000); Julius H. Schoeps, *Bilder der Judenfeindschaft: Antisemitismus, Vorurteile und Mythen* (Augsburg: Bechtermünz, 1999); Oliver Moody, "'Judensau' Shout in Anti-Semitic Attack," *The Times*, September 10, 2018.

47. Peter Pulzer, *The Rise of Political Anti-Semitism in Germany and Austria* (Cambridge, MA: Harvard University Press, 1988), 292.

48. Pulzer, *Rise of Political Anti-Semitism*, 319, 296.

49. Norman Cohn, *Warrant for Genocide: The Myth of the Jewish World Conspiracy and* The Protocols of the Elders of Zion (London: Serif, 1998), 15.

50. Cohn, *Warrant for Genocide*, 197.

51. Alfred Rosenberg, *Die Protokolle der Weisen von Zion und die jüdische Weltpolitik*, cited in Norman Cohn, *Warrant for Genocide*, 217; Adolf Hitler, *Mein Kampf*, trans. Ralph Mannheim (London: Pimlico, 1994), 294. For Hitler's demonization of Jews in *Mein Kampf*, see Felicity Rash, *The Language of Violence: Adolf Hitler's* Mein Kampf (New York: Peter Land, 2006).

52. Joseph Goebbels cited in Cohn, *Warrant for Genocide*, 225.

53. Randall L. Bytwerk, *Julius Streicher: Nazi Editor of the Notorious Nazi Newspaper* Der Stürmer (New York: Cooper Square Press, 2001), 106–107.

54. Bytwerk, *Julius Streicher*, 107.

55. See Hillel Kieval, "Representation and Knowledge in Medieval and Modern Accounts of Jewish Ritual Murder," *Jewish Social Studies* 1, no. 1 (1994–95): 52–72.

56. Bytwerk, *Julius Streicher*, 209. The special issue was reprinted in 1976 by the Louisiana-based White supremacist New Christian Crusade Church.

57. See David Biale, *Blood and Belief: The Circulation of a Symbol between Jews and Christians* (Berkeley: University of California Press, 2008).

58. Jeffrey Herf, *The Jewish Enemy: Nazi Propaganda during World War II and the Holocaust* (Cambridge, MA: Harvard University Press, 2006), 87.

59. Carl Schmitt, *The Leviathan in the State Theory of Thomas Hobbes: Meaning and Failure of a Political Symbol*, trans. George Schwab and Erna Hilfstein (Chicago: University of Chicago Press, 1996). For a discussion of von Leers, Schmitt, and others in this vein, see Biale, *Blood and Belief*, chap. 4.

60. Rash, *Language of Violence*, 130.

61. Louis W. Bondy, *Racketeers of Hatred: Julius Streicher and the Jew-Baiters' International* (London: N. Wolsey, 1946), 61.

62. *Der ewige Jude* (*The Eternal Jew*) can be viewed on the Australian War Memorial website at https://www.awm.gov.au/collection/F03328/.

63. Voigtländer and Voth, "Persecution Perpetuated."

64. See also Bernard Glassman, *Anti-Semitic Stereotypes without Jews: Images of the Jews in England, 1290–1700* (Detroit: Wayne State University Press, 1975).

11. Ambivalence

1. Arthur Schopenhauer, *The World as Will and Representation*, vol. 1, trans. E. F. J. Payne (New York: Dover, 1969), 481; Philip S. Kitcher, "Experimental Animals," *Philosophy and Public Affairs* 43, no. 4 (2015): 289.

2. T. J. Kasperbauer, *Subhuman: The Moral Psychology of Human Attitudes to Animals* (New York: Oxford University Press, 2018); Robert A. Brightman, *Grateful Prey: Rock Cree Human-Animal Relationships* (Los Angeles: University of California Press, 1993); Graham Harvey, *Animism: Respecting the Living World* (London: G. Hurst, 2017); John Knight, "The Anonymity of the Hunt: A Critique of Hunting as Sharing," *Current Anthropology* 53 (2012): 334–355. The example of the seal ritual is from Kent Flannery and Joyce Marcus, *The Creation of Inequality: How Our Prehistoric Ancestors Set the Stage for Monarchy, Slavery, and Empire* (Cambridge, MA: Harvard University Press, 2012).

3. Harvey, *Animism*, 145.

4. "Case No. 4:09 CV 05796 CW: Expert Report of Craig Haney, Ph.D., J.D.," Center for Constitutional Rights, https://ccrjustice.org/sites

312 NOTES TO PAGES 210–217

/default/files/attach/2015/07/Redacted_Haney%20Expert%20Report
.pdf, p. 17.

5. David Hume, *A Dissertation on the Passions; The Natural History of Religion* (New York: Oxford University Press, 2009), 40. See also Stewart Guthrie, *Faces in the Clouds: A New Theory of Religion* (New York: Oxford University Press, 1993); Harvey, *Animism*.

6. Randall Collins, *Violence: A Micro-Sociological Theory* (Princeton, NJ: Princeton University Press, 2008), 79–80.

7. S. L. A. Marshall, *Men against Fire: The Problem of Battle Command* (Washington, DC: Infantry Journal Press, 1947), 79.

8. Marshall, *Men against Fire*, 78.

9. See Felix Warneken and Michael Tomasello, "The Roots of Human Altruism," *British Journal of Psychology* 100, no. 3 (2011): 455–471.

10. David Grossman, *On Killing: The Psychological Cost of Learning to Kill in War and Society* (Boston: Back Bay, 2009), 86.

11. Harry Holbert Turney-High, *Primitive War: Its Practice and Concepts* (Columbia: University of South Carolina Press, 1949), 225.

12. Iranaeus Eibl-Eibesfeldt, *The Biology of Peace and War: Men, Animals, and Aggression* (London: Thames and Hudson, 1979), 100.

13. Fiery Cushman, Kurt Gray, Allison Gaffey, and Wendy Berry Mendes, "Simulating Murder: the Aversion to Harmful Action," *Emotion* 12, no. 1 (2012), 6.

14. Grossman, *On Killing*, 31. Marshall also said that military psychiatrists in the European theater during World War II "found that fear of killing, rather than fear of being killed, was the most common cause of battle failure." Marshall, *Men against Fire*, 78.

15. Ditte Marie Munch-Jurisic, "Perpetrator Abhorrence: Disgust as a Stop Sign," *Metaphilosophy* 45, no. 4 (2014): 270–287. See also Saira Mohamed, "Of Monsters and Men: Perpetrator Trauma and Mass Atrocity," *Columbia Law Review* 115, no. 5 (2015): 1157–1216.

16. Zygmunt Bauman, *Modernity and the Holocaust* (Ithaca, NY: Cornell University Press, 1989), 188.

17. Christopher Browning, *Ordinary Men: Reserve Police Battalion 101 and the Final Solution in Poland* (New York: Harper Perennial, 1998), 67–68.

18. Daniel Jonah Goldhagen, *Hitler's Willing Executioners: Ordinary Germans and the Holocaust* (New York: Knopf, 1996), 421, 201.

19. Hannah Arendt, *Eichmann in Jerusalem: A Report on the Banality of Evil* (New York: Penguin, 1994), 106.

20. Jason Anthony Riley, "Does YHWH Get His Hands Dirty? Reading Isaiah 63: 1–6 in Light of Depictions of Divine Postbattle Purification," in *Warfare, Ritual, and Symbol in Biblical and Modern Contexts*, ed. Brad E. Kelle, Frank Ritchel Ames, and Jacob L. Wright (Atlanta: Society of Biblical Literature, 2014), 243.

21. Num. 31:19–20 (New Revised Standard Version). See also the chapters by Kelle, Niditch, and Riley in Kelle, Ames, and Wright, *Warfare, Ritual, and Symbol.*

22. Susan Niditch, *War in the Hebrew Bible: A Study in the Ethics of Violence* (Oxford: Oxford University Press, 1995), 153.

23. Robert Parker, *Miasma: Pollution and Purification in Early Greek Religion* (Oxford: Clarendon Press, 1983).

24. William Warde Fowler, *The Religious Experience of the Roman People: From the Earliest Times to the Age of Augustus* (London: Macmillan, 1922), 97.

25. David J. Morris, *The Evil Hours: A Biography of Post-Traumatic Stress Disorder* (Boston: Houghton Mifflin, 2015); Bernard J. Verkamp, *The Moral Treatment of Returning Warriors in Early Medieval and Modern Times* (Scranton, PA: University of Scranton Press, 1993), 11.

26. Verkamp, *Moral Treatment of Returning Warriors.* For medieval Christian views on killing in combat, see also Robert Emmet Meagher, *Killing from the Inside Out: Moral Injury and Just War* (Eugene, OR: Cascade, 2014).

27. Cyril Daryll Forde, *Ethnography of the Yuma Indians* (Berkeley: University of California, 1931).

28. Leslie Spier, *Mohave Culture Items* (Museum of North Arizona Bulletin 28) (Flagstaff: Northern Arizona Society for Science and Art, 1955), 28–30.

29. Clifton B. Kroeber and Bernard L. Fontana, *Massacre on the Gila: An Account of the Last Major Battle between American Indians, with Reflections on the Origin of War* (Tucson: University of Arizona Press, 1987).

30. Eileen Jensen Krige, *The Social System of the Zulus* (Pietermaritzburg: Shuter and Shooter, 1965), 276–277.

31. H. E. Rawson, *The Life of a South African Tribe* (Neuchatel: Imprimerie Attinger Freres, 1913).

32. For the use of drugs in combat, see Lukasz Kamienski, *Shooting Up: A History of Drugs in Warfare* (London: Hurst, 2016).

33. W. Goldschmidt, "The Inducement of Military Conflict in Tribal Societies," in *The Social Dynamics of Peace and Conflict: Culture in International*

Security, ed. Robert A. Rubinstein and Mary Lecron Foster (Boulder, CO: Westview Press, 1994), 47–65.

34. See Paul Roscoe, "Intelligence, Coalitional Killing, and the Antecedents of War," *American Anthropologist* 109, no. 3 (2007): 485–495.

35. The literature is huge. For example, see M. H. Johnson, S. Dziurawiec, H. Ellis, and J. Morton, "Newborns' Preferential Tracking of Face-Like Stimuli and Its Subsequent Decline," *Cognition* 40, no. 1–2 (1991): 1–19; Catherine J. Mondloch, Terry L. Lewis, D. Robert Budreau, Daphne Maurer, James Dannemiller, Benjamin Stephens, and Kathleen Kleiner-Gathercoal, "Face Perception during Early Infancy," *Psychological Science* 10, no. 5: (1999): 419–422; H. D. Ellis and S. De Schonen, "The Development of Face Processing Skills" [and Discussion], *Philosophical Transactions of the Royal Society of London Series B, Biological Sciences* 335, no. 1273 (1992): 105–111; Mark H. Johnson, "Subcortical Face Processing," *Nature Reviews Neuroscience* 6 (2005): 766–774; Jennifer J. Richler, Olivia Cheung, and Isabel Gauthier, "Holistic Processing Predicts Face Recognition," *Psychological Science* 22, no. 4 (2011): 464–471. For unborn babies' responsiveness to faces, see Vincent M. Reid, Kirsty Dunn, Robert J. Young, Johnson Amu, Tim Donovan, and Nadja Reissland, "The Human Fetus Preferentially Engages with Face-Like Visual Stimuli," *Current Biology* 27, no. 12 (2017): 1825–1828; Takahiko Koike, Hiroki C. Tanabe, Shuntaro Okazaki, Eri Nakagawa, Akihiro T. Sasaki, Koji Shimada, Sho K. Sugawara, Hakura K. Takahashi, Kazufumi Yoshihara, Jorge Bosch-Bayard, and Norihito Sadato, "Neural Substrates of Shared Attention as Social Memory: A Hyperscanning Functional Magnetic Resonance Imaging Study," *Neuroimage* 125 (2015): 401–412.

36. For responses to facial disfigurement, see Marjorie Gehrhardt, *The Men with Broken Faces: The "Gueules Cassées" of the First World War* (New York: Peter Lang, 2015). For the notion of "seeing human" and its neurological basis, see Anthony I. Jack, Abigail Dawson, and Megan E. Norr, "Seeing Human: Distinct and Overlapping Neural Signatures Associated with Two Forms of Dehumanization," *Neuroimage* 79 (2013): 313–328. See also Emmanuel Lévinas, *Ethics and Infinity: Conversations with Phillipe Nemo*, trans. Richard A. Cohen (Pittsburgh: Duquesne University Press, 1985).

37. Grossman, *On Killing*, 128.

38. Raul Hilberg, *The Anatomy of the Holocaust: Selected Works from a Life of Scholarship* (London: Berghahn, 1985), 19.

39. Richard Rhodes, *Masters of Death: The SS-Einsatzgruppen and the Invention of the Holocaust* (New York: Alfred A. Knopf, 2002), 152–153.

40. Tzvetan Todorov, *Facing the Extreme: Moral Life in the Concentration Camps*, trans. Arthur Denner and Abigail Pollak (New York: Henry Holt, 1996), 161–162. See also Nestar Russell, *Understanding Willing Participants: Milgram's Obedience Experiments and the Holocaust*, vol. 2 (New York: Palgrave Macmillan, 2018).

41. Russell, *Understanding Willing Participants*, 245.

42. Heinrich Himmler, "Speech of the Reichsfuehrer-SS Heinrich Himmler at Kharkow, April 1943," in United States Office of Chief of Counsel for the Prosecution of Axis Criminality, *Nazi Conspiracy and Aggression*, vol. 4 (Washington, DC: United States Printing Office, 1946), 574.

12. Making Monsters

1. Morgan Godwyn, *The Negro's and Indians Advocate Suing for Their Admission into the Church* (Whitefish, MT: Kessinger Publishing, 2003), 14–15.

2. Godwyn, *Negro's and Indians Advocate*, 13–14.

3. Godwyn, *Negro's and Indians Advocate*, 30.

4. Godwyn, *Negro's and Indians Advocate*, 40.

5. Stanley Cavell, "Skepticism and the Problem of Others," in *The Claim of Reason: Wittgenstein, Skepticism, Morality, and Tragedy* (New York: Oxford University Press, 1999), 375.

6. Cavell, "Skepticism and the Problem of Others," 375.

7. Cavell "Skepticism and the Problem of Others," 375.

8. Kwame Anthony Appiah, *Experiments in Ethics* (Cambridge, MA: Harvard University Press, 2014), 144.

9. Kate Manne, *Down Girl: The Logic of Misogyny* (New York: Oxford University Press, 2018), 143.

10. Manne, *Down Girl*, 163–164.

11. See also Johannes Lang, "Questioning Dehumanization: Intersubjective Dimensions of Violence in the Nazi Concentration and Death Camps," *Holocaust and Genocide Studies* 24, no. 2 (2010): 225–246; Paul

Bloom, "The Root of All Cruelty?," *New Yorker*, November 27, 2017; Harriet Over, "Seven Challenges for the Dehumanization Hypothesis," *Perspectives on Psychological Science* 16, no. 1 (2021): 3–13. 3

12. Heinrich Himmler, *Der Untermensch*, trans. Hermann Feuer and Bulat Sultanov (SS Office: Berlin 1942), http://www.holocaustresearchproject.org/holoprelude/deruntermensch.html.

13. Cited in David D. Gilmore, *Monsters: Evil Beings, Mythical Beasts, and All Manner of Imaginary Terrors* (Philadelphia: University of Pennsylvania Press, 2003), 60.

14. For example, Linn Normand, *Demonization in International Politics: A Barrier to Peace in the Israeli-Palestinian Conflict* (New York: Palgrave Macmillan, 2016); Michael Paul Rogin, *Ronald Reagan, the Movie, and Other Episodes in Political Demonology* (Berkeley: University of California Press, 1987).

15. Hugh Raffles, *Insectopedia* (New York: Vintage, 2010), 145. The quoted material is from Jakob Döpler's 1693 *Theatrum Punarum* and Jodocus Damhouder's (1562) *Praxis Rerum Criminalium*. See E. P. Evans, *The Criminal Prosecution and Capital Punishment of Animals: The Lost History of Europe's Animal Trials* (Boston: Faber and Faber, 1987).

16. Eugen Bleuler, "Vortrag über Ambivalenz," *Zentralblatt für Psychoanalyse* 1 (1910): 266–268; Sigmund Freud, "The Dynamics of Transference," in *The Standard Edition of the Complete Psychological Works of Sigmund Freud*, vol. 12, trans. James Strachey (London: Hogarth Press and Institute of Psycho-Analysis, 1958): 97–108.

17. Sigmund Freud, "Totem and Taboo," in *The Standard Edition of the Complete Psychological Works of Sigmund Freud*, vol. 12, trans. James Strachey (London: Hogarth Press and Institute of Psycho-Analysis, 1958), 21–22.

18. Sigmund Freud, *Totem and Taboo*, in *The Standard Edition of the Complete Psychological Works of Sigmund Freud*, vol. 13, trans. James Strachey (London: Hogarth Press and Institute of Psycho-Analysis, 1953), 28.

19. Freud, *Totem and Taboo*, 30.

20. You may have noticed that I use the words "belief," "representation," and even "conception," more or less interchangeably in this book. I use all of them in a theoretically low-key manner. However, a more thoroughgoing analysis of the cognitive processes underpinning dehumanization may well need to pull these three things apart and characterize them more precisely. In this connection, Eric Schwitzgebel may be correct in arguing that the contradictory mental state that drives dehumanization is not best characterized in terms of the dehumanizer

entertaining incompatible *beliefs*. Eric Schwitzgebel, "Believing in Monsters: David Livingstone Smith on the Subhuman," *Nautilus*, September 11, 2020, https://nautil.us/blog/believing-in-monsters-david -livingstone-smith-on-the-subhuman.

21. See, for example, F. Castelli, F. Happé, U. Frith, and C. Frith, "Movement and Mind: A Functional Imaging Study of Perception and Interpretation of Complex Intentional Movement Patterns," *NeuroImage* 3, no. 12 (2000): 314–325; R. Desimone and J. Duncan, "Neural Mechanisms of Selective Visual Attention," *Annual Revue of Neuroscience* 18 (1995): 193–222.

22. David Brion Davis, *The Problem of Slavery in the Age of Emancipation* (New York: Alfred A. Knopf, 2014), 18.

23. Adrian Bridge, "Romanians Vent Old Hatreds against Gypsies: The Villagers of Hadereni are Defiant about Their Murder of 'Vermin,'" *The Independent*, October 19, 1993.

24. Sigmund Freud, "The Uncanny," in *The Standard Edition of the Complete Psychological Works of Sigmund Freud*, vol. 17, trans. James Strachey (London: Hogarth Press and Institute of Psycho-Analysis, 1955), 218.

25. Ernst Jentsch, "On the Psychology of the Uncanny," *Angelaki: Journal of the Theoretical Humanities* 2, no. 1 (1997): 12.

26. Jentsch, "On the Psychology of the Uncanny," 12.

27. Masahiro Mori, "The Uncanny Valley," trans. Karl F. MacDorman and Nori Kagegi, *Robotics and Automation Magazine* (June 2012): 98–100. See also, for example, Chin Chang Ho and Karl F. MacDorman, "Revisiting the Uncanny Valley Theory: Developing and Validating an Alternative to the Godspeed Indices," *Computers in Human Behavior* 26, no. 6 (2010): 1508–1518; Shensheng Wang, Scott O. Lilienfeld, and Philippe Rochat, "The Uncanny Valley: Existence and Explanations," *Review of General Psychology* 19, no. 3 (2015): 393–407; Jasia Reichardt, *Robots: Fact, Fiction* (New York: Studio Books, 1978).

28. Mori, "Uncanny Valley," 100.

29. Plato, *The Republic*, ed. G. R. F. Ferrari, trans. Tom Griffith (Cambridge: Cambridge University Press, 2000), 136.

30. There are numerous interpretations of what is going on in Plato's account. See, for example, Rana Saadi Liebert, "Pity and Disgust in Plato's *Republic:* The Case of Leontius," *Classical Philology* 108, no. 3 (2013): 179–201.

31. Arthur Machen, *The House of Souls* (New York: Alfred A. Knopf, 1922), 116.

32. Mary Douglas, *Purity and Danger: An Analysis of Concepts of Pollution and Taboo* (New York: Routledge, 1966), 44–45.

33. Johann Chapoutot, *The Law of Blood: Thinking and Acting as a Nazi*, trans. Miranda Richmond Mouillot (Cambridge, MA: Harvard University Press, 2018), 1–3.

34. Daniel Jonah Goldhagen, *Worse Than War: Genocide, Exterminationism, and the Ongoing Assault on Humanity* (New York: Public Affairs, 2009), 319–320.

35. Goldhagen, *Worse Than War*, 320.

36. Noël Carroll, *The Philosophy of Horror, or Paradoxes of the Heart* (New York: Routledge, 1990), 44. Note that Carroll, drawing on Douglas, holds that there are also other ways that a being can be cognitively threatening—by being formless, incomplete, or interstitial. I do not discuss these other kinds of cognitive threat because they are not pertinent to the theory of dehumanization.

37. Carroll, *Philosophy of Horror*, 33.

38. See Tommy J. Curry, *The Man-Not: Race, Class, Gender and the Dilemmas of Black Manhood* (Philadelphia: Temple University Press, 2017).

13. Last Words and Loose Ends

1. See Charlotte Witt's fascinating discussion of Aristotle's notion of "deformed" kinds in her *Ways of Being: Potentiality and Actuality in Aristotle's Metaphysics* (Ithaca, NY: Cornell University Press, 2003).

2. Kathleen Parker, "To Understand What a Weird, Wicked World We Live in, Look at These Abortion Laws," *Washington Post*, February 1, 2019.

3. Michael Spielman, "Is Dehumanization Always Intrinsically Unjust?," *Abort73.com*, February 23, 2017, https://abort73.com/blog/is_dehumani zation_always_intrinsically_unjust/.

4. Spielman, "Is Dehumanization Always Intrinsically Unjust?"

5. Joshua Trachtenberg, *The Devil and the Jews: The Medieval Conception of the Jew and Its Relation to Modern Anti-Semitism* (Philadelphia: Jewish Publication Society, 1983), 60.

6. For a detailed history, see Norman Cohn, *Warrant for Genocide: The Myth of the Jewish World Conspiracy and* The Protocols of the Elders of Zion (London: Serif, 1998).

7. Adam Waytz, Kelly Marie Hoffman, and Sophie Trawalter, "A Super-humanization Bias in Whites' Perceptions of Blacks," *Social Psychological and Personality Science* 6, no. 3 (2014): 352–359.

8. Adam Waytz, Kelly Marie Hoffman, and Sophie Trawalter, "The Racial Bias Embedded in Darren Wilson's Testimony," *Washington Post*, November 26, 2014.

9. John Paul Wilson, Kurt Hugenberg, and Nicholas Rule, "Racial Bias in Judgments of Physical Size and Formidability: From Size to Threat," *Journal of Personality and Social Psychology* 113, no. 1 (2017): 59.

10. Wilson, Hugenberg, and Rule, "Racial Bias in Judgments of Physical Size," 59.

11. Phillip Atiba Goff, Matthew Christian Jackson, Brooke Allison, Lewis Di Leone, Carmen Marie Culotta, and Natalie DiTomasso, "The Essence of Innocence: Consequences of Dehumanizing Black Children," *Journal of Personality and Social Psychology* 106, no. 4 (2014): 526–545.

12. Noël Carroll, *The Philosophy of Horror, or Paradoxes of the Heart* (New York: Routledge, 1990), 34.

13. Wes Craven, *A Nightmare on Elm Street.* Script. http://nightmareonelm streetfilms.com/Files/nightmare-on-elm-street-script.pdf.

14. Mary Douglas, *Purity and Danger: An Analysis of Concepts of Pollution and Taboo* (New York: Routledge, 1966), 49.

15. Johann Chapoutot, *The Law of Blood: Thinking and Acting as a Nazi*, trans. Miranda Richmond Mouillot (Cambridge, MA: Harvard University Press, 2018), 31.

16. Hinton Rowan Helper, *Nojoque: A Question for a Continent* (New York: George W. Carleton, 1867), 81.

17. Orlando Patterson, *Rituals of Blood: Consequences of Slavery in Two American Centuries* (New York: Civitas, 1998), 211–212.

18. Mia Bay, *The White Image in the Black Mind: African-American Ideas about White People, 1830–1925* (New York: Oxford University Press, 2000), 119.

19. David Brion Davis, *The Problem of Slavery in the Age of Emancipation* (New York: Alfred A. Knopf, 2014), 10.

20. Douglas, *Purity and Danger*, 49.

21. Frederick Douglass, "The Horrors of Slavery and England's Duty to Free the Bondsman," In *The Frederick Douglass Papers*, ser. 1, vol. 1, ed. John W. Blassingame (New Haven, CT: Yale University Press, 1985), 371.

22. Leon F. Litwack, *Trouble in Mind: Black Southerners in the Age of Jim Crow* (New York: Vintage, 1998), 331.

23. Joel Williamson, *A Rage for Order: Black-White Relations in the American South since Emancipation* (New York: Oxford University Press, 1986).

24. Amy Louise Wood, *Lynching and Spectacle: Witnessing Racial Violence in America, 1890–1940* (Durham, NC: University of North Carolina Press, 2011), 8.

25. Patterson, *Rituals of Blood*.

26. Patterson, *Rituals of Blood*, 202.

27. Patterson, *Rituals of Blood*, 213.

INDEX

African philosophy, 115
Agassiz, Louis, 45
ambivalence, 236–238
anti-Semitism. *See* Jewish people
Appiah, Kwame Anthony, 229, 257
Aquinas, Thomas, 126
Arendt, Hannah, 184, 217
Aristotle and Aristotelianism, on barbarians, 74–75, 259, 292n13; conception of soul, 76, 145; great chain of being, 109, 115; humanness, 125, 126; normative conception of the natural, 122; preformationism, 260
Armenians, 98
Aryan race, blood defilement of, 60, 61–63; distinguished from Jews, 56–57, 274; as essentialized kind, 155; as humans, 55; and Jewish conspiracy, 31; in Nazi ideology, 200, 271; in "The Operated Jew," 85, 88
Asheim, Steven F., 58
assembled kinds, 142–143
Augustine, 179–180
Auschwitz, 1, 11, 223, 270
Aztecs, 115

Bach-Zelewski, Erich von dem, 222, 223
Bacteria, 56, 108, 203
Bandura, Albert, 33
Bar-Tal, Daniel, 13
Bauman, Zygmunt, 215
Bible, and dehumanization of Black people, 6, 44–45; Genesis, 114, 117;

Gospel of John, 178; Leviticus, 120; in "The Operated Goy" (Friedlaender), 87; punishment of Jews, 188; ritual purification in, 218
Birth of a Nation, 7
Black people, animalistic slurs against, 235; in *Black No More*, 90–92, 93, 96; blood of, 59, 62; enslaved, 33, 110, 146, 226–228, 272; genetics, 77; lynching of, 2–5, 11, 253, 274–276; as monsters, 36, 268, 271–272; Nazi view of, 271; as primitive, 76, 120; racial essence of, 81–82, 96–98; rule of hypodescent, 62; as subhuman animals, 3–4, 5–9, 19, 25, 29, 39–49, 52–53, 226–231, 272–274; superhumanization of, 31–32, 265–268; and theories of ideology, 164, 167
Bleuler, Eugen, 236
blood. *See* race
Blumenkranz, Bernhard, 195
Boaz, Rachel, 59
Boehm, Christopher, 135
Borkum Hymn, 88, 294–295n12
Boyle, Robert, 59
Bradfisch, Otto, 50
Brown, Michael, 266
Browning, Christopher, 215–216
bubonic plague, 191–192, 202–204
Bühler, Hans, 58
Bukimi. *See* uncanniness
Byers, John, 171
Bytwerk, Randall, 200–201

Carroll, Charles, 44–45
Carroll, Noël, 253–254, 257, 268